FORTUNE ADVISER 2000
FIRST PRINTING 1999
ISSN 1096-1070
ISBN 1-883013-69-0

FORTUNE ADVISER STAFF:
EDITORIAL DIRECTOR: JOE MCGOWAN
EDITOR: VALERIE J. MARCHANT
DESIGNER: LAURA IERARDI, LCI DESIGN
COPY EDITOR: EDITH FIROOZI FRIED
EDITORIAL OPERATIONS: DAVID V. RILE

SPECIAL THANKS TO: JULIE CRESWELL, CAROL GWINN, JOAN HOFFMAN, RIK KIRKLAND, AND MARGERY PETERS

TIME INC. HOME ENTERTAINMENT
PRESIDENT: STUART HOTCHKISS
DIRECTOR, CONTINUITIES AND SINGLE SALES: DAVID ARFINE
DIRECTOR, CONTINUITIES AND RETENTION: MICHAEL BARRETT
DIRECTOR, NEW PRODUCTS: ALICIA LONGOBARDO
DIRECTOR, LICENSING: RISA TURKEN
GROUP PRODUCT MANAGER: JENNIFER MCLYMAN
PRODUCT MANAGERS: ROBERTA HARRIS, CARLOS JIMENEZ, KENNETH MAEHLUM, ANDRE OKOLOWITZ
MANAGER, RETAIL AND NEW MARKETS: TOM MIFSUD
ASSOCIATE PRODUCT MANAGERS: DARIA RAEHSE, DENNIS SHEEHAN, MEREDITH SHELLEY, BILL TOTTEN,
NIKI VISWANATHAN, LAUREN ZASLANSKY, CHERYL ZUKOWSKI
ASSISTANT PRODUCT MANAGERS: VICTORIA ALFONSO, JENNIFER DOWELL, ANN GILLESPIE
EDITORIAL OPERATIONS DIRECTOR: JOHN CALVANO
BOOK PRODUCTION MANAGER: JESSICA MCGRATH
ASSISTANT BOOK PRODUCTION MANAGER: JONATHAN POLSKY
BOOK PRODUCTION COORDINATOR: KRISTEN LIZZI
FULFILLMENT MANAGER: RICHARD PEREZ
FINANCIAL DIRECTOR: TRICIA GRIFFIN
FINANCIAL MANAGER: ROBERT DENTE
ASSISTANT FINANCIAL MANAGER: STEVEN SANDONATO

WE WELCOME YOUR COMMENTS AND SUGGESTIONS ABOUT FORTUNE BOOKS. PLEASE WRITE US AT:

FORTUNE BOOKS
ATTENTION: BOOK EDITORS
P.O. BOX 11016
DES MOINES, IA 50336-1016

IF YOU WOULD LIKE TO ORDER ANY OF OUR HARD COVER COLLECTOR EDITION BOOKS, PLEASE CALL US AT
1-800-327-6388 (MONDAY THROUGH FRIDAY, 7:00 AM–8:00 PM, OR SATURDAY, 7:00 AM–6:00 PM).

TO ORDER FORTUNE MAGAZINE, PLEASE CALL (800) 621-8000.

CONTENTS

FOR SALE ONLINE: YOU

BY JERRY USEEM

● ● ●

*The new way to look for a job is also the
new way for companies like Cisco,
Marriott, Motorola, and Prudential to
recruit top managers.*

● ● ●

Zalee Harris' husband was sure she had lost it. Here it was, just before Christmas, and she'd been laid off from her six-figure job at the telecom company in Tysons Corner, Va., where she'd worked for seven years. Now she was refusing to use the outplacement service or even to touch the Help Wanted section. Instead, Zalee was insisting, "The Internet is going to find me a job while I'm sleeping."

"Oh, my God," Joseph Harris told her, "we're going to be bankrupt by March."

Not quite. Zalee, built her own home page on the Web with photograph, résumé, and statement of purpose. She registered the address in search engines like Yahoo and WebCrawler. She bought contact-management software to keep track of employment leads. She posted her résumé on some 30 Internet job boards. Boom! In just over a month, she received more than 50 inquiries from headhunters and employers. On Jan. 18, just a day after a headhunter spotted her résumé on the CareerMosaic Website, Cable & Wireless offered her a job as a senior project manager—comparable with her old one, only this time her responsibilities would span 47 countries.

It isn't too often that the labor market undergoes a fundamental shift. Usually it takes something pretty big, along the lines of an industrial revolution or a baby boom. But if the new face of job hunting is a Web interface, as it appears to be, that's big. "Digital résumés, digital employment advertising, digital résumé searches—it's a rebuilding of the infrastructure," says Intel Chairman Andy Grove. "It's almost following e-mail in its growth."

Putting the online job market in a league with e-mail is a heady comparison. But consider: In January 1998, 17% of FORTUNE Global 500 companies were actively recruiting on the Net, according to research firm iLogos.com in Ottawa. Just a year later, that figure was 45%. Forrester Research in Cambridge, Mass., projects that employer spending on online recruiting will mushroom from $105 million in 1998 to $1.7 billion in 2003—roughly triple the projections Forrester made in 1997. By mid-1999 an estimated 2.5 million résumés were online, and a thriving economy of at least 28,500 job boards, such as Monster.com, HotJobs.com, and CareerMosaic (which has a partnership with fortune.com), were bringing employers and candidates together.

NOW AND IN THE FUTURE

True, the Net in its current incarnation affects only the first step—alerting employer and candidate to each other's presence—of a multistep hiring process that depends on human contact. After connecting electronically with the headhunter, Zalee Harris still needed to put on a suit and present her corporeal self to Cable & Wireless for interviews.

But extrapolate a bit, and it's not hard to imagine a future in which employers electronically screen for candidates' "soft" attributes, direct potential hires to a special Website for skills testing, conduct background checks over the Net, interview candidates via a videolink, and manage it all with Web-based software. It's not hard to imagine, because all those services currently exist, or will very soon (FutureStep for screening, Qwiztek.com for testing, PeopleWise for background checks, SearchLINC for video, and any number of packages for the back end). When those services are bundled, as they undoubtedly will be, we'll have much more than the electrification of newspaper classifieds.

Fine, you say, but who besides techies and the uncommonly geeky would consider pounding the pavement virtually? Well, according to a poll conducted by *Weddle's*, a newsletter and Website about e-recruitment, fully 65% of online job-seekers hail from nontechnical professions. Among them: Bobby Beck, a 37-year-old truck driver who wanted a job that would get him home to North Texas more than a couple of days a month. He logged on to layover.com, where truckers can apply for multiple jobs by

A TRUE TALENT EXCHANGE

Employers, meanwhile, are beguiled by the low cost, high speed, and wide reach of hiring online. One human resources pro speaks of "my previous HR life, before the Internet." Bruce Hatz, a corporate staffing manager at Hewlett-Packard, is even more direct: "It's dramatically more effective than any medium ever known. The Web is the future of recruiting."

If he's right, some profound changes are in the offing. Besides shifting huge sums of money within the $17-billion-a-year recruiting industry, online recruiting will touch the lives of the millions of people who change jobs each year, as well as anyone who has ever considered doing so—namely, you.

In the process, it threatens to accelerate, perhaps into hyper-drive, this decade's key job trends: compulsive job hopping, flexible hiring, and the evolution of an increasingly efficient labor market. By disseminating compensation information, it may strip companies of their sovereignty in setting salaries. The Internet threatens, in short, to erupt into a true talent exchange—a full-blown electronic marketplace.

Employers today aren't content merely to post openings on job boards and wait for résumés to roll in. Instead they venture forth and stalk. "You have to think in competitive intelligence terms," counsels Michael Foster, CEO of AIRS, a training and software company in Hanover, N.H., that teaches online-recruiting tactics. "As people interact with each other online, they leave traces that recruiters can find." Some e-cruiters lurk on Internet newsgroups, where workers gather to discuss everything from database administration to dating. They watch to see who says the smartest stuff, then make their approach by e-mail. Others use the Net to track workers around the globe. Hewlett-Packard has built technology to process résumés written in many languages—soon to include Asian characters—and deposit them in a centralized database, searchable by any Hewlett-Packard manager. At last count, it contained about 150,000 résumés.

The Website of Inacom, a 12,000-employee computer-services firm in Omaha, features a game called the TechnoChallenge that

TOP TEN ONLINE JOB SITES

• ● •

SITE	UNIQUE VISITORS IN 3/99
1. Monster.com	2,137,000
2. CareerPath.com	1,111,000
3. CareerMosaic.com	965,000
4. Jobsearch.org	726,000
5. HeadHunter.net	576,000
6. NationJob.com	366,000
7. HotJobs.com	344,000
8. Net-Temps.com	268,000
9. Dice.com	258,000
10. CareerBuilder.com	256,000

FORTUNE TABLE/SOURCE: MEDIA METRIX

combines flashy graphics with a series of technical questions. To play, contestants must enter their name, profession, and contact information—ostensibly to qualify for a drawing for a $1,500 prize if they score 100,000 points or more. What most don't know is that they're also being screened for potential employment at Inacom. "Anyone who scores 90% and above, we go after," says VP of technical recruiting Eva Fujan.

AGGRESSIVE CISCO

———————————— ● ————————————

More aggressive than any online employer is Cisco Systems. The $10-billion-a-year networking company hires 66% of its people and receives 81% of its résumés via the Net. Its Website is a Venus's-flytrap of attractions. Visitors can fill a shopping cart with job openings that interest them or join the Make Friends @ Cisco program, which connects them with a real-life person from the department in which they want to work. If they don't have a résumé handy, Cisco's Profiler is a simple, humorous interface that will help them build one. And because roughly 90% of "suspects" (as the IT team calls early-stage job prospects) log in from their current employer, there's an Oh No! My Boss Is Coming button, which quickly fills the screen with "Seven Habits of a Successful Employee." (No. 2 is "Embrace change.") Soon there will be a "virtual tour" of Cisco's San Jose campus. The whole kit gets prominent play on the company's home page, thereby ensnaring curious passersby.

"Cisco has turned this into a machine," says John Sullivan, director of human resource studies at San Francisco State University. Barbara Beck, Cisco's longtime chief of HR, diligently measures the machine's output. Her studies, for instance, indicate that Cisco's cost per hire is $6,556, vs. an industry average of $10,800. Its in-house staff of recruiters has remained steady at around 100 even as the company's annual rate of hiring has risen from 2,000 to 8,000 people.

But the most important statistic, says Beck, is 45 days: the average time it takes Cisco to fill an open job—down from 113 days three years ago. (A study by iLogos.com indicates that, on average, using the Net shaves 20 days off a company's hiring cycle.) For Cisco, whose current job openings fill a 463-page book, that's precious time.

How avidly does Cisco pursue candidates online? It has software that tracks where visitors to its Website go after leaving. It then places employment banner ads on those sites. Cisco's banners incorporate a domain-name reader, so that they appear only on the browsers of people who might be interested in working at Cisco—say, engineers at high-tech powerhouses like 3Com, Lucent, and Nortel. Of course, Cisco also subscribes to a number of job boards. In the world of e-cruiting, that's where the real action is.

THE MONSTER BOARD

Ground zero of this world is, oddly enough, the former epicenter of the minicomputer revolution: 5 Clocktower Place in Maynard, Mass., where Digital Equipment Corp. once made its home. Inside, amid purple carpets and lime-green chairs, you'll find an 11-foot statue of an ungainly and snaggletoothed beast named Trumpasaurus. And nearby you'll also find the closest thing this nascent industry has to an iconic figure.

That figure is Jeff Taylor, a contentious and goateed 38-year-old who in summer 1994 perplexed staffers at his Boston-area ad agency by launching an Internet site he called the Monster Board. The idea was straightforward: Job candidates who logged on could (1) post their résumé for viewing by employers, and (2) search a database of job openings, all free. Employers, for their part, paid for access to the résumés and for the right to post job openings. Taylor was zealously plugging the Monster Board's Web address—the 454th dot.com site, he proudly notes—in radio spots before anyone really knew what the Web was.

Truncated now to Monster.com, Taylor's creation has become a byword for the entire find-a-job-on-the-Net phenomenon, with a database of 226,000 job openings and 1.5 million résumés, and projected 1999 revenues of $90 million—perhaps a third of all employer spending on online-recruitment advertising.

Once Taylor has passed the obligatory moment of pained reflection, he launches into a hyperkinetic oration about how Monster.com will supposedly reinvent job hunting as we know it. "For 100 years we've had the 'job announcement' strategy," he says. "Whether it's nailed to a tree in the center of town, or in the Help Wanted section of the newspaper, it's a matter of hiring whoever happens to be actively looking at the moment."

In its place, Taylor submits, will be a world in which employers build long-term electronic relationships with candidates years before they actually need them (dubbed just-in-time recruiting, or JITR, by industry analyst John Sumser of Interbiznet.com in Mill Valley, Calif.) and in which employees keep their credentials in play more or less constantly via a sort of personal online-marketing module. They become active yet passive lookers, perhaps content with their station in life but always on the watch for that dream job. "I think there's going to be 20, 30, 40 million résumés in [databases] in the U.S.," says Taylor, who begins to describe his plan for a desktop "career operating system, not unlike Intuit," that will manage people's ongoing chore of making sure they are optimally employed.

Another radical business idea Taylor embraces is the human auction—in which workers sell themselves to the highest bidder.

ONLINE JOB HUNTING
BY THE NUMBERS

● ● ●

2.5 million	Estimated number of résumés posted on the Internet
28,500	Estimated number of Websites that offer job-posting services
65%	Percentage of online job seekers who are not engineers or computer professionals
$105 million	Amount employers spent on online recruiting, 1998
$1.7 billion	Amount employers will spend on online recruiting, 2003 (proj.)
17%	Percentage of FORTUNE Global 500 companies actively recruiting on the Internet, January 1998
45%	Percentage of FORTUNE Global 500 companies actively recruiting on the Internet, January 1999
81%	Percentage of résumés Cisco Systems receives via the Web
66%	Percentage of new hires at Cisco who come from the Web
68	Days shaved off Cisco's hiring cycle by using the Internet

FORTUNE TABLE, AS OF 7/6/99

The concept has met with equal parts enthusiasm and derision. Enthusiasm, because it looks like the consummation of what pundits have long predicted our labor market would become: a frictionless clearing-house in which employers enlist free-agent workers on an as-needed basis, Hollywood-style. Derision, because the whole concept strikes some as far-fetched—despite the fact that a team of 16 software types have already tried to auction themselves off on eBay for $3.1 million. Taylor's idea is for workers to profile their skills, name an opening price, then put themselves on the block for one, three, or five days (though they're under no obligation to accept any offer).

A FLUID MARKET

The proliferation of such market makers will almost certainly result in a labor market that is more fluid than ever, perhaps even coming to resemble in some ways a Chicago Mercantile Exchange for people. But clearly the commodities market analogy has limits. Soybeans don't insist on working in the Bay Area only. A barrel of petroleum doesn't need to be cajoled from its current position. Pork bellies needn't be closely inspected to make sure they can get along with the other pork bellies.

Which is to say that any marketplace where the goods are sentient beings has friction that other markets don't. You can be sure, too, that companies will do everything in their power to increase that friction, erecting new barriers to employee movement. Vesting periods for stock options, for instance, are getting longer. "Retention" has become the HR buzzword du jour. Other times the handcuffs are not so golden: More than a few companies have quietly hired full-time "salvagers" to patrol Internet job boards for their own employees' résumés.

A frictionless marketplace also requires truth in labeling, and résumés are notoriously untruthful. But set aside such concerns for a moment and assume that the Net will make hiring and job seeking, at the very least, more market-like. What happens then?

Despite companies' best efforts at retention, job hopping could accelerate. The "price" of an employee may become more objective, specific, and market-driven. Pay disparities may widen too. As the forces of supply and demand make themselves felt more quickly through the ether, top performers will command top dollars. "The value differential between top and average talent is enormous, close to 100 to one," says Bob Proctor of McKinsey & Co.

Of course, a few things are missing from this vision. Training, for instance. The fact is, most people who have skills to sell on the open marketplace acquired them through conventional, open-ended relationships with employers. By treating workers as fixed constellations of skills—as opposed to dynamic beings who can be taught things—an electronic mart might allocate people with wonderful efficiency in the short term but underinvest in them over the long haul.

One thing's for sure: Employees who learn online tactics now will be well prepared, whatever happens. Zalee Harris, for one, still has her personal Web page (http://members.aol.com/_ht_a/zaleharris/ZOPS.html). "Just in case something happens," she laughs, "I'm up and running."

●●●

THE PERILS OF CULTURE CONFLICT

BY MATT SEIGEL

● ● ●

Every society, be it a tropical isle or an Exxon, develops a distinctive culture. Your advancement or even survival at work depends on figuring out whether you fit in.

● ● ●

On the Micronesian island of Pohnpei, one measure of a man's status is his ability to contribute enormous yams to the village feasts. If someone does this consistently, his fellow villagers will praise both his skill as a farmer and the supernatural powers at his command, and often he will be elevated to a titled position. Contributing foods other than yams might be nice, but wouldn't enhance his status. All that matters is yam size.

Using labor-intensive techniques, the men of Pohnpei sometimes cultivate yams exceeding nine feet in length and requiring up to 12 people to carry them. Frequently the yams are adorned with leaves, and the biggest ones have to be held together with mud so they don't collapse in pieces. These "show yams" are rarely eaten.

Many Pacific islanders attach ceremonial significance to yams. Some emphasize size; others emphasize number and quality. But even Western cultures have their "yams"—things that are valued less for their inherent qualities than for the meaning the culture assigns them. Nations do this, and, yes, so do corporations. Especially in an era of entrepreneurship like ours, in which companies are as different from one another as their individualistic founders, identifying the yams of a particular company's culture before you sign on is now a matter of career survival.

Kathy Wheeler learned this the hard way in 1992, when she left Hewlett-Packard for Apple Computer. An engineer by training, Wheeler was one of three managers running a 40-person product-design team at HP when she was recruited. Wheeler liked HP, but the Apple job promised her sole responsibility for a product team and a corresponding bump in salary.

Though Apple's headquarters was just two miles from Wheeler's old office, to hear Wheeler tell it, she might as well have moved to Pohnpei. Wheeler had felt comfortable with the "yams" of HP culture: collaboration, consensus seeking, rock-solid engineering ability. Those were the qualities HP prized, and Wheeler had them big. At Apple, she says, everything was different. Suddenly she encountered a culture that exalted heroes and admired slick user interfaces. Those who got ahead were not for the most part the most skilled engineers but rather the "evangelists"—brash marketers of Apple products to the outside world. Before long, Wheeler says, she was deeply unhappy. "When you're used to being valued for one set of accomplishments," she says, "and what's actually being valued are accomplishments you either don't feel comfortable with or just aren't able to deliver on, the discomfort is pretty profound." Fourteen months after arriving at Apple, Wheeler returned to HP, notwithstanding Apple's efforts to keep her.

FIGURING OUT A CULTURE

Many job hunters don't spend enough time selecting for culture because they're not quite sure what it is. A corporate culture can be defined succinctly as a set of behaviors or qualities that are valued not because competition forces all successful companies to value them, but simply because, well, because that's the way things are.

One way to figure out the culture of a corporation, says Jennifer Chatman of the University of California at Berkeley's Haas School of Business, is to identify the personality traits and behaviors that those who thrive in the company have in common. Such traits will emerge in evolutionary fashion, says Dan Cable of the University of North Carolina's Kenan-Flagler Business School. As we all know, managers tend to hire others like themselves and employees tend to accept jobs at places where they expect to feel comfortable. At the same time, employees who don't hit it off with their bosses quit at higher rates, and those who fit in splendidly get promoted faster. Moreover, the personal values of the ones who stay the longest have more time to be molded by mentors, fellow employees, training programs, and company reward systems. Gradually, from the actions of all these forces, a culture emerges: an agglomeration of values and practices that are shared by anyone who matters at the firm.

For example, true to Wheeler's experience, Hewlett-Packard has elevated egalitarianism to something of a fetish. Everyone, including the CEO, works in a cubicle, and every company car in the U.S., the CEO's included, is a Ford Taurus. As HR directors can tell you, a well-defined culture can be a hindrance to a firm if the market changes underneath it and the culture fails to keep pace. Susan Bowick, HP's head of HR, says the company's commitment to decision by consensus has been a disadvantage in some of the fast-moving markets the firm has entered.

One measure of the importance of culture at a company is the amount of time its senior executives spend worrying about it. Shaping the company culture, says Dave Arnold of Heidrick & Struggles, a top headhunting firm, is "one of the main missions facing most top human resources executives today." Rob Goffee and Gareth Jones, both British professors of organizational behavior, have recently published a book offering a new typology of firm cultures. In *The Character of a Corporation* (HarperCollins), they set up a two-by-two matrix in which a company's degrees of sociability and solidarity are rated. Sociability is general friendliness among employees, while solidarity is the more hard-headed kind of cooperation that even people who don't like one another demonstrate when they have an overriding goal. Goffee and Jones see certain personality types fitting into particular culture types—for example, high-sociability but low-solidarity cultures attract extroverts with "low needs for structure or certainty."

Company culture is at least as important for employees as it is for managers. That's because many managers despair of ever changing a company's culture from the top down, but canny employees are free to select a company whose culture is compatible with their personal values. Doing so, says Chatman, can make a big difference in their careers. In a study of accounting firms she conducted, Chatman found that new employees whose personalities suited the firm's culture were about 20% less likely to leave their jobs in the first three years than those whose values-sorting test results suggested a poor fit. They also performed better and were more satisfied with their work.

TWO-PART TASK

———————————●———————————

Employees interested in achieving a good match face a two-part task. First, they must figure out their workplace priorities—those values and traits most basic to their identities, whether by birth or upbringing. Second, they must identify the companies where those qualities are most abundant and prized.

You can address the first task by making a list of the ten values that are most characteristic of your ideal workplace and the ten that are least characteristic.

The second task is tougher, since companies won't always be completely candid about their cultures. Still, even before you decide to apply for a job at a particular company, you can make some educated guesses about its culture just on the basis of its business strategy, says Ed Gubman of Hewitt Associates. For instance, if you're a "people person," service-oriented companies such as Nordstrom or Home Depot are better bets than efficiency-obsessed commodity producers like Cargill.

But don't, Chatman warns, fall into the trap of stereotyping a culture on the basis of its firm's industry. When Chatman studied the accounting profession in the mid-1980s, the employees of Touche Ross (now Deloitte & Touche) picked informality as their firm's No. 1 value among Chatman's 54 items. At Arthur Andersen, informality ranked dead last. How much more varied can you get?

Company Websites are a rich source of clues, say career experts. You also might want to see whether reports on the companies you're curious about have been published by Wet Feet Press (www.wetfeet.com) or Vault Reports (www.vaultreports.com). The two services sell company dossiers geared to job applicants.

When it comes time to visit a company, bear in mind that you can learn a lot just from nonverbal artifacts: What do the work spaces look like? How are employees dressed? Most important, what are they doing—standing around chatting, or sitting alone in their offices? The most telling artifact of all is the company's com-

WHAT DO YOU VALUE AT WORK?

● ● ●

The 54 items listed below cover the full range of personal and institutional values you'd be likely to encounter at any company. Professor Jennifer Chatman and others use this list to study cultural preferences. Divide it into two groups: the 27 that would be the most evident in your ideal workplace, and the 27 that would be the least. Keep halving the groups until you have a rank ordering, then fill in the numbers of your top and bottom ten choices. Test your fit at a firm by seeing whether the company's values match your top and bottom ten.

TOP TEN CHOICES

☐ ☐ ☐ ☐ ☐ ☐ ☐ ☐ ☐ ☐

BOTTOM TEN CHOICES

☐ ☐ ☐ ☐ ☐ ☐ ☐ ☐ ☐ ☐

THE CHOICE MENU

You Are: 1. Flexible. 2. Adaptable. 3. Innovative. 4. Able to seize opportunities. 5. Willing to experiment. 6. Risk-taking. 7. Careful. 8. Autonomy-seeking. 9. Comfortable with rules. 10. Analytical. 11. Attentive to detail. 12. Precise. 13. Team-oriented. 14. Ready to share information. 15. People-oriented. 16. Easygoing. 17. Calm. 18. Supportive. 19. Aggressive. 20. Decisive. 21. Action-oriented. 22. Eager to take initiative. 23. Reflective. 24. Achievement-oriented. 25. Demanding. 26. Comfortable with individual responsibility. 27. Comfortable with conflict. 28. Competitive. 29. Highly organized. 30. Results-oriented. 31. Interested in making friends at work. 32. Collaborative. 33. Eager to fit in with colleagues. 34. Enthusiastic about the job.

Your Company Offers: 35. Stability. 36. Predictability. 37. High expectations of performance. 38. Opportunities for professional growth. 39. High pay for good performance. 40. Job security. 41. Praise for good performance. 42. A clear guiding philosophy. 43. A low level of conflict. 44. An emphasis on quality. 45. A good reputation. 46. Respect for the individual's rights. 47. Tolerance. 48. Informality. 49. Fairness. 50. A unitary culture throughout the organization. 51. A sense of social responsibility. 52. Long hours. 53. Relative freedom from rules. 54. The opportunity to be distinctive, or different from others.

pensation system. Does it pay people for performing well over a long period, or is compensation tagged to yearly or quarterly goals?

For more nuanced information, make sure you interview people at all levels—especially peers—in every department where you might be spending significant amounts of time. And don't forget to speak with former employees who were at your level. Other good information sources are the company's suppliers and its corporate customers. But before all that are questions you should put to practically everyone you talk with about the company: What kind of people seem to succeed there? What particular aspects of their behavior are celebrated? And what sorts of behavior bring failure? The answers will tell you volumes about the firm's culture.

Before you walk into an interview, try to prepare other questions that will ferret out whether the firm shares your top ten and bottom ten priorities. Career counselor John McDorman urges clients to ask questions that call for examples, since the answers can't be easily faked. For instance, if you're particularly concerned about work-life balance, you might ask your interviewer to tell about a time when an employee's personal commitments conflicted with the immediate needs of the company, and how that dilemma was resolved. George Bailey, formerly of Watson Wyatt, recommends another line of questioning that's often fruitful. Especially if you're a manager, ask how the yearly budget is handled: It's a case study in how the firm resolves conflict. And Chatman advises job seekers to ask about the company's founders, its early history, and its folklore. Firms, like people, often reflect their formative experiences, even many years later.

Chatman recalls a Federal Express folk tale about a delivery guy who had been given the wrong key to a FedEx drop box. So he loaded it into his truck and took it back to the station, where they were able to pry it open and get the contents to their destination the following day. At FedEx, this employee is remembered as a hero. At the U.S. Postal Service, Chatman suggests, someone who uprooted a mailbox from a sidewalk would probably be regarded as a lunatic, if not a felon.

● ● ●

SHOULD YOU GO OUT ON YOUR OWN?

BY ANNE FISHER

• ● •

Answers to these six questions
are as important to your success
as venture capital.

• ● •

Great business ideas will always find backers, even in down markets, because venture capitalists have nightmares about missing out on, say, the next Intel. But here's another thing that doesn't change: Startups are risky. Even if you have the best product or service and the most brilliant business plan the world has yet seen—and you do, don't you?—entrepreneurs and the experts who advise them say you can be tripped up by failing to do some serious reflecting of a more subjective kind. Before you hand in your notice and clean out your desk, ponder the following questions. They could keep you from making a wrenching and expensive mistake.

1. Do you have the right personality for running your own business?

In her book *Working Solo* (Wiley), longtime entrepreneur and counselor to the self-employed Terri Lonier offers a wealth of hardheaded practical wisdom—beginning with a 25-question quiz designed to make you take a good look at yourself. Some key points: How prepared are you to lower your standard of living for a while, if need be? Are you good at making quick decisions, or do you need lots of time to mull things over? Are you resilient when things go wrong? Can you admit to yourself that you don't know something you need to know, and are you able to ask for help?

"Not everyone is cut out to be self-employed," says Lonier, whose Website, www.workingsolo.com, offers a monthly e-mail newsletter of tips for entrepreneurs. "You really have to be ruthless in assessing your strengths and weaknesses, and in thinking about why you want to do this in the first place. If you yearn to be on your own mostly because you're unhappy in your current position, you might be better off looking for another job instead."

2. Are you willing to do a lot of everything?

"In a big company you may be an expert in your field—say, marketing or manufacturing—and take for granted how much you have relied on other people's skills in other areas. But in a small business, especially in the critical early stages, you have to understand it all yourself," says Fred Thomas, president of the U.S. Small Business Administration's SCORE program. (SCORE connects fledgling entrepreneurs with seasoned veterans who give free business advice. For a SCORE chapter near you, call 800-634-0245.) Thomas notes that the staggering time commitment involved in running a new company is often enough to send former senior managers running back to the corporate fold.

3. Do you think of "sell" as a four-letter word?

David Birch, founder and head of the Cambridge, Mass., economic research firm Cognetics, has been studying and advising small businesses for many years. He says the most often overlooked cause of small-business failure is many entrepreneurs' lack of experience in sales, or any taste for it. "Especially in the critical first year or two, you're so enthused that you tend to assume people will want what you've got," says Birch. "But the idea that you have to sell to get revenue is alien to many people"—especially if they come from a highly structured corporate environment.

4. Can you stomach nonstop networking after the workday is done?

Or, to put it another way, are you adept at selling not just your product or service but yourself? Skill at schmoozing is, of course, valuable in any job, but for small-business owners it can mean the difference between thriving and starving. In most corporations a wealth of connections—with customers, actual or potential employees and colleagues, vendors, suppliers, and financial backers—is already in place when you walk in the door. To run your own business effectively, though, you have to spin that complex web of relationships yourself.

Many people find that they loathe doing this because it tends to involve long evenings of listening to speeches at rubber-chicken dinners, serving on trade association committees, and giving up free time to charm a lot of people you may not even like. Still, for one-person businesses, networking can be a sanity saver.

5. Is your family 100% behind you?

Over and over again, successful small-business people and the folks who advise them say that opposition from a spouse, or resentment from kids who wonder why you're never home anymore, can burden a new business to the breaking point. So find out what they think.

6. Are you prepared to wait for success?

Tom Culley, a former McKinsey consultant who has been involved in dozens of startups in Brazil and the U.S., has written a wonderfully clear-eyed book called *Beating the Odds in Small Business* (Fireside/Simon & Schuster). Culley has seen countless small-business owners give up in frustration when they don't achieve instant wealth. "Fast growth and quick riches seem to be all you read about," says Culley, "but the reality is that the entrepreneurs in those stories are like lottery winners. Sure, this could happen to you. But only a fool would count on it." He adds, "It takes years of grueling work to build a profitable company. My rule is: Survival first, then success—however long it takes you."

Linda McCormack who started Pixellence, a Web-page design firm in Glen Head, N.Y., agrees. "If I were to give just one piece of advice to somebody starting a company, it would be 'Don't give up' " she says. "It's always the really discouraging day when you feel you should pack it in that the phone rings, and it's somebody you gave your business card to six months ago and forgot about, and everything turns around. You've got to be willing to hang in there." Or as Culley puts it, "Slow ain't sexy, but it sure beats falling on your face."

●○●

TAKING CHARGE
IN A TEMP WORLD

BY ANN HARRINGTON

•●•

*Worry about employability, not about
employment.*

•●•

FORTUNE's Ann Harrington talks to John A. Thompson, the co-author of *The Portable Executive: Building Your Own Job Security From Corporate Dependency to Self-Direction* (Simon & Schuster).

Are people better prepared to be downsized than they were in the early '90s?

They are clearly better prepared. A couple of things have happened. Those caught in previous downsizing cycles haven't given up their networks, so they don't have to start over again. Second, they understand that their next job is going to come from their skill-set base. And the Web search process makes looking a lot more efficient and expands one's ability to see opportunities. You can get information about whole industries very, very quickly. Before, you had to write letters. You had to search around or go to some specialist. Now you can pretty much get it on your own.

What would you advise those who face a downsizing or fear their job is no longer secure?

Everyone should see himself or herself as "a personal service business entity," not as an employee. Basically you are a business, offering the company, your client, a valued service. If you're a long-term employee of a company and the company is going through change, you should look at how what you have to offer can help it make the change, so that you will continue to be vital to it. If what you have to offer is not what it is going to need after the change, then you should look at yourself and say, How do I have to change? You do not have to worry about employment. You have to worry about employability. If you're employable, you'll find a job.

What is portability?

Portability is a state of mind, not a state of employment. It's a belief in yourself and your value, and a commitment to maintaining skills that have value. Twenty-five years ago, when I was in public accounting, CPE—continuing professional education—was forced on us. In fact, the profession fought it. Now CPE is an absolute necessity in every single job.

Would people still prefer to stay at one company?

Everybody would love to go to one company, find his greatest challenge in life, have a job for life, and retire. The problem is that companies can't afford that today. Even if they had all the money in the world, they couldn't afford it, because the needs of companies change so rapidly. Technology comes in, and the product changes. That's why you're seeing companies hiring here and letting go there. It's not just downsizing. It's a realignment of responsibilities.

Why do you say that a flattened company structure is ideal for the portable executive?

A flattened structure means that whenever something comes up that is out of the ordinary, companies don't have the people within the organization to do it. So they've got to find the resources outside.

Might they even be the same people who were squeezed out in the flattening?

They could be. A big part of the trend is bringing the retirees back. Major insurance companies, for example, have a whole network of retired adjusters. Contingency teams are set up so that if there's a big hurricane, for instance, the insurers just call them up, put them on an airplane, send them to work for two or three weeks, and then bring them back. It's an emergency network and exactly what portability is all about.

Are you likely to work all night on a report if you have been hired for only six months?

I was in public accounting for 35 years. I worked 14, 15 hours a day on client matters. I was not employed by the client. If I lost the client, it wasn't the end of my life. Still, I did it. That model of professional commitment is the model the portable executive is adopting. I get my next assignment by doing a great job with this assignment. That is a basic tenet of professional services.

Do companies view managers differently?
Yes. They're looking to them to bring their skills to the table and not have to be guided. And to be "leaders." Leadership is taking more responsibility to get the job done, based on one's ability to build a group of people. You see, no manager is supposed to be able to do what has to be done today—he doesn't have the skills. But because a manager is dependent on the people around him, he's expected to pull together those skills. Twenty-five, 30 years ago, the bosses knew more than the workers. When you had trouble on the floor, the vice president of engineering was down there tinkering, and the laborers stood around looking at him because he knew more than they did. But today when the computer shuts down, the boss doesn't know how to fix it. He hopes to God the worker does. So the job of a middle manager, which had been to supervise a bunch of relatively unskilled people, is now to build a team of skilled people. You're so interdependent, you're forced to be a "leader."

Do you now think there is going to be enough work for middle managers in the future?
I think there's going to be a huge market for them. On the one hand, technology is supposed to make our lives simpler. On the other hand, much of technology doesn't satisfy our needs. And it takes a human to figure it out. So where the manager comes in is in showing how you marry technology with human endeavor. The middle manager who was basically a supervisor has disappeared. Now the middle manager is the manager of the technology and business interface.

SUCCESS SECRET:
A HIGH EMOTIONAL IQ

BY ANNE FISHER

● ● ●

Emotional intelligence is more
essential than ever, and yours may be
in need of some improvement.

● ● ●

What separates people who do well in life from people who fail or who simply never seem to get very far, despite obvious smarts and skills? FORTUNE's Anne Fisher talks to psychologist Daniel Goleman, who, in his groundbreaking 1995 bestseller, *Emotional Intelligence,* drew on a wealth of new research to argue persuasively that what we usually think of as intelligence—as measured by IQ—is far less important as a predictor of a person's path in life than one's supply of attributes he calls emotional intelligence. Those attributes include self-awareness, impulse control, persistence, confidence and self-motivation, empathy, and social deftness. Now Goleman has written a sequel, *Working With Emotional Intelligence* (Bantam), that zeroes in on how these qualities or the lack of them can make or break your career.

In era that seems preoccupied with technology and technical skills, why place a premium on "soft" stuff like emotional intelligence? How important is it really?
The data that argue for taking it seriously are based on studies of tens of thousands of working people, in every kind of professional field, and the research distills precisely which qualities mark a star performer. The rules for work are changing, and we're all being judged, whether we know it or not, by a new yardstick—not just how smart we are and what technical skills we have, which employers see as givens, but increasingly by how well we handle ourselves and one another. In times of extremely rapid and unpredictable change, like right now, emotional intelligence more and more comes to determine who gets promoted and who gets passed over—or even who gets laid off and who doesn't.

This is true at every level of the organization. When corporations hire MBAs, the three most desired capabilities are communication skills, interpersonal skills, and initiative—all elements of emotional intelligence. And the higher you go up the corporate ranks, the more these things matter.

How do you know that?

We've been able to quantify it in a couple of ways. I did one study where I gathered from HR training and development specialists their competence models—which are essentially lists of the most desired traits—for 181 jobs in 121 companies worldwide, with their combined work force numbering in the millions. Once we separated out the purely technical skills from the emotional competencies, and compared their relative importance, we found that two out of three of the abilities considered vital for success were emotional competencies like trustworthiness, adaptability, and a talent for collaboration.

That finding has been supported by other in-depth studies showing that emotional competencies are twice as important to people's success today as raw intelligence or technical know-how. And in any kind of managing or leadership position, emotional intelligence is of paramount importance. Often when you see people get promoted on the basis of technical ability and then fail in that new job, it's because they were promoted for essentially the wrong reason. They lack emotional competencies that are crucial at that higher level. More and more companies are realizing this and altering how they train and promote people accordingly.

Which emotional competency is most important to someone who has or wants to get a high-level executive job?

It's hard to single out one trait as most important, because different aspects of emotional intelligence come into play depending on the circumstances. But one distinguishing characteristic is, How persuasive are you? Can you get "buy-in" for your ideas from the people around you? The most effective leaders have very finely honed political awareness and ability. The word "political" is loaded, I know, because it carries negative connotations of empty charm, manipulativeness, or someone who is good at managing up but not down and is really interested only in his or her own gain. But "political" in the sense I mean is a knack for articulating a mission or a goal and knowing how to bring everyone on board to get it accomplished. Can you take the pulse of a group, understand its unspoken currents of thought and concerns, and communicate with people in terms they can understand and embrace? That is great leadership. And it takes huge social intelligence, including a strongly developed sense of empathy.

Beyond taking a quiz like the accompanying one we've devised, how can a person gauge his or her own EQ?

It's very tough to measure our own emotional intelligence, because most of us don't have a good sense of how we come across to other people, and that is much of what ultimately matters here. What you really need is to have someone else, or preferably a cross section of people you work with, rate you on the various components, such as trustworthiness, reliability, flexibility, how good you are in a crisis, and how open you are to new ideas and new ways of doing things. This is why 360-degree performance evaluations are so helpful. A 360, in which you are getting honest feedback from people above, below, and beside you, can give you a very clear sense of where you need to improve. The areas to focus on especially are the ones where your boss and your peers see you very differently from how you see yourself.

What about people who work for companies that don't offer 360-degree evaluations?

Clearly it will take a little more work on your part, but you can set up your own. Pick some people whose judgment you respect—including perhaps your immediate boss, a couple of peers who are neither your best buddies nor biased in any other obvious way, and maybe one or two people below you in the organization who have worked closely with you. Ask them to rate you according to the quiz, or use the more detailed list from the book. You may be very surprised by their answers and by how much the score they give you varies from the score you give yourself. You want to be on the lookout especially for points of agreement, areas where, for instance, your boss and your subor-

WHAT'S YOUR EQ AT WORK

• ● •

Answering the following 25 questions will allow you to rate your social skills and self-awareness. EQ, the social equivalent of IQ, is complex, in no small part because it depends on some pretty slippery variables—including your innate compatibility, or lack thereof, with the people who happen to be your co-workers. But if you want to get a rough idea of how your EQ stacks up, this quiz will help.

As honestly as you can, estimate how you rate in the eyes of peers, bosses, and subordinates on each of the following traits, on a scale of one to four, with four representing strong agreement, and one, strong disagreement.

_____ I usually stay composed, positive, and unflappable even in trying moments.

_____ I can think clearly and stay focused on the task at hand under pressure.

_____ I am able to admit my own mistakes.

_____ I usually or always meet commitments and keep promises.

_____ I hold myself accountable for meeting my goals.

_____ I'm organized and careful in my work.

_____ I regularly seek out fresh ideas from a wide variety of sources.

_____ I'm good at generating new ideas.

_____ I can smoothly handle multiple demands and changing priorities.

_____ I'm results-oriented, with a strong drive to meet my objectives.

_____ I like to set challenging goals and take calculated risks to reach them.

_____ I'm always trying to learn how to improve my performance, including asking advice from people younger than I am.

_____ I readily make sacrifices to meet an important organizational goal.

_____ The company's mission is something I understand and can identify with.

_____ The values of my team—or of our division or department, or the company—influence my decisions and clarify the choices I make.

_____ I actively seek out opportunities to further the overall goals of the organization, and enlist others to help me.

_____ I pursue goals beyond what's required or expected of me in my current job.

_____ Obstacles and setbacks may delay me a little, but they don't stop me.

_____ Cutting through red tape and bending outdated rules are sometimes necessary.

_____ I seek fresh perspectives, even if that means trying something totally new.

_____ My impulses or distressing emotions don't often get the best of me at work.

_____ I can change tactics quickly when circumstances change.

_____ Pursuing new information is my best bet for cutting down on uncertainty and finding ways to do things better.

_____ I usually don't attribute setbacks to a personal flaw (mine or someone else's).

_____ I operate from an expectation of success rather than a fear of failure.

A score below 70 indicates a problem. If your total is somewhere in the basement, don't despair: EQ is not unimprovable. "Emotional intelligence can be learned, and in fact we are each building it, in varying degrees, throughout life. It's sometimes called maturity," says Daniel Goleman. "EQ is nothing more or less than a collection of tools that we can sharpen to help ensure our own survival."

dinates all see the same shortcoming in you. Maybe nobody thinks you listen very well, or everybody more or less agrees that you tend to lose your temper pretty easily. Whatever the specific problem, that's where you need to direct your attention.

Let's suppose I give myself a high rating on, for example, being open to new ideas—yet my colleagues see me as rigid and inflexible. How do I go about fixing that?
You can do it. Emotional intelligence is not a fixed quantity, and in varying degrees we're all increasing it as we go through life. To change a particular tendency, what you need at the outset is motivation. You have to want to do it, not just because someone tells you that you should but because you see the importance of it. Most shortcomings in emotional intelligence are the result of habits of mind that are deeply rooted because they are learned very early in life. For example, a reluctance to consider new ideas may come from some experience in your childhood that taught you that new ideas are too dangerous or risky, that if you go out on a limb you may fall off and get hurt.

There are two basic steps in transforming any mental habit. The first is to notice when you are falling into it. Monitor yourself. The next time someone proposes something new and you catch yourself automatically thinking "No," stop and think again. Jot down some notes, if that helps you. Why does this particular idea make you uncomfortable? What's the context of the discussion? What are the emotions that go along with resisting the idea? Do you feel threatened by it in some way? Why? Don't judge yourself or tear yourself down. Just try to analyze your own reaction to the situation.

What's the second step?
Practice a different response. This will feel strange at first, and it is a real effort, because you are dismantling an old habit and building a new one. You might even deliberately set up a situation where a lot of new ideas will be thrown at you—for instance, call a meeting with the express purpose of getting your team to brainstorm about different ways of doing things. Then concentrate on keeping your mind open to what people suggest. It does take time

for new mental habits to form. It doesn't happen instantly. But by being aware, you can do a little better each time you try.

It helps to have some support. Many executives hire a coach to help them alter a specific behavior. A more practical approach for most people is to find a role model in your own workplace, a colleague who is especially strong in a trait you'd like to develop, and emulate that person. Watch how he or she handles a given situation, and see how closely you can adapt your own style. As you feel you're getting better at the competency you're trying to develop, ask the people around you for feedback. You might even encourage a colleague to give you a signal when he or she sees you slipping back into your old habit.

— • ● • —

ASK ANNIE:
ADVICE ABOUT WORK

● ● ●

FORTUNE's *Anne Fisher answers questions
about polish, high-tech job searches,
the importance of considerate exits,
working at home, good manners,
discretion—and more.*

● ● ●

WHY CHARM SCHOOL?

●

Dear Annie: After promoting me twice in the past three years, my boss just told me he wants to send me to an executive coach. This is fine, but I am a little uneasy because I'm not sure what I'm supposed to be getting out of the experience. When I asked for details, I got a vague answer about needing "polish." How can I make sure I learn the right stuff? *Onward & Upward*

Dear O&U: It sounds as if you're being sent to the kind of coaching that human resources types refer to, half-jokingly, as "charm school." If so, it's not surprising that your boss is being evasive about the reasons for it. "Often a boss can't exactly put his or her finger on what it is you are lacking—or else he or she knows precisely but is afraid of offending you by spelling it out," says Debra Benton, who coaches senior executives at companies like Mattel, Gillette, PepsiCo, Du Pont, Hewlett-Packard, and AT&T. She is the author of a fascinating book, *Secrets of a CEO Coach: Your Personal Training Guide to Thinking Like a Leader and Acting Like a CEO* (McGraw-Hill). Relax: "What it means," says Benton, "is that you're being groomed for a bigger job. So think of it as a compliment." It can also be a substantial investment. Benton charges $7,500 a day for her services.

Benton has boiled down what superiors want to see to a list of five. The first one, which Benton calls "executive presence," may be what your boss means when he says "polish": "It's the impact you have when you walk into a room, a collection of subtle—you might almost say subliminal—visual cues, including everything from how your clothes fit to how you walk. These things may seem trivial, but they're not." It's nearly impossible to evaluate one's own "presence," so let the coach do it for you.

And bear in mind the four other most common reasons you might need charm school: (1) "executive maturity," defined as the "political savvy and diplomacy to deal effectively with people"; (2) team leadership, including managing upward in the organization; (3) social ability ("you may be either too buttoned-up or not buttoned-up enough") and (4) technical orientation, meaning that you tend to "intellectualize facts rather than selling ideas."

JOB HUNTING IN TECH LAND

———————————●———————————

Dear Annie: I'm in my mid-30s and have done well in both sales and management for the past 15 years. But I've always worked for consumer-goods companies, and now I'd like to reposition myself in high technology. I have no computer-programming or systems-analysis skills, and no real interest in becoming a techie. Is it unrealistic to try making this switch? *Thinking Ahead*

Dear Thinking: You are wise not to aspire to geekhood since, in your mid-30s with zero computer background, you'd find yourself playing a demoralizing game of catch-up with people fresh out of school. However, according to the American Electronics Association, there are now over 152,000 technology companies in the U.S., 74% more than in 1990; and the industry has created 617,000 new jobs since 1994. Happily for you, not all those jobs are earmarked for programmers or systems experts. In fact, say many headhunters, sales and management experience is a great asset, because it implies that—unlike most techies—you actually understand how to communicate with fellow humans, including customers.

You will need to get some basic knowledge of computer systems. Subscribe to computer magazines so that you know what's out there and can speak—or at least approximate—the lingo. Take a few computer courses. Or better yet, suggests Dave Opton, executive director of Exec-U-Net (www.execunet.com), an Internet recruiting network for senior executives, "get the nearest 'wired' teenager to sit down with you and show you the ropes. Learning directly from someone who is a savvy user is by far the fastest, easiest, and most entertaining way to go." All the while, think about ways in which technology might be made more user-friendly—how it might, for example, make salespeople's jobs simpler or more effective. Having done that, says Joseph J. Carideo, a senior partner at executive search firm Thorndike Deland in New York City, "you can offer high-tech employers your expertise in sales and management and say, 'I think I know what your customer wants' "—even if the customer doesn't necessarily know it yet.

In your job search, Carideo recommends looking beyond huge established employers and reaching out to e-commerce startups instead. "I've had e-commerce companies come to me looking for a CEO and saying, 'We don't care about tech experience, we need someone who can manage,' " he says. "In a few years it'll be different, but right now e-commerce is the Wild West. It's wide open to anyone who's smart and willing to take a bit of a risk."

EXITING GRACEFULLY

Dear Annie: I am in my mid-20s and work as the only project developer at a small software company, responsible for total project management and training. I've just accepted a new job that doesn't start until the end of next month. At that point I'll be right in the middle of a big project here. How much notice should I give my boss that I am leaving? Is the standard two weeks enough? **Scorpio**

Dear Scorpio: Are you kidding? As soon as you finish reading this, get up and go into your boss' office, close the door, and tell him that he'd better start looking for somebody to replace you. It's always wise to make as graceful and considerate an exit as possible, unless you enjoy the smell of smoke from burning bridges.You have lots of working years ahead of you, and it would be a shame to start cultivating enemies so early.

DECENT ENGLISH

Dear Annie: I'm not your average FORTUNE reader—I teach English at a state university—but I wonder whether you can help me out. I'm teaching a course in business English this semester, and I find that my students are very quick to disparage the importance of writing as a business skill. Can you give me a realistic view of how useful it is to be able to communicate well in a business environment? *Sisyphus*

Dear Sisyphus: Gary Blake, who runs the Communication Workshop in Port Washington, N.Y. (www.writingworkshop.com), has this to say: "When I go around the country talking with big corporate clients, I am astounded at the number of managers who bewail the fact that nobody who works for them can write a simple paragraph. You can have the greatest ideas in the world, but they're no good to your company, or your career, if you can't express them clearly and persuasively."

Paula Goodman, a vice president and senior recruiter at Citigroup in New York City, finds that strong writing skills are "a tiebreaker. If I have two job candidates in front of me, equally qualified except that one can write well and the other can't, I'll hire the one who can—every time." Want statistics? A recent survey by Robert Half International of the 1,000 largest employers in the U.S. reported that 96% say employees must have good communication skills to get ahead.

HOPING TO WORK AT HOME

Dear Annie: I think that my job is perfect for telecommuting, but my boss has shot down the idea when colleagues of mine have proposed it in the past. He says he doesn't believe that anyone can work effectively from home. Any suggestions on how I might change his mind? *Cubicle Rat*

Dear C.R.: As home computers, fax machines, and handy new phone technology make telecommuting more practical, the ranks of at-home workers are growing by 15% a year. Apart from the hassles this spares workers (one survey found that the average telecommuter has dispensed with 90 minutes a day of travel time), there is some evidence that employers are finding the arrangement highly cost-effective. A study from the Society for Human Resource Management found that a person who works at home just two days a week saves his or her employer between $6,000 and $12,000 a year in office-space requirements, equipment costs, turnover, and increased productivity.

To overcome your boss' skepticism, you are going to have to build a strong case based on your own situation, beginning with a written schedule detailing how you plan to spend your days at home. Don't forget to say what's in it for your company. If, for instance, you really believe that you can concentrate better and produce higher-quality work without the noise and other distractions from surrounding cubicles, be sure to stress that. And at the outset you could offer to telecommute just one day a week for a couple of months—an eight-day trial that's essentially risk-free.

Gil Gordon, a consultant who helps companies set up telecommuting programs, suggests you seek out others in your company who are working from home and encourage your boss to talk with their bosses about how it's going: "Your manager might be more open and receptive to what his peers have to say than he is to you." For more tips on how to start telecommuting, including answers to specific questions your boss might raise, take a look at Gordon's Website, www.gilgordon.com. BellSouth's www.bellsouth.com/workathome is another useful site. During the '96 Olympics, the Atlanta-based company encouraged its employees to work at home to reduce downtown traffic jams. About 2,500 of them have barely set foot in the office since.

WOMEN NEED MENTORS

Dear Annie: My company recently started a mentoring program pairing women and minorities with more senior people. How important is having a mentor, really? And wouldn't it be better to find my own, rather than having one assigned to me? *Skeptical*

Dear Skeptical: "It's incredibly important to have a mentor, or a series of them," says Y&R CEO Linda Srere. "I've had the same one for 15 years, and I actually just called him for advice last week." Claire Farley, president of Texaco's oil and gas exploration unit, calls having mentors "an essential part of success. I've never met a CEO who didn't have several along the way." Among the invaluable boosts mentors can give you, Farley says, is preparing you for higher levels of responsibility "by giving you a 'sneak preview' of what it means to have power—removing some of the mystery. And by sharing their own experiences with you, and giving you objective criticism and support, mentors really help you stretch."

As you suspect, you are far better off finding your own mentor than being assigned one. Chemistry counts here, as it does in any other close relationship. Ideally, you and a potential mentor should gravitate toward each other. "Find someone who has qualities you admire, tell that person what you admire about him or her, and ask whether he or she can tell you how to develop the same qualities," suggests Srere.

THANK-YOU NOTES

Dear Annie: A while back you wrote a column about the importance of sending handwritten thank-you notes. But I am still wondering—if I send thank-you notes to both the human resources person and the hiring manager who helped me get my new job, won't it seem like kissing up or overdoing it? **Mike**

Dear Mike: No. Bill Young, an executive-communications coach at the Strickland Group in New York City, attributes your reluctance to a widespread form of testosterone poisoning: "It's some kind of macho thing. Tough guys never say thank you." Adds Young "It's really unfortunate that commonsense politeness is so often lost in the sharp-elbowed, almost barbaric competitiveness of so many companies today. It's important to thank people properly, with a short note, and I strongly encourage all my clients not to forget." Nobody will think you're kissing up. They'll just think your mama raised you right.

TOO MANY DRINKS

Dear Annie: At my company's annual holiday party a couple of months ago, I drank a lot more than usual, and late in the evening, I was dancing with the wife of a colleague and we got a little carried away. This was a mutual attraction that we acted on in a moment of stupidity, but it is keeping me awake at night because her husband has just been promoted and is now my boss. I have no idea whether she ever told him about "us," but what if she did? Should I say anything to him? Or just pretend it never happened and hope for the best? Or start job-hunting now? *Sweating Bullets*

Dear S.B.: For crying out loud, why say anything? If your boss' wife has kept mum about this, um, incident, you'd be doing no one any favors by bringing it to his attention. You may simply have gotten away with a big corporate faux pas here—now just let it die, and get back to work. Let me, though, propose a good rule: Drink alcohol only when you are among friends—and corporate politics being what they are, most people have far fewer of them at an office party than they think they do.

CHAPTER TWO

• ● •

LESSONS FROM
THE TOP

VIACOM: SUMNER REDSTONE'S REMARKABLE RIDE

BY MARC GUNTHER

• ● •

Sumner Redstone led a revival at
Blockbuster video, silenced his
critics, and became the richest mogul in
entertainment.

• ● •

Why is it, exactly, that people have always underestimated Sumner Redstone? Could it be that he spent most of his life away from the media glare, running a not-very-glamorous chain of movie theaters in Boston? Could it be that his company, Viacom, began as a hodgepodge of cable systems and TV reruns? Or could it be that Redstone himself can't match the charisma of a Ted Turner, the creative spark of a Michael Eisner, the buccaneering spirit of a Rupert Murdoch, or the analytical candlepower of a Gerald Levin? In an industry that worships youth, the fact that Redstone is considered the senior citizen of the crowd surely hasn't helped his cause. Nor has his bluster, his habit of wearing cheap suits, or his occasional malapropisms.

Never mind. Those who underestimated Redstone missed the mark. During a lifetime of savvy investing, shrewd dealmaking, and old-fashioned hard work, Redstone has made more money from the entertainment business than anyone else alive. By the spring of 1999 he had about $9 billion of Viacom shares, plus another $1 billion or so in National Amusements, his privately held theater chain.

These numbers only hint at Redstone's remarkable life story, though. He grew up during the Depression, in a tenement where the bathroom was down the hall. He made himself into an academic superstar at some of the nation's finest schools. He helped crack Japanese codes during World War II. There was the now-famous Boston hotel fire that nearly killed him but instead only galvanized his ambition. He was 63—an age when most executives shop for a retirement home—when he bought Viacom.

THE MAN'S RELENTLESS

To those who don't know him, the latest chapter in Redstone's story may be the most surprising. A few years ago Viacom, especially its Blockbuster Video unit, was in trouble. Redstone's reputation sank along with the company's stock. "Everybody treated me as if I was stupid," he says. "It hurt me a lot." Another 73-year-old might have walked away. Redstone couldn't. He hurled himself at the problems, camping out in Blockbuster's Dallas headquarters until he had remade its business model, fixed its distribution and marketing woes, and found a new CEO for the unit. "Whenever you have a catastrophic situation, you'd better be on top of it," Redstone says.

This may point to a final reason that the Viacom chairman and chief executive has not received the full credit that he is due. His success didn't spring from a brilliant vision, a creative break-through, or a bold bet on technology as much as from his sheer tenacity. This is a man who works all the time and operates in only one mode: relentless. "It's his job, his life, his hobby—everything is the company," says Philippe Dauman, one of Viacom's two deputy chairmen. "If he had the time," sighs his daughter and business partner, Shari, "he would be involved in every single aspect of everything that goes on everywhere." There's no line between work and play, weekday and weekend, the company and the man. "Viacom is me," Redstone says. "I'm Viacom. That marriage is eternal, forever."

Certainly Redstone has seen to it that he'll run the company for as long as he likes. In spring 1999 he controlled 67% of the voting stock and 28% of the shares outstanding at Viacom, which owns the Paramount movie and TV studios; the MTV, Nickelodeon, and VH-1 cable networks; Blockbuster; Showtime Networks; 19 TV stations; half the UPN network; Simon & Schuster consumer publishing; Paramount theme parks; and 80% of Spelling Enter-tainment. This ebullient grandfather runs a company that lives off the young—kids who watch Nickelodeon, teenagers glued to MTV, fans of *Beverly Hills 90210*, and the under-40 crowd that dominates moviegoing and video rentals.

Just about all those businesses are thriving. By far the most powerful engines driving Viacom are its high-margin cable networks, which have enjoyed double-digit earnings gains as they have expanded globally during the 1990s. Paramount has become the best-run major studio in Hollywood, releasing a string of winners while minimizing financial risk in a tough business. And Blockbuster has been revitalized. To the unwieldy, debt-burdened giant created by its 1993 merger with Paramount, Redstone brought a much needed focus and discipline. By selling a smorgasbord of assets, including Madison Square Garden, cable systems, radio stations, and a videogame company, Redstone slashed debt from $11 billion to about $4 billion. His best deal was the sale of Simon & Schuster's educational, professional, and reference publishing businesses to Pearson for $4.6 billion; no analyst expected them to fetch that much.

Even after shedding assets, Viacom brought in revenues of $12.1 billion in 1998, up 13% over the prior year's, and operating income of $1.19 billion, up 31%, excluding a one-time charge for Blockbuster. Gordon Crawford, senior vice president of Capital Research & Management and a longtime Viacom investor, says that with MTV and Nickelodeon leading the way, there's no reason Viacom itself can't grow 15% to 20% a year for the next decade. "There's a big, long-term, global opportunity there," he says. The stock tripled from October 1997 to April 1998, reaching $90 before a split that took effect March 31.

AND HE MUST WIN

For Redstone, that's sweet vindication. It's not about the money; while his net worth rises by $200 million with every dollar gain in the stock price, he has never sold a share and is mostly uninterested in the things money can buy. What drives him, more than anything, is winning. He looks at the stock price as a very public scorecard. "This is a guy who gets up every day and needs to win," says deputy chairman Tom Dooley. "He has to win a battle. He has to win an argument. He has to see the stock go up." This is why work doesn't wear him down. It charges him up, stimulates

VIACOM HAS PAID OFF FOR LONGTIME SHAREHOLDERS

• • •

While Blockbuster and Paramount contribute the lion's share of Viacom's revenues, cable networks MTV and Nickelodeon are growing faster and driving the stock price.

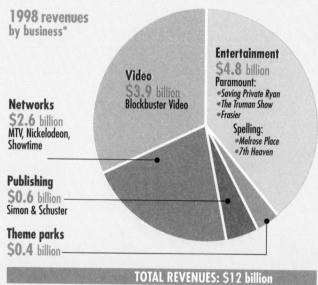

1998 revenues by business*

Video
$3.9 billion
Blockbuster Video

Entertainment
$4.8 billion
Paramount:
• Saving Private Ryan
• The Truman Show
• Frasier
Spelling:
• Melrose Place
• 7th Heaven

Networks
$2.6 billion
MTV, Nickelodeon, Showtime

Publishing
$0.6 billion
Simon & Schuster

Theme parks
$0.4 billion

TOTAL REVENUES: $12 billion

FORTUNE CHARTS
* Includes intracompany transfers.

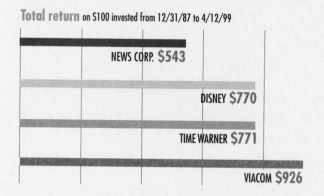

Total return on $100 invested from 12/31/87 to 4/12/99

NEWS CORP. $543

DISNEY $770

TIME WARNER $771

VIACOM $926

his brain, and even seems to retard the aging process. He isn't a classic workaholic or a drone—he's a happy warrior. "Sumner is the youngest man I know," says Sherry Lansing, chairman of the Paramount movie studio.

Redstone is one of those self-made men whose confidence runs so deep that they seem immune to ordinary self-doubt. It's not a trait that leads to self-awareness, but it's probably good for business. "Optimism can be a driving force for a company," he says. "And what is optimism? It's confidence in your ability." Redstone does have more reasons than most people to believe in himself. Take that 1979 hotel fire, which left him with severe burns over nearly half his body, including both legs. Doctors feared he'd die, then predicted he'd never walk, and later worried he'd lose an arm to an infection. But he is now hampered only by a right arm that hangs loosely from his shoulder and a gnarled hand with purplish skin.

There's a lesson there, he declares with his usual gusto: "Staying the course. Hanging in there. Refusing to drop. Having the confidence I could make it. Saying I'd walk when they said I couldn't. Today I'm running as fast as I could ever run on the tennis court."

Redstone has been running since childhood. His father, Max Rothstein, who changed the family name, rose from poverty to own nightclubs and drive-ins, and gave Sumner his first taste of show business. But the real driver in the family was Sumner's mother, Belle. "My mother was very tough," he recalls. He finished first in his class at the brutally competitive Boston Latin school, sped through Harvard in $2^1/2$ years, and then joined his professor of Japanese, Edwin Reischauer, on an elite code-cracking team that deciphered Japanese communications during World War II. After Harvard Law School and several top-rung legal jobs in Washington, D.C., Redstone decided to go home to Boston to join his father in the theater business.

It was there that Redstone learned the mantra that would guide him at Viacom: Content is king. As an owner of lowly drive-ins, National Amusements was getting only second-run fare from Hollywood. Putting his legal skills to work, as he is wont to do, Redstone sued the studios and got access to their most popular pictures. He also became a big investor in Hollywood; he bought shares in Twentieth Century Fox, Columbia, MGM/UA, and Loews, amassing the war chest he needed to launch his hostile, highly leveraged takeover bid for Viacom, then a little-known cable, broadcast, and syndication company.

Stepping onto a bigger stage for the first time, Redstone was greeted with catcalls. The old Viacom management dismissed him as a "two-bit theater operator from Boston," recalls Tom Dooley, a holdover from the old regime. Redstone has been trying to prove himself ever since. In the late 1980s, his lenders pressured him to reduce debt by selling MTV and Nickelodeon, which were then money losers. But content is king, remember, so he sold cable systems instead. During the epic takeover battle for Paramount, Redstone was cast as the underdog to the tough and brilliant Barry Diller. When Redstone persevered, taking on another huge load of debt, his detractors said that, swept up by emotion, he'd overpaid. Finally, when Redstone fired his popular CEO, Frank Biondi, and ran into problems at Blockbuster, he was derided as too old, too out of touch, and too domineering to run a modern media giant—"razzmatazz Redstone, the foolish boss of a bloated empire," as one financial columnist described him. Nothing delights him more now than having proved his critics wrong.

HE FOCUSES ON THE BIG PICTURE AND THE LONG TERM

In early 1999 the Viacom brain trust—Redstone, Dauman, and Dooley; MTV Networks CEO Tom Freston; and Jonathan Dolgen, who runs the Paramount movie and TV studios—operated informally, loudly debating issues and cracking jokes, with nary a PowerPoint presentation in sight. They "sometimes act like a dysfunctional family, but they are a family," an insider says. Redstone relies most closely on Dauman, who represented him as a partner in a Wall Street law firm before joining Viacom, and Dooley, an outgoing native of Brooklyn who rose up through finance. They're in and out of his office all day and on call the rest of the time. Los Angeles-based Dolgen and Freston, as operators of Viacom's biggest businesses, get more rope, although they too stay in touch.

What no one is permitted to do is put parochial interests ahead of Viacom's. For example, Redstone forced Paramount to make movies developed by MTV and Nickelodeon even though both sides resisted at first. While some friction remains, the partnership has paid off: Paramount and MTV have made a string of profitable movies, while Nickelodeon's *Rugrats* movie, which cost about $25 million to make, has grossed just under $100 million. Redstone touted the arrangements to investors at private briefings during a Salomon Smith Barney investment conference. "The MTV and Nickelodeon people have taken their low-cost model from the cable networks and brought it to Hollywood," he says. When costs can't be held down, Paramount likes to spread the risk; by co-financing expensive pictures, the studio has never lost more than $25 million on a movie, according to Redstone.

But Redstone admits that making movies is Viacom's toughest business. Its best, by far, are the cable networks, with their strong brands, low costs, and margins of better than 30%. Nickelodeon dominates viewing among kids; MTV has become the top-rated cable network among 12- to 24-year-olds; and VH-1, the newly energized music channel for baby-boomers, has greatly increased its ratings and ad sales. Growing, too, are the company's newer cable networks, such as TV Land, an oldies channel, and Comedy Central, home to the gross-out cartoon hit *South Park*. Overseas, MTV and Nickelodeon are turning profitable after a decade of losses, during which they built distribution and established their brands. "Anybody who ignores the fact that 96% of the world's eyeballs are outside the U.S. is going to pay for it," Redstone says. "We're on the case." By mid-1999, MTV was reaching about 282 million homes in 82 foreign territories, nearly four times as many as it reached in the U.S.; the channel generated $250 million in revenue and $41 million in operating income in 1998, despite the economic turmoil in Asia.

Incidentally, Viacom's global strategy, which is aimed at generating big money five or ten years from now, is evidence that Redstone, remains a long-term thinker. For all his fretting over the stock price, he's been willing to sacrifice short-term results to build value over time, whether by investing $400 million in animation for Nickelodeon or pouring more than $400 million, by the spring of 1999, into hapless UPN.

BUT HE'S NOT INTERESTED IN MONEY

———————————•———————————

Will Redstone ever step aside? It's not likely, given his passion for the job. [When this book went to press, Viacom had announced its plan to buy CBS Corp., forming the world's second-largest media company. The 76-year-old Redstone was expected to run the combined companies if the merger was completed.] In 1998, Redstone took his first vacation in years, a trip to the Caribbean island of Anguilla; the first thing he did upon arrival was get the hotel to install a new phone with a longer cord, "so that while I could enjoy looking at the water, I could be on the phone talking to the company." Even then, he says, "after three days I had a tough time." He is close to his grandchildren but otherwise has few interests outside Viacom. He loves to eat well, and he enjoys tennis, but that's about it. He still lives in the suburban home he bought years ago for $43,000. "He has almost zero interest in money and the tangible things that money can buy," says Dauman.

Indeed, ask him what he wants out of life, beyond Viacom, and he describes an ideal morning in Los Angeles. "To me, staying in a bungalow at the Beverly Hills Hotel, walking out and being surrounded by flowers, and then going down the path to play tennis—that's the height of my material aspirations," Redstone says. "Then I get in the car to go to the studio."

———————•●•———————

THE JACK AND HERB SHOW: CREATING GREAT COMPANIES

BY JOHN HUEY AND GEOFFREY COLVIN

— • ● • —

General Electric CEO Jack Welch and
Southwest Airlines CEO Herb Kelleher talk
about their companies.

— • ● • —

You've been in this job 17 years, Jack, and yet you're still bursting with energy. What makes you so energized?

Jack Welch: I have the greatest job in the world. We go from broadcasting, engines, plastics, the power system—anything you want, we've got a game going. So from an intellectual standpoint, you're learning every day.

We get a great kick out of the fact that we have made this company think outside itself. We want people who get up every morning with a passion about finding a better way: from their associate in the office, from another company. We're constantly on the search. We've designed a culture that gets people to look outside the company, and we've designed a reward system that's aligned with that.

I get a sheet every week of stock optionees who've cashed options. This year we will see $1.6 billion in employee gains in stock options; $1.2 billion of that will be below any senior-management level. Some 40% of our optionees make $70,000 or less. If they got a thousand shares each of the past five years, they would today have a gain of $800,000. In five years they've gotten about 12 times their annual salary. That's a kick.

How do you encourage fun in a business where you've got people's lives in your hands every day?

Kelleher: There's something we call professional terminalism. Professionalism is being very good at what you do in a very modest way. That's the way our people are: They're results-oriented. Whether it's the best safety record in the world, the best customer service record in the world, the youngest jet fleet, or lower fares, our people are really focused.

GE has an informality that belies the image that most people would have of a huge, massive, financially driven global company. How does that work?

Welch: Informality gives you speed. It takes the crap out of the business equation, the pontificating. I can remember 20 years ago in this company when you went to a meeting, the lights went down, you read a script, you gave your pitch, and you got the hell out of the room. That was the game. Today you're in there having an open dialogue with self-confident people, real exchanges about real things.

Giving people self-confidence is by far the most important thing that I can do. Because then they will act. I tell people, if this place is stifling you, shake it, shake it, break it. Check the system, because it wants to be a bureaucracy. And if it doesn't work, get the hell out. If GE can't give you what you want, go get it somewhere else.

What's your advice, Herb, to someone who wants a job at Southwest, given that you can hire so few of the many who apply for a job there?

Kelleher: If you're an altruistic, outgoing person who likes to serve others and enjoys working with a team, we want you. If you're the kind of person who enjoys a more secure, more regimented, more inflexible, more rule-governed type of environment, that doesn't mean that you're a bad person, but we're probably incompatible.

Is it true that you should be prepared to tell a joke in the job interview?

Kelleher: No, that's not true. But it is true that we will say to someone, Tell us how humor helped you get around one of the more difficult situations in your life.

People think it's kind of crazy, Jack, but we had a pilot-applicant class one day and we said, We don't interview you in suits; put on some Southwest Airlines shorts. Now, you may think that seems kind of quirky and aberrational—irrational, even. But the ones who were delighted to do it because they thought it was a lark—those were the ones we hired.

You both run huge companies. How do you renew a big organization, renew your own spirit? And most important, what do you do to renew the sense of purpose of your employees?

Kelleher: The way we accomplish that is that we constantly tell our employees to think small and act small, and we'll get bigger. Think big, be complacent, be cocky, and we'll get smaller.

One way we avoid complacency is that we reject the idea of long-range planning. We say, Do strategic planning, define what you are, and then get back together soon to define whether you need to change that. And have the alacrity of a puma. Because this plan about what we're going to do ten years from now will almost certainly be invalidated in the next six months.

Welch: You need to believe that you are a learning institution and to constantly challenge everything you have. I was at Crotonville [the New York State site of GE's Leadership Development Center] on a Monday night after the Asian crisis. I said, How many people can raise their hand and say they predicted the crisis? Not one hand went up, including mine. I said, What does that tell you? All of this crap you planned for is meaningless, basically. What's important is that you're agile, in your thinking and in your action.

You've also got to use the strength of a big company, and reduce its weaknesses. For example, a big company doesn't communicate as well as a small company. There's no chance. A big company moves more slowly. We think we're the fastest elephant at the dance, but we are an elephant. What a big company's balance sheet allows it to do: keep playing. We've made $10 billion to $15 billion of acquisitions every year for the past five years. Most don't even make the papers. A billion here, a billion there, two billion here.

You're doing a total-quality thing ten or 15 years after the rest of corporate America did it, Jack. Why are you doing it, and why now?

Welch: There was only one guy in the whole country who hated quality more than me. I always believed quality would come from just operating well and fast, and all these slogans were nonsense.

The guy who hated quality more was Larry Bossidy. He hated quality totally. Then he left GE and went to AlliedSignal. In order to resurrect AlliedSignal, Larry went out, saw Motorola, and did some stuff on Six Sigma. And he called me one day and he said, "Jack, this ain't b.s.—this is real stuff, this is really great stuff."

We poll 10,000 employees every year. In '95 they came back and said, We desperately need a quality issue. So Six Sigma was something we adopted then. The results are fantastic. We're going to get $1.2 billion of gain this year. For years our operating margin was never over ten. It's been improving, and it's going to be 16.7 this year. Our working-capital turns were four for 35 years. It will be nine this year.

Finally, what keeps you guys awake at night?

Kelleher: What keeps me awake are the intangibles. It's the intangibles that are the hardest thing for a competitor to imitate. You can get airplanes, you can get ticket counter space, you can get tugs, you can get baggage conveyors. But the spirit of Southwest is the most difficult thing to emulate.

So my biggest concern is that somehow, through maladroitness, through inattention, through misunderstanding, we lose the esprit de corps, the culture, the spirit. If we ever do lose that, we will have lost our most valuable competitive asset.

Welch: People don't realize that 10% of our company is owned by our employees, including production workers, who own some $2 billion worth. It is an incredible feeling of responsibility to take their savings and their life and have something go wrong with it.

MEG WHITMAN
MUSCLES EBAY UPTOWN
BY DANIEL ROTH

●─●─●

*eBay is moving away from Beanie Baby
swap meets toward big-ticket, revenue-
boosting auctions.*

●─●─●

On April 20, 1999, Meg Whitman, CEO of eBay, found herself in Washington before a group of 210 journalists and guests in the ballroom of the National Press Club. The moderator introduced her by quoting a recent *New York Times* story about her wildly popular auction Website: "Millions of people have begun embracing the online auction," he read, "an Internet phenomenon that in a matter of months has captivated the nation's bargain hunters and spawned a market for nostalgia."

It was the perfect setup for Whitman, who trotted out stories about how eBay had changed customers' lives: the woman with diabetes and lupus who, after being forced out of a job, reconnected with society by trading over eBay; the struggling antique-shop owner who rescued her business by selling on eBay; the couple in Curtis, Neb., who saved their entire town by persuading neighbors to sell over eBay. The significance of eBay, Whitman explained, goes far beyond commerce: "People are not only buying and selling, they're ... using the bulletin boards, the chat rooms, and the eBay Cafe to meet new friends and establish new relationships ... As one eBay user put it, 'eBay and its cyber-incredible world is bringing people together to do a lot more than trading goods. We are trading our hearts.' "

Six days later Whitman traded something far less warm and fuzzy—$260 million in eBay stock in exchange for Butterfield & Butterfield, a 134-year-old auction house in San Francisco. The deal made sense to Wall Street: Though the diabetic woman and the Curtis couple make for great PR, their average auction closes at only about $47, of which eBay's cut is about $3; the average Butterfield & Butterfield auction closes at $1,400, of which the house's cut is almost $400. Buying into the high-end auction business might not add to the cyber-incredible chatter in the eBay Cafe, but it sure promises to boost eBay's business.

On news of the Butterfield & Butterfield acquisition, reaction was split. Stock traders applauded, sending eBay stock up 4%, but Internet message boards lit up with protests. Referring to founder Pierre Omidyar, now eBay's chairman, someone wrote: "The Average Guy and Average Girl made this behemoth what it is. This is the thanks you get, kids. You made it possible for eBay to become what it wants to become."

HYPE THE TOUCHY-FEELY
OR PLEASE THE WALL STREET TYPES?

Increasingly, it seems, eBay is a company at war with itself. The swap fest that has been endlessly touted as the Internet's happiest marketplace ("People go gonzo over eBay," declared *USA Today*) is fast evolving into something rather different. While Whitman continues to hype eBay's touchy-feely communitarianism, she's quietly and rapidly overhauling the company in service of a goal the staunchest capitalist would understand: pleasing Wall Street.

In the spring of 1999, Whitman systematically imposed control on eBay's famously anarchic, free-form environment. She is gearing the site increasingly to big-ticket items and big sellers (eBay takes an average 6% fee on sales), even at the risk of alienating small ones. For example, Whitman is encouraging real-world store owners to expand their sales via eBay. She has introduced a PowerSeller program that gives extra customer support to big vendors—even as middling and smallish users complain loudly about the lack of support available to them. And in addition to the Butterfield purchase, in mid-May Whitman bought automobile auctioneer Kruse International; the two old-world auctioneers give eBay a steady supply of high-ticket goods and an army of appraisers to perform a function eBay customers have long performed on their own.

All the while, Whitman has worked to sanitize eBay's public image, going so far as to maintain decorum by suspending some users for posting too many messages trashing eBay. By the rules of the old economy, these are perfectly predictable—and seemingly sound—moves for a newly public company to make. What business wouldn't like to attract people with deeper pockets or squelch disruptive customers? Indeed, eBay's stock seems to tick up every time Whitman makes an announcement. But eBay isn't an old-economy business; its growth has come about through a kind of spontaneous generation unheard of in the pre-Internet age. In fact, eBay may provide an excellent test of just how successfully management practices that were developed under the old rules can be applied under the new.

GOING GANGBUSTERS

By those old rules, eBay is going gangbusters: From 1995 until late 1998, the company did no national marketing or advertising whatsoever. Nevertheless, almost purely by word of mouth, it had 3.8 million registered users at the end of March 1999 and grew from 289,000 items listed for sale at the end of 1996 to 2.2 million by the summer of 1999. Fueled by the apparently infinite American desire to buy, sell, and talk about Beanie Babies, old coins, and other cultural flotsam, eBay has become one of the few profitable Internet companies, expected to net $24 million in 1999 on $170 million in revenue. In the first three months of 1999, eBayers bought and sold $541 million of goods; by the end of the year, $2.7 billion worth of goods should trade hands over eBay, making it the largest consumer-commerce site on the Web. By comparison, Amazon.com is expected to sell $1.4 billion in books, music, and auctioned goods in 1999.

Wall Street loves eBay's numbers. But Richard Zandi, an analyst at Salomon Smith Barney, calculates that by 2009 eBay will have to sell $212 billion of goods a year to live up to its current value. To put this in perspective, that's almost 60% more than what the world's biggest retailer, Wal-Mart, sold in 1998.

For Whitman, that's some serious pressure. Which makes it, depending on how you assess the situation, all the more inevitable or all the more nerve-racking that she is moving eBay away from its roots. Whitman is fond of attributing eBay's success to what she calls the "network effect," essentially an escalating cycle in which sellers attract buyers and vice versa. The question is, By altering the size and composition of the network, is she undermining it? Can she keep eBay faithful to its roots and still live up to Wall Street's expectations? And do those roots even matter anymore?

EBAY'S BEGINNINGS

To understand where eBay came from, you have to meet Pierre Omidyar. Sitting in his San Jose office, decorated with Pez dispensers and books on collecting them, Omidyar is wearing a short-sleeved shirt batiked with cave drawings and has a long, black ponytail. As eBay's chairman, Omidyar has the primary day-to-day function of vetting big ideas. He is the picture of calm, commercially oblivious computerdom. Born in France, he grew up in Bethesda, Md., and early on started toying with computers. After college he moved west to work as a programmer. In 1992 he started (and two years later he left) a company called eShop, an early e-commerce site later bought by Microsoft. By the time he reached communications-software maker General Magic in 1995, Omidyar was the stereotypical antiauthoritarian, libertarian programmer. And he was starting to have a bad feeling about what the Internet—then in its infancy—was becoming.

In summer 1995, Omidyar's girlfriend, a Pez-dispenser collector, complained that it was hard to find like-minded souls to buy from and sell to. Omidyar saw the vacuum as an opportunity not only to score points with his spouse-to-be but also to develop a possible antidote to the corporate infiltration of the Internet.

"I came from the anticommercial side," he recalls.

When eBay launched on Labor Day 1995, it was an efficient market and little else. Omidyar made no guarantees about the goods being sold, took no responsibility, and settled no disputes. The system was simple: Users went on and bid for items. There were no fees, no registration, no search engine—and for the first month, no customers.

EBAY'S STOCK OUTSTRIPPED THE FIELD

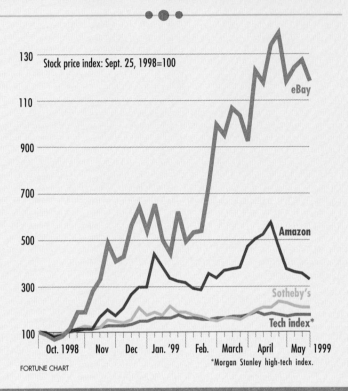

Stock price index: Sept. 25, 1998=100

130
110
900
700
500
300
100

eBay

Amazon

Sotheby's

Tech index*

Oct. 1998 Nov Dec Jan. '99 Feb. March April May 1999

FORTUNE CHART

*Morgan Stanley high-tech index.

The business took off almost in spite of its creator. Omidyar's sole attempt at marketing was to list eBay on the National Center for Supercomputing Applications' What's Cool site. That was enough: People started piling onto eBay so fast that by February 1996, Omidyar had to institute a fee to recoup his rising Internet service provider costs. By the end of March, eBay turned a profit.

The business worked much as it does now—a seller describes his item, sets a minimum bid, and chooses how long the auction will last, between three and ten days. Before the auction, eBay charges a listing fee ranging from 25 cents to $2, and later it takes a cut of the final price, starting at 5% for the first $25 and sliding down to 1.25% as the price exceeds $1,000. Although eBay gets only an average 6 cents for every dollar's worth of goods that trade hands, 5 cents of that is gross profit, thanks to a completely automated system.

In 1996, eBay still had one problem: There was no way to make sure what you were buying was real or that you'd get it after you paid for it. The anonymity and physical distance between buyers and sellers on the Internet encouraged counterfeiting and fraud. In the end, it was the eBayers themselves who found a solution. In message-board postings to Omidyar, they suggested he set up a system for buyers and sellers to rate each other. That became the Feedback Forum, a sort of peer-reviewed credit-reporting system. Buyers and sellers rate each other and comment on how their business together went. (A recent posting: "Honest & Trustworthy— FANTASTIC person to do business with—asset to eBay!!") Get negative feedback, and buyers know to avoid you.

The Feedback Forum proved to be the missing element in the formula; what Whitman would later call the eBay "community" finally took shape. "As high tech as eBay is, the closest analogue to what they've created is the original small-town market," says Peter Kollock, a UCLA sociology professor who has been studying eBay for the past two years. "It's a market that relies on identity and reputation for risk management."

Another force in eBay's evolution was the message boards Omidyar created as a way of encouraging users to answer one another's questions. By mid-1996 about 5,000 people were using eBay (then called AuctionWeb); one of the most visible and entertaining was a former mural painter in tiny West Rutland, Vt. Under the handle "Uncle Griff," Jimmy Griffith spent his days and nights coaching newcomers through the system and lecturing others on what he felt was proper online-auction protocol. He'd pepper his postings with pieces of Uncle Griff's fictional biography: that he was a fiftysomething, cross-dressing dairy farmer in West Upperbuttcrack, Vt., and that he still lived with his mother, despite her untimely death 30 years before. "It was silly," Griffith explains, "but my hero is Judith Martin, Miss Manners. I was trying to further her idea of etiquette, only extending it to the way people behave online."

Omidyar brought on Griffith as eBay's first customer-support rep. It was more than just an odd hire: By offering Uncle Griff a position at eBay, Omidyar was paying homage to his users. Not only would their auctions feed the business, but they themselves would build the infrastructure that supported it.

Under this banner of self-reliance, Griffith established eBay East, which would be a main customer-support center for the next several years. He handpicked an enthusiastic, if unlikely, team of local waitresses, school-cafeteria cooks, and housewives; together they personally answered hundreds of queries a day from eBay users, guiding them through the auction process, sorting out glitches in the system.

Back in San Jose, Omidyar and Jeff Skoll—who had joined eBay as president in 1996—devoted their efforts to eBay's computers. The community would grow itself, Omidyar's thinking went, as long as the system worked. And grow it did. By 1997 the company was doubling every three months, far too quickly for Omidyar and Skoll to handle. By mid-1997, without help from outside, the two had built one of the most visited sites on the Web, with more than 150,000 users bidding on 794,000 auctions each day. The average eBay shopper was spending nearly 3½ hours a month on eBay, longer than the average shopper on any other site. The tide of hype began to rise: GOING ONCE. GOING TWICE. CYBERSOLD, gushed *Business Week*. It was one of many such headlines.

In June 1997, Omidyar and Skoll took the eBay business plan to Benchmark Capital and got a $4.5 million check for 22% of the company. Benchmark also promised to find seasoned managers to help run eBay.

ENTER MEG WHITMAN

———————————◆———————————

"What you see of eBay today is the tip of the iceberg," says Whitman, nibbling on a fruit salad in her San Jose office. Three Teletubbies bake in the sunlight on her windowsill. "Today [the merchandise] is largely collectible, largely under $300. What we are starting to see—and we really look to our users here, we call them our army of entrepreneurs—is that they are starting to put much more practical items on the site."

Our army. It's an appropriate choice of metaphor. When Benchmark persuaded Whitman to leave her job heading Hasbro's preschool division (after stints at Disney and Procter & Gamble, and one as CEO of FTD), eBay was a ragtag band of sellers hawking stuff from their basements. Whitman, a Princeton economics grad with a Harvard MBA, considers it her job to whip that mob into shape. Like any seasoned sergeant, she seems willing to sacrifice a few troops along the way.

Soon after joining eBay in February 1998, Whitman started building her ranks. Significantly, in a company that had always disdained advertising, one of her first moves was to snag Pepsi's head of marketing, Brian Swette, to oversee eBay's embryonic marketing group. Then, in preparation for the IPO, she started making changes to the site. eBay's gray-and-white face was dressed up with bright primary colors, and a bizarre anthropomorphic apple was added by way of a mascot.

In September 1998, Whitman walled off all firearm and pornography auctions in separate, age-restricted sites. With the dirty laundry safely hidden away, she was ready for the road show. She took eBay public on Sept. 24.

The stock single-handedly revived the market for Internet IPOs. On its first day of trading, the stock went from a split-adjusted $6 a share to $18.08. Suddenly eBay's top executives were multimillionaires With riches came the magnifying lens of the public eye. Articles began to appear about rampant rifle, grenade, and pistol sales at eBay. Worse, the articles warned of escalating fraud at the company. *SmartMoney* called Internet auctions the "perfect venue for scams." The National Consumers League's Internet Fraud Watch declared auction fraud the No. 1 problem on the Web.

Omidyar and Skoll had long insisted that the fraud problem at eBay was minuscule—just 27 reported cases out of every million auctions—and that if users would just use the Feedback Forum, the site would police itself. But Whitman was convinced this laissez-faire policy wasn't cutting it with the public, and in mid-December of 1998—over the objections of Omidyar and Skoll—she decided to take action.

"eBay comes from the roots of an open, sort of libertarian, point of view," she says. "It's a bit of a Vermont thing. Like, let's not get government too involved here. We had to make a seminal decision: Were we going to be more proactive to make eBay a safe place to trade or not?" She got her way. In January 1999 the company announced a "comprehensive trust and safety program." eBay granted buyers free Lloyd's of London insurance for purchases up to $200, less a $25 deductible. Sellers got a chance to pay $5 and have their identity verified by credit-rating agency Equifax, and eBay promised tougher action against shill bidders and deadbeat bidders. Whitman also banned firearm sales altogether and banished even pinup calendars and risqué postcards to the Adults Only area.

NEW: TOP-DOWN DECISION

While the changes were mostly toothless, they marked a major shift in eBay policy. For the first time, the company was making top-down decisions instead of letting them boil up from below. That top-down pattern would become common. In February 1999 a major server crashed, which was routine at the time and is still all too common. The site was paralyzed for hours. When it finally came back up, outraged eBayers started venting on the support board. eBay responded first by suspending the customers for 24 hours, then by killing the live board completely, freezing access to instant customer support. Whitman has declined to resurrect the live board and recently allowed a new round of suspensions on another eBay board. Those have fueled online conspiracy theories that run from the paranoid (that eBay would kick low-dollar vendors off the system) to the plausible (that it would replace the Feedback Forum with Equifax).

To the old-guard populist users, Whitman's moves smacked of authority flexing its muscles—strictly *verboten* in the Internet pioneer world and a long way from that "very open, honest, friendly environment" that she likes to talk about in the national media. But nothing drove home eBay's willingness to break with its past more than the announcement that came next: Customer support was being shifted to a new corporate facility in Salt Lake City. The new facility, just now opening, will be staffed by a temp agency. eBay East will survive for now, but Uncle Griff's online advice has

already taken on a distinct corporate drone: It features an itali-
cized lawyerly disclaimer that *"eBay is not liable or responsible for any
type of damage or loss caused … by the information below."* Griffith now
divides his time between Rutland and San Jose. "Things change,"
he shrugs.

GOAL: ATTRACTING A NEW TYPE OF SELLER

For her part, Whitman prefers to see the shift as part of an
inevitable maturation, as eBay looks to attract a new type of
seller whose main concern is getting the highest possible price.
"eBay started with individuals selling to one another," she says, but
it's moving on to serve as a distribution channel even for traditional stores and businesses: "When you walk through your
neighborhood, you always see the small shops and wonder how
they survive. Well, a lot of them now keep their storefront, [but]
the real money is made on eBay."

In Whitman's drive to make eBay a conduit for merchants,
some of eBay's old clientele is finding that doing business on the
site has become a trying, unhappy experience. A two-year veteran, who requested anonymity, persuaded her husband to give up
his job to help her sell full-time over eBay. As the company grew,
she grew with it. She grosses $120,000 a year on the site and says
she pays eBay $1,000 a month in listing fees. But now, she says,
eBay is ignoring her in favor of a fancier breed of client. Even
though she has been enlisted in the PowerSeller customer-service
program for big-ticket sellers, her e-mail and phone calls regularly go unanswered. So why not go to Amazon? Because she still
gets the highest price for her auctions at eBay—a function of the
"network effect" that Whitman says creates a kind of snowball
phenomenon as both sellers and buyers seek out the largest market under one roof. "This might be one of those businesses where
the big actually get bigger through the natural benefit of a larger
market," says Whitman. In other words, eBay got there first, and
there's no stopping it now.

HOME DEPOT RENOVATES

BY ROY S. JOHNSON

● ● ●

*The world's biggest home improvement
retailer keeps getting bigger. Now
CEO Arthur Blank wants to be
your contractor, and more.*

● ● ●

Home Depot is growing like angry crabgrass these days. Its monstrous orange crates are already as much Americana as the Golden Arches. At the beginning of 1999 two new stores were opening every week. By 2001 the landscape will be covered with 1,350 Depot centers—three times as many as in 1996. Arthur Blank, the company's CEO and president as well as one of its founders, was at lunch at the close of 1998 with Chairman, former CEO, and fellow-founder Bernie Marcus, when he started doing the math in his head. The two men had always visited every new store in the nation. Blank said, "Do you realize we'll open stores this year that we'll never see? There's no way we'll see every single store anymore."

It's a nice problem to have. And it's a far cry from the problem Wall Street thought Home Depot had only a couple of years ago. Back then the stock hit a lull after sizzling for more than a decade—largely because of a perception that Home Depot just couldn't grow much bigger.

Surprise! Sales were a record $30.2 billion for the fiscal year ended January 1998, 25.1% ahead of the previous year. And yet, Home Depot is at "one of the most critical times in our history," says Blank. The question isn't how many stores can Home Depot build before we can all walk to one, but rather how Blank will confront the challenges of rapid growth. For instance:

● Can Home Depot maintain its high customer-service standards while absorbing about 150,000 new employees—the company calls them "associates"—into its unique culture over the next couple of years?

• Can the company penetrate and dominate new markets, like the $216 billion professional maintenance industry, while keeping core customers from growing bored with existing stores?

• Can Blank—and this may be his most critical test—cultivate future leaders who are as fervent about the company's purpose as its founders?

Blank has already taken steps to address each challenge, and he says he's confident. But he's a numbers guy at heart, so he's also a realist. "The next ten years for the company are going to be much more complicated than the last ten years," he confesses. "The reality is, if Bernie has succeeded, then I'll be—and I don't mean this at all disrespectfully—a better CEO than he was; and if I end up succeeding, the next CEO will be better than me."

So far, results are solid, surprisingly so to some investors. When we last visited Home Depot, in March 1996, Wall Street wasn't buying. The company's stock had been—and these were our words—"flat as a two-by-four," up only 0.7% over three years. Now Wall Street is one happy shopper. What changed? Just this: the strongest housing market ever and (in no small part on account of the Depot folks themselves) a wave of empowered boomers who feel more comfortable with a hammer than they have any right to be.

Between March 1996 and November 1998, Home Depot's stock increased 177%, compared with 65.3% for the S&P 500. By the following summer the stock was closing in around 64. "They're a great lesson in how to build a successful company," says analyst Skip Helm of Chicago's William Blair & Co. "They had the best mousetrap, and the marketplace was huge."

THE CUSTOMER WANTS EVERYTHING

Home Depot also helped create the marketplace. Its emphasis on service and education eliminated much of the mystery surrounding things like drains, decks, and caulking. So much so that a lot of us go to the Depot these days the way we go to the grocery store—not because we're hungry but just because, well, you always need something, right? One of my co-workers says she walked into a Depot one day with no intention of buying anything but walked out with a bag of rocks. "Hey, they were on sale," she says. "And they came in three colors!"

With people like this walking around, you can believe that between 1990 and 1998, annual average household spending in Home Depot stores jumped 141%, from $191 to $462. That dropped the number of households needed to support a single store like, well, a bag of rocks—from 154,000 to 93,000 in the same period. Those changes fuel the meteoric growth in the number of Depot stores. Simply put, with more people spending more, you need more places for them to go. By the end of 1998 the typical Depot was generating $43 million in annual sales, up from $29 million in 1990.

"We're in the business of making people's dreams come true," Blank says. "Housing is still the biggest investment most Americans have, and rates of homeownership [65%] are as high as they've ever been. Home's where people live and raise their families. I don't see any limits to the number of stores we can build. I feel confident, with the dollars on the table, that we can continue to grow the core business." Blank and Marcus go so far as to argue that even a turn in the economic weather wouldn't dampen their growth much: When people aren't buying new houses, the thinking goes, they fix up their old ones instead.

Home Depot succeeded where others faltered by being the first on the block (now almost every block) to recognize just what the core customer wanted: everything. They built radical "big box" stores (the typical new store is 108,000 square feet) and loaded them with every imaginable home product, under one humongous roof. Nothing fancy, just rows and rows of building materials and good old-fashioned toolbox stuff. Then they hired carpenters, plumbers, contractors, and other industry professionals to stroll the aisles in bright-orange aprons with their names handwritten on the front, and drilled them in the founders' mantra: This is a service business, not a discount hardware store. Help customers solve their problems, don't just sell them a wrench. "It's not what we [Marcus and Blank] do, it's what happens in the stores," says Marcus. "He who gives the best service wins."

As any homeowner knows, the best time to conduct a major maintenance or renovation is before you're forced to, say, by an upstairs shower leaking into the living room. Similarly, Blank is moving his own way just as the foundation seems as if it has never been more sound. What do you do when you feel you're outgrowing your home? Build an addition, naturally. So Blank expanded Home Depot's traditional do-it-yourself market to include major home renovation projects ($40 billion annually) and to appeal to housing professionals, such as managers of major apartment and condominium complexes and hotel chains, who together spend about $216 billion every year. To penetrate these segments, Home Depot is stretching the company in several intriguing new directions, each offering new opportunities as well as real risks. "It seems Arthur's intent on making his own mark," says Helm, the analyst. "As much credit as we give him for being a big part of the company's success, Bernie still gets most of the credit. Now [Arthur's] in position to make his own mark, and the pace of activity and innovation has accelerated."

THE CUSTOMER ENJOYS ONE-STOP RENOVATING

A warning: Home Depot's glitzy Expo Design Centers are not for the weak of credit card. The 88,000-square-foot store in Davie, Fla., contains, for example, 20 complete kitchens fitted with fancy appliances and accented with exotic tiles, lighting, and stone floors; dozens of finished baths with whirlpools and brass faucets; a ceiling crowded with gleaming chandeliers; a room decorated with antiques (yes, they're for sale); a $5,000 Sub-Zero refrigerator, a $7,500 Dacor range, $8,000 gas grills by Wolf and Viking, and an $8,500 Aquatic whirlpool bath. "Where Home Depot stops, we start," says Bryant Scott, president of the Expo division. Actually, Expo and Home Depot share about 10% of the same inventory, but that's it. Expo contains dozens of unusual tiles, hundreds of bathroom and door fixtures, scores of patterns and materials for window treatments, floors, and carpets. You can even get your face done in tiles on your bathroom floor."

Just as the "big box" concept was radical for its day, Expo is breaking new ground. It's a one-stop-shopping venue for major renovations, which usually require homeowners to find trustworthy contractors and designers, then make separate trips to buy tiles, plumbing materials, drapes, appliances, and the like. You can get all that at Expo. Additionally, industry-certified designers and project managers oversee the entire project from beginning to end. Goodbye, general contractor.

In seven years of trial and mostly error, Home Depot toyed with the size of the new stores and the mix of products and services, integrating customer suggestions along the way. At the end of 1997 Blank gave Expo the go-ahead. The company will build as many as 400 of the centers by 2005. Blank predicts Expo will produce "the same [growth] phenomenon" that marked Depot's rise—only faster.

In early 1998 he shook up Home Depot's management structure by creating an additional layer of executives—four group presidents—between the six division heads and the CEO. Then he bucked tradition by filling two of the powerful new posts with outsiders: direct-marketing expert Jeff Cohen, 40, and retail veteran David Suliteanu, 44, a former Macy executive. Feathers were ruffled; egos were bruised. "There was some tension," says Scott, the Expo president, a Depot veteran who now reports to Suliteanu rather than Blank. "In truth, there isn't much difference. David's great to work with, and Bernie's and Arthur's doors are still open."

Blank defused much of the potential damage by emphasizing the new guys' unique skills, then wisely putting them in charge of portions of the business outside the company's core. "We acquired certain expertise we didn't have in the company," he says. "And what I've told people is that their presence frees [group presidents] Larry [Mercer, who heads operations] and Bill [Hamlin, merchandising head] to focus on the mother ship, the core business. We can't take our eye off the ball. If we do, someone could run away with it."

Cohen is overseeing projects that could significantly improve the way Home Depot serves customers. The company now owns Maintenance Warehouse/America, the nation's top direct-mail marketer of maintenance and repair products to lodging and multifamily-lodging managers. The $130 million company distinguished itself by promising next-day delivery. "There are tremendous cost efficiencies in phone ordering," says Cohen. The real jewel here may be the company's telephone capabilities. Home Depot also now own National Blinds, a $70 million catalog company specializing in window coverings and wallpaper. Again, its true value is its phone magic. Because it sells all its products by telephone, operators follow a strict script designed to ensure that the customer gets the right product in the right size and the right color. Cohen is also trying to determine how best to introduce Internet sales to the company, which has so far resisted the tempting lure of the World Wide Web. "Customers are buying in a whole variety of ways, and it's pushing us," admits Blank. "We need to find ways to be there when the customer's looking for us, even in the middle of the night. We're not there yet."

MORE PRODUCTS FOR EVERYONE

None of these new initiatives will create an economic windfall anytime soon. It costs about $20 million to build an Expo, $5 million more than a Home Depot. Quick calculations tell you the company could spend as much as $17 billion in upcoming years building new stores alone. Moreover, Expo's prospects are no bubble bath. The Depot folks like to tell you their business is largely immune to economic viruses—"Rain or shine, we've been able to do well," says Marcus—but with its reliance on consumers with $30,000 to $50,000 to spend on a project, Expo is particularly vulnerable. A significant and extended downturn in the economy, and we'll be putting off those new kitchens and baths, at least for a while. All the more reason why Blank, despite his enthusiasm for Expo and other projects, recognizes that Depot's regular customers are its foundation. "The DIYer is the essence of our business," says Blank. "They're 70% of our business, and our success has been being able to bring them through the continuum of being a light shopper to a serious one.'"

Here's where Pat Farrah comes in. He's the last of the original founders. Heck, he really invented the "big box" concept before he left Home Depot in 1985 and returned to California to be near his children and "retire," having already made a fortune. Now, his kids grown up, he's back with a vengeance as a senior vice president and the company's chief merchandiser. "I've had my retirement, and I'm tanned," he said during a visit to an Atlanta store. "Now I'll just drop dead in the aisles." In 1979, Home Depot carried about 12,000 different products. That number rose to over 45,000, and Farrah can probably tell you about every one of them.

With its extensive store network and huge traffic volume, Home Depot is now an alluring distribution network for companies whose products are not typically available at retail. Some are small items, like the Zep line of commercial cleaning and pesticide products once available only through wholesalers. "We're providing companies with incremental income by getting their products to consumers they never reached," Farrah says. Other products are created with well-known vendors, "branded," and sold only at the Depot. An example: a line of Scotts lawn mowers produced by Deere, known for its riding mowers and heavy agricultural and construction equipment.

Farrah's pride and joy is a line of professional power tools called Rigid, which are sold only at Home Depot stores. In an Atlanta store, the products are prominently displayed up front. The line is produced at a plant in Paris, Tenn., that was set for extinction last year when Sears, for which it produced the company's popular Craftsman line, decided to build the tools overseas instead. More than 400 jobs were going to be lost—until Farrah, Marcus, and Blank got wind of it. For 15 years, Marcus had tried to do a deal with the plant to produce professional-quality tools, but the facility's contract with Sears forbade its working with a competitor. So when Sears bolted, Depot rode in, cut the deal, and kept the plant open.

"BERNIEANDARTHUR"

For Blank it was critical that Home Depot not lose its stride during the CEO transition, because the move was viewed with some trepidation in many circles—largely because Arthur Blank, quite simply, just wasn't Bernie Marcus. Even now, Compare the CEOs is a popular game around the water coolers at the Depot.

Marcus remains to many the company's poster boy. He's gregarious, charismatic, and outgoing—a favorite uncle. He's called Mr. Outside, mostly for the legendary road shows he still conducts when he visits stores and meets with managers. Blank is Mr. Inside, the financial guy who amazes board members at meetings by citing sales figures from various stores with nary a note in front of him. He's an engaging conversationalist with a genuine smile and hearty laugh. No one, though, calls Blank gregarious. He speaks softly at times, but it doesn't hide his passion for the things that engage him. "He's a pretty complicated guy," says one former senior-level Home Depot employee. "That can make some people uncomfortable."

Marcus, in contrast, is the Pied Piper. He's regularly recognized by happy shareholders as he visits stores across the U.S. "Hey, I've got your stock!" a woman yelled recently as she spotted Marcus in a mall, looking as if she'd seen an apparition. Another ex-Depot manager offers a succinct description of each man's impact on the company's culture: "Bernie's the carrot," he says. "Arthur's the stick."

Perhaps so. But Blank just may turn out to be the very guy Home Depot needs right now—someone who can see the trees (the new initiatives under way or being tested) and the forest (overall store growth) without losing sight of either.

Blank considers having Marcus remain active a plus. In fact, they've worked together for so long that it's hard to distinguish where the CEO ends and the chairman begins. (Talk to enough folks in the company, and you begin to think the place is run by someone named Bernieandarthur.) Blank is clearly in charge, with classic CEO duties. He manages daily operations and maps the company's strategic vision. Marcus does what he does best—sell. Blank still regularly seeks Marcus' counsel, usually during their monthly dinners alone in one of their offices. Blank brings a list of questions and concerns, and says he shares all of the details regarding the company's operations. "I never make that list based on the fact that I'm CEO and therefore he's not entitled to know things," says Blank. The discussions aren't all centered on business, though. The two men rarely depart without sparring over the treacherous minefield of politics. Marcus, the son of Russian immigrants from Newark, N.J., is a Republican; Blank, whose working-class parents ran a pharmacy in Queens, N.Y., is a Democrat. They're both softies when it comes to underprivileged kids, the environment, health care, the arts, and the mentally disabled, and each has established a charitable foundation to support programs aimed at some of those areas. "We're both moderate, so we agree on social issues like gun control and abortion," says Marcus, smiling now. "As for candidates, we go our separate ways."

The challenge for Home Depot remains simple: Can Home Depot do it all? And can it continue to make Wall Street believe? Much will depend upon Blank's leadership. Home Depot empowers its employees—from group presidents to store personnel—to make decisions without clearing each one through management. Even at the risk of making a mistake. "People here ask for forgiveness more than they ask permission," says Cohen. Adds Blank: "Everyone's role here is to develop people behind them who are even better than they are for the business going forward, because our business is not going to get any easier."

CHAPTER THREE

• ● •

SMART INVESTING

QUESTIONS EVERY MUTUAL FUND SHOULD ANSWER

BY MATT SIEGEL

• ◉ •

*So you've decided to try to beat the market,
not just copy it. You've chosen the kinds of
mutual funds you want to invest in.
What else do you need to know?*

• ◉ •

Mutual funds play a prominent role in the financial planning strategies of millions of investors. The allure of expert management and a chance to beat the market attracted $477 billion in mutual fund investments in 1998, according to the Investment Company Institute in Washington, D.C. But achieving solid returns requires more wisdom than you're likely to extract from the Sunday business page. Once you've found several mutual funds that interest you, ask questions. Here's what else you need to know:

1. What are the fund's expenses?

The key number to look for is the expense ratio (found in the prospectus), which gives you the year's management expenses plus the so-called 12b-1 (or marketing) fee as a fraction of fund assets. Different types of funds will have higher or lower ratios, but the point is to make sure that your fund is at or below the average for its category. (For a large-cap U.S. fund, the average is 1.2%; for a small-cap, it's 1.4%.) The catch: Loads—fees paid to brokers when you enter or exit a fund—are not included in the expense ratio, and they can be big. So ask yourself one question: Is your broker's advice worth the load? If not, go with a no-load fund.

2. What is the turnover rate?

That's purchases or sales for the year (whichever is less), divided by assets. You want a low turnover, in part because heavy sales tend to generate taxable capital gains, which will drag down returns significantly. True, IRA and 401(k) investors don't have to worry about taxes. But everyone gets hit by turnover-related trading costs. Again, the type of mutual fund makes a difference. In 1998, U.S. large-cap growth funds averaged a 97% turnover rate, and large-cap value funds a 65% one.

3. What is the investment style?
Somewhere in its prospectus, its Statement of Additional Information (which you should ask for), or its ads, the fund should clearly state its investment philosophy. What size companies does it invest in? Does it bet on sectors, or just select companies based on their numbers? But don't take the fund's word for it. Morningstar and Value Line analyze fund holdings in order to classify funds by style. If your mutual fund has careened from one label to another over the years, demand an explanation.

4. Who manages the fund (and how long has he or she been doing it)?
You want a manager who has been following the fund's investment style for a long time. If the manager is new to this particular fund, you can scrutinize his or her record with a prior fund (and ignore this fund's past performance). But remember, the performance of many funds may look great during a record-breaking stock market, so trace the manager's involvement with a fund as far back as possible. Also, avoid someone who is managing a slew of other portfolios. (Ask the fund, or Morningstar can sell you a list.)

5. What is the fund's policy toward holding cash?
Funds rarely commit to a cash policy, but you can get a general sense by looking at data on prior years' cash holdings. If a fund has been keeping over 10% in cash for more than a few months, ask why (unless you don't mind paying equity-sized management fees for a bunch of T-bills).

6. What are the returns?
Investors nearly always fixate too much on returns. If you must have a number, go way back—five years, or even longer if possible. A good fund should consistently avoid the bottom of the

rankings, even if it never blows the doors off. Of course, returns are useless unless they're adjusted for style and risk. That means comparing your fund with an appropriate index, not necessarily with the S&P. (Your fund will suggest one it considers appropriate.) You can also look at risk-adjusted rankings, such as Morningstar's "star" ratings.

Maybe you should find out, too, how your domestic funds performed in the most recent lackluster markets, such as July–September 1998.

7. What is the fund's standard deviation?
This statistical measure of risk, which has become a very popular yardstick lately, is an indicator of a fund's volatility. Standard deviation tells you how much a fund's short-term results vary from its long-term average; the higher the standard deviation, the more the fund's results jump around. The beauty of standard deviation is that it's an absolute number that allows for volatility comparisons among funds and across asset classes. It can tell you, for example, that a corporate bond fund with a standard deviation of 10.8 is more volatile than a high-yield bond fund with a standard deviation of 4.9 and less volatile than a global stock fund with a standard deviation of 20.7. Knowing that, you can make rational decisions about how much risk you're willing to accept for the returns you're trying to get.

OWNING MORE FUNDS WON'T MAKE YOU MERRIER

BY MARIA ATANASOV

● ● ●

Having six to ten funds gives you
good diversification. Having more
just gives you a headache.

● ● ●

One of the dumbest things that smart people do with mutual funds is buying too many of them. It's easy to see how it happens. You put your annual IRA contribution, say, into the fund that currently has the strongest record and rosiest outlook. Then next year, when you're ready to save again, you invest in the fund with the most impressive history and most promising forecast. Before you know it, you've got a large portfolio of funds that have no logical connection except that they were all once top performers. You become less an investor in mutual funds than a collector.

A recent study by Boston-based Kobren Insight Group suggests that this syndrome is even more common than many fund advisers suspected. Among investors who had more than $500,000 in fund investments (the size of the median FORTUNE subscriber's investment portfolio), some 78% had at least ten funds and a gregarious 45% had more than 15.

HOW MANY TO MINIMIZE RISK?

●

That's probably too many. The only reason to own multiple funds is to lower your portfolio's risk by holding funds that react differently to the same market stimulus. But according to Catherine Voss Sanders, publisher of *Morningstar Investor*, you can get most of the risk-reducing benefit of diversification with just four funds, each owning a markedly different class of securities, such as large- and small-cap domestic stocks, foreign stocks, and fixed income. Slicing these classes even finer—say, by splitting your domestic stock funds into growth and value groups—diminishes benefits. Finally, says Voss Sanders, "after ten to 12 funds, you get only a marginal reduction of volatility."

The reason: once you get beyond the basic asset classes, fund holdings start to overlap. Says Voss Sanders: "You're not diversified just because you have a small-company fund and an aggressive-growth fund." Such funds would probably own many similar stocks, and naturally their performances would tend to be highly correlated. You can check your funds' correlation—or R2—with major indexes such as the S&P 500 in the Quicktake reports on Morningstar's Web page, www.morningstar.net. (Look in the report's modern portfolio theory section.) If any of your funds have correlations greater than 85% with a single index, you are getting little diversification benefit from owning more than one of them.

SHOULD YOU SELL SOME?

So should you just sell your duplicative funds and rearrange your funds into a more theoretically pure portfolio? Not without looking carefully. If you've been accumulating shares of many funds for a while already, odds are you have a goodly chunk of unrealized gains in your portfolio. Cashing in your winners to build a more reasonably diversified portfolio would have a definite cost—namely, taxes on the gains you realize in the process. (Obviously, this is not a problem for funds you hold in a 401(k) or other tax-sheltered investment.) Still, says financial planner Bob Cohen of Framingham, Mass., the benefits of pursuing a more streamlined investment strategy can frequently offset the tax price. "I tell investors, 'Let's pretend you don't own any funds. If you were starting from scratch, what would be in your first portfolio?'" If the ideal portfolio is enough of an improvement over the current mishmash, it may be worth the taxes.

And as for the next time you're tempted to salt away some new savings, save yourself some trouble. Add the money to funds you already own.

INVESTING ADVICE FOR WOMEN

BY AMY KOVER

● ● ●

There's a lot of investing advice out there
that's targeted at women. Some of it is
silly and some worthwhile.

● ● ●

"Close your eyes. Take a moment to remember when you were a child," the psychologist intones. "What was your first experience with money? Was it a good experience?"

A group meditation class? A therapy session? No, it's the kick-off of an investment seminar that Michelle Smith and her mother, Corinne, financial planners at Paine Webber, organized for about 40 women early in 1999.

While the Smiths' approach may be unusual, they are far from alone in targeting investment advice specifically to a female audience. In the past seven years the number of books, seminars, investing programs, television shows, and magazines designed to help women "get smart" about money (as it's frequently put) has exploded. More than 20 investing books included the word "woman" or "women" in their titles this past year or so, as opposed to just four in 1992. *Worth* magazine put out a women's investing supplement called *Equity*. (Sample story line: "The history of women is told through the history of handbags.") Says Deena Katz, president of Evensky Brown & Katz, a financial-planning firm in Coral Gables, Fla.: "Everyone is pandering to the women's market these days."

This is really no surprise. Whether it's to sell jeans to black teens or cruises to homosexuals, segmented marketing is everywhere. And now that women work and earn more than ever before, the financial industry naturally wants to tap into those dollars. Moreover, several trends having to do with women started to coalesce around 1992—Supreme Court Justice Clarence Thomas' confirmation hearings, the Year of the Woman that saw an unprecedented six women elected to the U.S. Senate, a groundbreaking survey by Oppenheimer Funds showing that women felt alienated by financial advisers. "When you have an investing seminar just for women, it allows their concerns to be the focus," says Louis "P.J." Patierno, a financial planner in Colorado.

The problem is that with so much "pandering"—or at least segmented marketing—going on, women's financial materials can range from worthwhile to offensive. As Melissa Moss, who heads up the Women's Consumer Network, points out, "Women don't want to be talked down to, nor do they want to feel ghettoized." But even if the material is superb, do women need a special approach? "There's nothing in men's genes that makes them better at investing than women," jokes Alexandra Armstrong, a well-known Washington, D.C., financial planner. Nor is there any reason women as well as men can't pick up a basic investment primer. Money is supposed to be gender-neutral, after all. Microsoft will perform just as well in a woman's portfolio as in a man's.

WOMEN *ARE* DIFFERENT FROM MEN!

But there are demographic differences between men and women that can affect financial decisions. For one thing, women probably need to be saving more money. They live an average of about six years longer than men. At the same time, because of their work history—women tend to hold service-sector jobs, work for small companies, or drop in and out of the labor force, all situations that make it difficult to accumulate much of a retirement nest egg—relatively few qualify for pensions, and those who do receive only half as much as men, on average. In the end women wind up living longer, but with less money to live on.

Despite their need for higher savings, a fear of risk often prevents women from investing as aggressively as they should. Only 5% of female decision-makers surveyed by the Investment Company Institute in 1995 were willing to take substantial risk for the prospect of substantial returns, compared with 11% of the men. Along the same lines, a study conducted from 1996 to 1998 by Long Island University's National Center for Women and Retirement Research showed that among households with income of at least $30,000, 87% of women owned CDs in their retirement plans, vs. just 52% of men. Safe but low-growth products like CDs can barely beat inflation, let alone earn a decent return over time. And Oppenheimer has found that "advisers assumed that women were more conservative and would sell them government bonds," says CEO Bridget Macaskill. "What they really should have been doing was encouraging women to be more aggressive."

Now throw in one more twist: Women's longer life spans, added to the rising divorce rate, mean that nine out of ten women will wind up in charge of their family's finances, generally because there's no man around. Often they are not well equipped to do this: Only 12% of the women who have partners have sole responsibility for their family's investments, according to the Oppenheimer survey. The result is a client base with money and no idea how to invest it.

GIMMICKS, PSYCHOBABBLE, SALE PITCHES

———————————————●———————————————

With statistics like these floating around, special financial planning for women is a good idea—if it's done right. What are some of the programs doing wrong? For one thing, they rely on cheesy gimmicks. Helen Rothlein, a financial adviser at Prudential Securities, links her program to girl stuff, holding seminars at Saks Fifth Avenue or Sotheby's. Similarly, Geri Eisenman Zolna, an adviser at American Express, likes to schedule female client-appreciation nights at restaurants. "If I were to market to men, it might be at Madison Square Garden," she says. For a $2,000 minimum investment, American Express also proffers useless freebies such as a ProcrastiMeter—a little cardboard slide rule–type scale that allegedly measures your readiness for retirement.

And women's financial materials often suffer from an overload of psychobabble. Many seminars hand out quizzes reminiscent of the "Are you a true romantic?" tests in *Cosmopolitan*. Among the true-or-false questions posed by the Smiths of Paine Webber: "If I get good at money, it'll be harder to find someone to love me." Then there are the breathless books. In *Prince Charming Isn't Coming*, author Barbara Stanny writes that her book "is about waking up, reclaiming our power, remembering we can fly." (As the daughter

A GUIDE TO THE GUIDES

● ● ●

From brokerage firms to book publishers, companies of all sorts want to win over women with financial advice "for her." Some understand what women need—vital information delivered in a straightforward fashion. Others are clueless, shoveling out more dopey marketing gimmicks than solid data. Here's how a few stack up:

CLUED IN

Citibank In a brochure titled *Money Matters for Women*, financial planner Ann Diamond explains how to unload debt and start saving.

Merrill Lynch Both novices and experts can find help here. *You and Your Money* spells out financial definitions. *A Woman's Guide to Wealth and Management* has advice for entrepreneurs.

Oppenheimer Funds The first big fund company to focus on women, it has the most comprehensive assortment of products. Most notable: *A Woman's Guide to Investing*, a no-nonsense book that also works for men.

Women's Institute for a Secure Retirement (WISER) This nonprofit translates legal mumbo-jumbo regarding Social Security, IRAs, and much more.

of the "R" in H&R Block, Stanny never worried about money until a financial disaster hit.)

Another offensive approach: vendors that push their own products. Salomon Smith Barney ran a seminar for women about breast cancer that featured companies specializing in medical technology for women—ones that Salomon just happened to follow. "We monitored individual trading in some of these stocks, and there was a huge jump right after the luncheon," says Mindy Ross, head of targeted marketing at Salomon.

It Takes Money, Honey Don't judge this book by its cover. Author Georgette Mosbacher provides a wealth of resources. Sample: how to get into mutual funds cheap.

CLUELESS

American Express Invest $2,000, and Amex will throw in a ProcrastiMeter that supposedly measures how much to save for retirement. Gee, thanks.

Putnam Funds Rather than enlisting a financial pro, Putnam went for image: Gail Buckner, ex–CNBC talking head, is its Women and Investing spokesperson.

Salomon Smith Barney Its new *Women in Transition* brochure has lots of slick advertisements and glib sound bites. Too bad it comes up short on real information.

A Girl Needs Cash: Banish the White Knight Myth and Take Charge of Your Financial Life Authors Joan Perry and Dolores Barclay are as euphemistic about money as some people are about sex. Their term for an investment portfolio? "Money machine."

Our Money, Ourselves Who needs to know what a stock is, anyway? Authors C. Diane Ealy and Kay Lesh prefer to devote a chapter to the "spiritual nature" of money.

Luckily, not every program is full of girlie gimmicks and sales pitches. Oppenheimer has put together several solid women-oriented programs since its 1992 report. Its book *A Woman's Guide to Investing* lays out the demographic differences between men and women and then provides clear advice—applicable to both genders—on such topics as managing a household budget and calculating total return. "Our goal isn't to speak to women differently, but to speak to them more loudly," says Cathleen Stahl, head of women's programs at Oppenheimer.

GETTING STARTED

———————————●———————————

Some books, like *Suddenly Single*, by Kerry Hannon and *Ernst & Young's Financial Planning for Women*, break down advice according to different life events—marriage, childbirth, divorce. "Life stages seem like a logical, noncondescending way to present this information," says financial planner Armstrong. *It Takes Money, Honey*, by Georgette Mosbacher (ex-wife of former Commerce Secretary Robert Mosbacher), although wrapped in a deceptively tarty cover, is a good guide to other materials, telling readers everything from how to reach the American Academy of Matrimonial Lawyers to the cheapest way to get into a mutual fund.

Another solid resource guide: *The Women's Consumer Network*. Founded by Moss, a longtime Washington public policy wonk, the network uncovers good financial deals—say, banks that offer the lowest mortgage rates—and tries to negotiate benefits like lower mutual fund fees for its members.

Of course, women are perfectly capable of learning to invest without using girls-only material. For instance, women in investment clubs usually get started the same way as their male counterparts—by following the investment basics recommended by the National Association of Investors Corp. and boning up on articles in the *Wall Street Journal*, FORTUNE, and other business publications. These women's clubs enjoyed an average return of 17.9% in 1997, beating the returns of both mixed and men-only clubs (17.3% and 15.6%, respectively). And what do these women think of female-oriented advice? "I attended a women's seminar run by a male broker once," says Mary Reynolds, an accountant whose North Carolina club racked up an average 22% annual gain over the past six years. "He handled it in a way that made these women completely dependent on him. He had some of these little old ladies wrapped around his finger."

Necessary or not, cheesy or classy, investing advice geared to women is probably only a temporary phenomenon. Women in their 20s and 30s are already demonstrating much more financial independence than their mothers. For one thing, they're working more—twice as many women ages 20 to 34 are in the work force now as in 1970. And with fewer companies offering defined-benefit pension plans, most Gen X women receive 401(k) sign-up forms within their first year of employment. That means they have to make investment decisions almost from the moment they begin earning money. There's lots of anecdotal evidence as well. "My first client was a woman who lived on Lake Shore Drive in Chicago and didn't know how to write a check to pay the assessment on her condo," says planner Katz. "Thank goodness I don't ever see that anymore."

All of that is fine with women in the investing business. "If there is one thing I would love," says Oppenheimer CEO Macaskill, "it's for our program to self-destruct." Until then, the books and seminars will keep coming, and probably should. But—please—lose the pink wrappings and swoony therapists.

WHY SMART INVESTORS ASPIRE TO BE AVERAGE

BY SHELLY BRANCH

●—●—●

They know there are just a few points to remember and that they are not hard to understand.

●—●—●

A few years back Charley Ellis, founder of the financial consulting firm Greenwich Associates, asked two doctors what he might do to maximize his life span: "They huddled together, these two geniuses, and finally said, 'Well, you don't smoke and you don't drink, so here it is: Buckle up when riding in a car, and maybe take an aspirin every two days.'"

Ellis was stunned by the simple advice, but he shouldn't have been. This investing *penseur*—he's published nine financial classics and has taught at Harvard and Yale—has long believed that advice for mutual fund investors can be similarly boiled down. "Investing is dazzling in its complexity," says the courtly Ellis, "but the main messages are few and easy to understand."

Save regularly, he says. Write down and review your goals. Don't mistake brokers for your friends. But above all—counterintuitive as it may be in this CNBC-addled age—don't try to be above average.

This may sound odd coming from a man whose job is to help the world's biggest institutions set investment policy and select money managers (in other words, to make some of the same decisions that mutual fund investors do). But Ellis has his reasons. He points out that funds returned, on average, 15% annually from 1982 to 1997. That's worse than the S&P 500, as everyone knows, which returned over 19%. But the average mutual fund investor realized just 10%. How could shareholders do even worse than their funds? Habitually bad timing. People get excited by a hot market and buy at the top; then they despair when things turn cold, and sell at the bottom.

Ellis frets that individuals have been lulled into a kind of data trance. They're hooked on CNBC, Morningstar, TheStreet.com, and e-trading, and they confuse information about the immediate past with insight into the future. Says Ellis: "As investors, we run the risk of getting so connected to the specifics, the entertainment, and the fast nature of the details that we miss the main events."

A particularly misleading detail, says Ellis, is a fund's track record. Three, five, or even ten years of performance is not long enough to tell you whether the manager is brilliant or just lucky. Says Ellis: "Do I believe that John Neff, who ran Vanguard's Windsor fund, is a superior manager? Yes. But that's not based on his last five years there, but rather on his record of 31 years, in very difficult environments." As for average people's ability to pick future fund winners? "They don't have a chance in the world," he says.

PAY ATTENTION TO
THE "POWERFUL PLODDERS"

That observation frames Ellis' argument for index funds, which seek to mirror the returns of indexes such as the S&P 500. The majority of individual investors would do well, he contends, simply to put their money into those "powerful plodders," as he calls them. Ellis champions them not just because they are the ultimate "average" performers (remember, left to his own wiles, the typical fund investor falls way short of "average") but also because they are a bargain. Their annual expenses average about a fourth of the typical actively managed stock fund's 1.6%. That works out to a 1.2% annual head start in net performance. Also, because indexes replicate the market, they represent the summary of all investors' collected wisdom at any moment. "So the best capability in the world is yours for as little as 20 basis points," he says.

Ironically, the best way to beat the averages is to be willing to settle for average. If you can't see yourself settling, remember that one of Ellis' heroes, who is something of a successful money manager himself, has also been known to preach the merits of indexing for many investors. His name is Warren Buffett.

ONLINE INVESTING ISN'T JUST FOR GEEKS

BY KATRINA BROOKER

● ● ●

Millions of Americans are logging on to
the Net to research stocks, get great prices
on trades, and control their finances.

● ● ●

At the 1998 PC Expo trade conference in New York City,
Launny Steffens, vice chairman of Merrill Lynch, the world's
largest full-service brokerage, denounced online trading as a form
of gambling. "The do-it-yourself model of investing, centered on
Internet trading, should be regarded as a serious threat to
Americans' financial lives," he railed. Steffens can rant all he wants.
But four million investors (and counting) weren't listening—they
were too busy logging on to their online accounts.

Gone are the days when trading online was the domain of
techno-geeks. The hero of one online firm's television commercial
is a tow-truck driver, and that's no stretch. Now you're as likely
to find a plumber scouring the Web for stock tips as a computer
programmer. How are the newcomers faring? To find out, we
tagged along with a small crew: a cop, a housewife, and the family of an old-style professional broker. Truth be told, none seem
to miss the help of a traditional broker.

Just a few years ago people like this had not even heard of
online investing. There were only a few thousand investors in
cyberspace then, and just three online brokerages. "Even a year
and a half ago, people in our industry didn't think the Web could
compete," says Dan Leemon, chief strategist at Charles Schwab.
Now online brokers can hardly keep up with the crush of
investors logging on. By some estimates, 21 million people will
have online accounts by 2003. E*Trade, the second-largest online
broker, had over 550,000 accounts by the summer of 1999, up
from 20,000 in 1995, while Charles Schwab customers had 2.8
million online accounts, up from 336,000 four years before. They
now account for the majority of Schwab's total trading business.

By the close of 1998, Online brokers were handling some 253,000 trades a day—approximately 10% of all U.S. trading.

CHEAP AND EASY

What's got so many investors scurrying online? For starters, it's a lot easier now. "Trading online used to be a real hassle," says Julio Gomez, who runs Gomez Advisors, a research firm in Concord, Mass., that tracks online brokerages. In the old days you needed special software, an expensive computer, and lots of patience. Now it costs just a few hundred dollars for a computer with a high-speed modem that gets you online in a hurry.

What's more, investing online is cheap. There are now some 100 online brokers, and fierce competition has sparked a price war. From 1996 to the end of 1998, commissions for Web trades dropped 70%, from an average of $52.89 a trade to $15.75. (By way of contrast, full-service firms were charging between $300 and $500 a trade.) One deep-discount online broker, Web Street Securities, even offers Nasdaq trades free.

GOOD SERVICE TOO

The scramble also has forced the online brokers to clean up their act. Customers will not accept lousy service from anyone. They expect the firms with which they do business to give them access to, well, just about everything: research, financial news, charts of stock prices, technical graphs, even shares in IPOs. Discover Direct and DLJDirect hand over to retail customers what was once proprietary research that their parent companies, Morgan Stanley Dean Witter and Donaldson Lufkin & Jenrette, respectively, reserved for big institutional customers. Even Suretrade, a deep discounter, offers stock charts and consensus earnings estimates. On E*Trade's Website, investors can play a stock-picking game designed to hone their investing skills. These days, online investors have access to as much information about the market as any professional broker.

ONLINE INVESTOR PROFILES

THE FAMILY

In 1998, Taylor Davis, then 4 years old, stunned her parents at the dinner table by announcing, "I want to buy Kool-Aid stock." This was no precocious preschooler simply mimicking grown-up talk. Her mouth ringed orange with Kool-Aid, Taylor knew whereof she spoke: Every night for the past year and a half, she has clambered onto her father Duane's lap as he flips on the computer to review the Ameritrade online investing account he has set up in her name. In the Davis family, thanks to the Internet and $8 online trades, everybody is an investor.

Duane, an honest-to-God, real-world broker for First Union in Winston-Salem, N.C., used to be the only one in the family who cared about the stock market. His wife, Carol, was too busy getting her law degree and raising their two children. To the kids, the stock market was some far-off place where Dad went to work. But last year Duane decided that setting up an online account would be an affordable way to teach his family about the market. The plan worked. "When I was growing up, nobody talked about the market around the dinner table," says Duane Davis. "Now my kids are sitting there giving me stock tips."

At first, the Davis kids viewed online investing as just another computer game. Duane would sit them up on his lap and point to the screen as he clicked in orders to buy stock in their favorite haunts, McDonald's and Gymboree. After Duane took his 3-year-old son, Duane II, out to buy Nike sneakers, he then sat him at the computer and bought $200 of Nike stock for his account. They log on together every night, pulling up charts that show how the kids' portfolios have grown; each of the Davis children now has about $6,000 in online accounts. The family's goal is to invest enough money in 15 years to pay the kids' college tuition. It hasn't taken long for the kids to understand that this is no game.

Their mom, on the other hand, was wary of jumping into the market. Back when they were using real-world brokers, Carol let Duane do all the stock picking for her account. But when she helped him set up an organization for educating black investors (the

Coalition of Black Investors), she caught the bug. With a dozen buddies from her book club, she organized an investment club, Sisters Making Sense. Like Carol, none of the others in the club knew much about investing, but they were determined to learn without the help of a broker. Sisters Making Sense trades via an account on Ameritrade, the cheapest online broker the group could find.

As she started to learn, says Carol, "I fumbled around the Web a lot." Then, in August 1998, just a few months after the club was launched, Carol watched their $7,000 investment sink 10%. But Sisters Making Sense was saving for retirement, so they decided to ride out the market chaos and continued contributing $100 apiece every month to their account. Later their portfolio started to show a positive return.

Carol says she has now developed some savvy. She uses the Web to whip up stock charts and downloads research from sites like DBC.com (her favorite). In just seven months of online investing, Carol says, she learned more about the market than in ten years of living with a broker.

Still, the Davis family's main source of income is Duane's job as a full-service broker. Isn't he worried that his online hobby could steal his business? "A lot of people in my industry are afraid of online trading; I'm not one of them," he says, insisting there's room in the brokerage business for both types of services.

THE COP

Not long ago, Frank Brucato's heroes were the New York Rangers. Today, Brucato, a 29-year-old transit cop from the Bronx, has just one hero: Michael Dell. "Mikey Dell? I wish I was his son," gushes Brucato in a heavy Bronx accent, flashing Dell's price chart on his computer screen to point out how well the stock has done. These days Brucato's more likely to read stock reports on the Internet than to catch a game on TV. He even dreams of becoming a professional day trader. But Brucato's not giving up his day job just yet. Despite his enthusiasm, this cop's rookie year in the market makes a midnight patrol in New York City's subway system look like a cakewalk.

Brucato started investing online in October 1997, after the sergeant at his precinct told him how cheap it was and how much extra money he could make. Up until then, Brucato had never

WHICH ONLINE BROKER IS RIGHT FOR YOU?

● ● ●

With some 100 online brokers out there—all offering a wide range of prices and services—figuring out which to use can be overwhelming. To narrow it down, start by determining what kind of investor you are. Gomez Advisors, an online brokerage research firm, puts investors into three main categories: hyperactive traders, serious investors, and life-goal planners. On its Broker Scorecard (www.gomez.com), Gomez ranks the top 21 firms best suited to each. Here are some of its top picks for each investor type:

HYPERACTIVE TRADER

You want to trade every day—several times a day. You need cheap commissions, margin rates, fast execution, and real-time quotes.

Datek Online   www.datek.com
Research and services Account holders get free, unlimited real-time quotes, access to headline news, and stock charts.
How it rates Datek is a cheap trade. Plus, the site is easy to navigate.

Web Street Securities   www.webstreetsecurities.com
Research and services Its Trading Pit works like a real trading floor. News, charts are free; real-time quotes are not.
How it rates This is the fast-action site for trading junkies.

Suretrade   suretrade.com
Research and services News and charts are free. Customer service is accessible only via e-mail.
How it rates The ultimate in no-frills, bare-bones online trading.

even owned a mutual fund. But feeling flush with cash—he'd just inherited $30,000 from his grandparents—and intent on buying an engagement ring for his girlfriend and a house, Brucato bought a computer and opened an online brokerage account.

He followed his sergeant into two stocks, Mountain Energy and Physician Computer Network. He'd never heard of them

SERIOUS INVESTOR

You make five to ten trades a month, so price counts. But you also study the market. You need research, news, and tools to help you invest.

E*Trade www.etrade.com
Research and services Institutional research, free real-time quotes, access to IPOs, stock screening, and 16-hour-a-weekday customer service.
How it rates A serious investor's paradise. Its Website is dazzling.

DLJ Direct www.dljdirect.com
Research and services DLJ research, free real-time quotes, access to IPOs, stock screening, and great customer service.
How it rates Investors get all the frills, plus an easy-to-use Website.

Discover Brokerage Direct www.dbdirect.com
Research and services Round-the-clock customer service, institutional research, free quotes, and a customized Web page.
How it rates This discounter's Website is packed with investing tools.

LIFE-GOAL PLANNER

You're a long-term investor. You want help with financial planning and with your portfolio. Going online sounds cool, but you like a personal touch.

Fidelity www.fidelity.com
Research and services Round-the-clock customer service, Salomon Smith Barney research, investment advice from Peter Lynch.
How it rates Fidelity is not cheap, but you get what you pay for.

Charles Schwab www.schwab.com
Research and services Online seminars, access to Schwab branches, 24-hour customer service, free real-time quotes, access to IPOs.
How it rates The industry giant. You get lots of hand-holding.

before, but they were both cheap, trading under $5, and Brucato figured they had no place to go but up. At first he was cautious, investing only a few hundred dollars. But then he discovered the investor message boards. All over the Web, people claiming to be "insiders" insisted that these stocks were going to be up over 1,000% in the next six months. Messages hinted at big contract announcements just around the corner. To Brucato it sounded like easy money. "You ever see them playing three-card monte in Manhattan? Well, they get you because you think, 'How can I lose?' This is the same thing," he says.

If everything he'd read on the message boards were true, Brucato figured he could make a quick $200,000—enough to buy the ring and the house, and still have enough left over for stereo equipment and furniture. He poured in a total of $20,000. "Greed drove me," he says, shaking his head. Cheap stocks are usually cheap for a reason. Shortly after Brucato bought in, the stocks plunged in value—down to less than a penny apiece. By the end of that summer, officer Brucato had lost nearly two-thirds of his inheritance.

Looking back on his first year in the market makes Brucato shudder. "It was one big roll of the dice—and I rolled a seven," he says. Still, he was not scared off. Now he steers clear of penny stocks, message boards … and advice from his sergeant. Instead, he spends several hours a day online reading analyst reports and investor newsletters, and following price charts. He's started investing in options, hoping to piece his portfolio together again. In early October 1998, he bought options on both America Online and Donaldson Lufkin & Jenrette: He's an AOL subscriber, and he liked DLJ after reading a report about how interest-rate cuts would boost bank stocks. He sold his AOL contracts in late October for a $5,500 gain. And the value of his DLJ contracts tripled.

Despite the success, Brucato's moving warily. He eyed Dell for weeks. Even though he admired the stock—and the company's founder—he wouldn't buy until he got to know the computer industry better. What he had learned, you see, is that buying stocks is not so different from police work: "You're supposed to look around a little, not just jump into a situation without knowing what you're getting into. That's when it gets dangerous."

THE HOUSEWIFE

For most of her life, Joan Sherman had regular old dreams—you know, dreams about her children, her husband, her dogs. But toward the end of 1998, the 54-year-old homemaker from Pound Ridge, N.Y., started dreaming about the stock market. Once she dreamed about buying Western Digital; another time it was Merrill Lynch. It's not surprising that the stock market has seeped into her subconscious. After all, she spends her waking hours transfixed by it.

After 34 years as a suburban housewife, Joan Sherman has found her true calling: picking stocks. She says that thanks to her knack for timing the market, she has more than doubled her (and her husband's) retirement savings over the past two years. In the summer of 1998 she made a move that many financial pros would envy. Going mostly on gut instinct, she sold off most of her big positions (like Citicorp at $150, for a 50% return). She's now sitting on an enviable pile of cash.

Sherman once filled her days playing tennis matches at the country club and planting zucchini and string beans in her vegetable garden. Her husband, a tax accountant, had always been in charge of the finances. She'd never heard of trading volume, quarterly earnings, or a ticker symbol. But two years ago, Sherman's stockbroker persuaded her to buy Cendant. After the stock price fell, she decided she could do better by trading online on her own—without a broker. Almost immediately after she opened her account online, Sherman was hooked. The highs and the lows that you go through when you see your money disappear or grow—I love it," she beams. Now her racquet collects dust, and her garden is tangled with weeds. Sherman says she no longer has time for such trifles: "I'm playing with the big boys now."

Instead, Sherman spends hours a day at her computer, scouring for stock tips, checking charts, and reading research. Every morning she logs on to her account with Charles Schwab and checks the prices of 32 stocks on her tracking screen, a list of companies she owns or would like to own at the end of 1998. If nothing's going on there, she clicks on one of her 100-odd stock-related bookmarks. Most days she roams around investor forums like Silicon Investor and Motley Fool looking for a tip or two.

Some of her best ideas come from a fellow online investor, one James Taylor of Houston. They've never met face to face, but Sherman says Taylor is a wizard at using technical charts that track trading volume and price trends as a market forecast. He has given her such good tips that Sherman now pays him—$50 a month. At $600 a year, that's pretty close to what a broker would cost. But Sherman says she'd rather pay a fellow investor who doesn't make a commission on her trades—and who's also putting his money on the line, as it were.

Still, for all her frenetic vigilance, Sherman is a calm investor. It usually takes her days if not weeks of mulling a stock over before she buys. Part of her caution comes from weathering market upheaval; watching how quickly the market can turn has made her wary. Besides, Sherman says, it goes against her nature to overpay for anything. Years of training at Loehmann's and the Barneys warehouse sale have paid off. Buying a skirt and buying a stock, she says, are not that different: "[The market's] like shopping—when I go to Bloomingdale's, I want to get something wonderful, but I have to get it for the right price."

CHAPTER FOUR

•●•

YOUR FINANCES

THE NEW AGE OF FINANCIAL PLANNING

BY BETHANY MCLEAN

●●●

Once, financial planning meant paying
more than you could afford to a guy you
didn't like for advice you couldn't trust.
Now that guy wants to "empower" you.
Do you need this kind of love?

●●●

I'm flying to Miami to visit a man named Harold Evensky. "So what are you doing in Florida?" asks the passenger sitting next to me. When I tell him I'm going to interview this Evensky guy, I get a big surprise. "Harold Evensky!" exclaims my seatmate. "He's a legend!"

"Legend" might be an overstatement, but Evensky is a high-profile guy—the most widely recognized of that new breed of financial expert known as a financial adviser. He is constantly quoted in everything from the *Wall Street Journal* to *Modern Maturity*, and was anointed in 1998 by *SmartMoney* as the 22nd-most-powerful person in the mutual fund world. In 1996, he published a book entitled *Wealth Management*; in the fall of 1998 he testified before Congress about why mutual fund fees are too high; then he rolled out a software program called Harold Evensky's Sitting Duck Financial Planning System. "Harold is the philosophical leader of the industry," says Peter Moran, a principal at Turner Investment Partners. Adds Mark Hurley, CEO of Undiscovered Managers: "Everyone knows that Harold is a god."

In the beginning, in 1985, the god founded his own practice. After three years with Bache and a few more with Drexel Burnham Lambert, Evensky had had enough of cold-calling strangers and pushing product at them; he wanted to create a new, holistic kind of counseling, one that integrated every aspect of his clients' financial lives. Growth was slow in the early days; by 1990 Evensky and his partner, Peter Brown, had almost no assets. (That's when he persuaded Deena Katz, a Chicago-based financial planner, to join him;

they were married in 1991.) But today Evensky Brown Katz & Levitt manages some $400 million out of its gracious Coral Gables offices.

Evensky is an intense man, entrepreneurial, extremely well versed in the nitty-gritty of finance. He and his fellow pioneers are off to a pretty impressive start. They've already created an entirely new life form: a financial adviser with undivided loyalties; a warm, fuzzy, human-scale reproduction of the imposing corporate Cyclops that once ruled the business under the banners of American Express, Merrill Lynch, and Paine Webber. One question that now remains is whether this cuddly new being can carve out a secure place in the food chain. Another is, Do you need one?

In the old days, if you wanted investment advice, you turned to a full-service broker who helped himself to a fat commission, such as a load on a mutual fund. One, or even all, of the choices he offered you would be his company's products; if you wanted a no-load fund, you were on your own. Independent planners, however, combine the best of both worlds: advice and objectivity. They may specialize in an area, such as tax, estate, or retirement planning, but don't sell any proprietary products—so they're free to recommend whatever is best for you from a whole spectrum of investments. Slicker financial-planning firms may even offer one-stop shopping for managing every aspect of your finances, from tax management to estate planning, from employee benefits to long-term-care insurance.

Your planner earns her keep by charging a commission, an hourly fee, or a fee based on assets under management.

EMPATHY AND ENCOURAGEMENT

As advisers like Evensky have made it available, one-on-one custom-tailored financial planning has become one of the hottest products in financial services. Aging baby-boomers are finding themselves with more and more money—and, as investing gets increasingly complicated, with fewer ideas about what to do with it all. Indeed, a 1996 study by financial services research firm Dalbar found that 89% of respondents were likely to seek advice once their investable assets topped $100,000. Hoffman says that as of June

1998, there were roughly 30,000 financial advisers working in independent shops, more than double the number six years earlier.

Given the infancy of the business and the high percentage of free agents practicing it, it's hard to nail down the "typical" financial planner. Anyone can hang out a shingle, and the craft draws people of widely varying degrees of ethics, intelligence, and authority. It doesn't even have a standard credential yet, although the fairly rigorous CFP, or certified financial planner, seems to be the leading contender. Still, an upper tier does seem to be emerging—a sophisticated and articulate group of advisers, usually managing upwards of $100 million. If anyone represents that group, it's Harold Evensky.

Evensky's firm invests clients' money primarily in no-load or load-waived mutual funds and charges a fee—around 1%—based on assets under management. But in addition to the full array of financial services, Evensky's clients also get plenty of the softer, squishier stuff, like empathy and encouragement. Walk into the firm's offices, and it's as though you've walked into a financial health spa or a self-help group. Evensky and Katz are full-service healers, not only dispensing financial advice but also attending weddings and throwing around words like "coaching" and "quarterbacking" to describe their role. Evensky's favorite story is of an 80-year-old client—a physician who lived for his practice but was losing some $20,000 a year. Evensky determined that with Uncle Sam subsidizing the doctor's estate taxes, he could keep losing money and still leave his kids a substantial inheritance. Evensky told him to keep going: "It was the best news he had ever heard."

It should probably come as no surprise that the mechanics and vocabulary of psychotherapy have taken hold in the world of personal finance. In fact, this kind of feel-good evangelism is almost endemic to the new variety of financial planner. Ross Levin at Minneapolis' Accredited Investors waxes poetic about his duty: "My job is helping people marshal all their resources—financial, physical, and spiritual," he says. John Cammack, vice president of T. Rowe Price Associates, freely admits that working with financial planners is a great opportunity to let all his "'70s stuff" hang out. "Clarifying your goals in a capitalistic society is essential," he says. And California-based planner Cynthia Meyers—author of an article entitled "The Financial Planner as Artist"—looks forward to the day when planners will not only "quarterback" clients' relationships with their attorneys and CPAs but also serve as creative directors for their entire lives, linking them with marriage counselors, career specialists, and psychologists. "You can't have meaningful investments if they aren't tied to your life goals," she cautions. Meyers' proudest moment was encouraging a divorced 60-year-old woman to pursue a singing career. (Meyers sings too.)

Clearly, for Evensky, Meyers, and others in the business, the planning process isn't just about money. "Success is measured not by performance relative to other managers," says Evensky, "but rather by the client's success in meeting life goals." And Evensky beams sincerity even to jaded mutual fund pros. As Turner Partners' Moran says, "There's never an ulterior motive with Harold. It starts and ends with what's best for his clients."

PLANNERS DEMAND ATTENTION

O ne of the things helping the new planners realize their clients' "life goals" is that they're getting themselves taken seriously in the market. They've already begun exerting considerable influence in the world of finance. Take Charles Schwab. Schwab was the first company to provide advisers with one-stop shopping for no-load mutual funds (via Schwab's OneSource program) and with the necessary back-office technology. By the end of 1998 nearly 5,400 advisers were working through Schwab. They controlled some $130 billion, or 30%, of Schwab's $433 billion in assets, up from zero in 1987; Daniel Leemon, Schwab's chief strategy officer, says that by 2002 Schwab expects to have well over $300 billion in assets from advisers.

In response, the full-service brokerage firms have been forced to adjust by providing boomers with the customized, in-depth advice they crave. Or at least they're providing what looks like customized advice: Critics charge that it's still the same old prefab stuff, much of it pushing the same old proprietary product.

In the face of the planning movement, big brokers are also having a harder time holding on to employees. Planners working for the Merrills of the world have to split their earnings with the

AMERICAN EXPRESS: THE EMPIRE STRIKES BACK

● ● ●

American Express Financial Advisors is the crusty old patriarch of financial planning. Founded over a century ago and acquired by American Express in 1984, AEFA (as it's called internally) was at the close of 1998 managing almost $190 billion in assets and employing some 10,000 advisers, who serve more than two million clients.

AEFA, with headquarters in Minneapolis, does planning the old-fashioned way. It offers plans for between $400 and $15,000 (depending on complexity) and sells all the constituent proprietary products—Amex mutual funds, annuities, insurance. As far as AEFA is concerned, there is no competition; independent shops are still too small to worry about.

In many ways, AEFA has proved the validity of this attitude. It is enormously profitable—earnings are approaching $800 million per year—and it has posted better than 20% annual growth in earnings since 1984. AEFA says the redemption rate for its mutual funds runs about 8% to 10% annually, nearly half the industry rate. During the 1998 fall market crash, while much of the industry saw cash flowing out of its equity funds,

companies that hired them, while a self-employed adviser keeps 100% of his. Little wonder, then, that many talented brokers like Evensky are fleeing big firms to set up small, autonomous shops. Or that they're skipping the Merrill stage entirely: Ken Schapiro set up Condor Capital right out of college; now, ten years later and 33 years old, Schapiro manages over $200 million in a business he calls high tech, high touch, and low cost.

But of all the intramural stresses brought about by the rise of these new financial advisers, their clash with the mutual funds is perhaps the most complicated. On the one hand, funds want to cater to advisers, and over the past three years most major mutual fund companies have created entire units devoted to doing so.

AEFA clients used the downturn as a buying opportunity: AEFA equity funds had money coming in.

CEO Dave Hubers, a native Minnesotan who has worked at AEFA since he graduated from college in 1965, thinks that with more and more consumers demanding advice, his firm will continue to flourish. And he has no intention of conceding ground to Charles Schwab, Merrill Lynch, and their kind: "I'd rather have our deck to start from than theirs," he says. AEFA intends to double its field force by 2006, to 20,000 advisers.

But because AEFA pushes its proprietary products, many would-be competitors label it a dinosaur. Indeed, while AEFA grew from $20 billion in assets in 1984 to $190 billion by the end of 1998, Schwab grew from $5 billion to more than $430 billion in the same period—and there have been a number of high-profile cases of successful advisers fleeing AEFA and carrying their clients off with them. So AEFA is changing its ways: A new division, Amex Direct, lets clients buy non-AEFA products without consulting an adviser. And soon advisers will be able to select the degree of support service that they wish to receive from headquarters, based on how much independence they want. Will these moves keep the old behemoth nimble? According to William White, a consultant at Spectrem Group, "the jury is still out on how successful they will be."

On the other hand, the fund companies don't want to transform their businesses—or lower their profit margins—in order to satisfy the advisers.

Enter Evensky: "Without mutual funds," he says, "we wouldn't be in business. But they could do some things better." So in the fall of 1997, with that in mind, he and a group of successful, like-minded advisers—dubbed the Gang of 71 because 71 of them were involved—mailed a letter to the big mutual fund companies. The letter requested, among other things, lower fees. Evensky, who gets very agitated about fees, says that expense ratios on stock mutual funds increased 33% (on a dollar-weighted basis) between 1985 and 1997. But if fund sizes are going up, he asks, why aren't expenses going down? The Gang of 71 also asked for more tax-efficient management and better, more timely disclosure on exactly what stocks the funds are holding.

On Nov. 16, 1997, the day before some 150 fund companies and 1,600 advisers met in San Francisco at a Schwab's annual conference, the Gang of 71 and representatives from the fund companies sat down to talk. The Gang had assumed that they were the mutual fund companies' best customers—after all, they were sophisticated buy-and-hold investors who committed big sums of money. They were in for a nasty surprise. "The fund companies spit all over them," says Don Phillips, CEO of Morningstar. Evensky concedes as much, adding that "most mutual funds see us as a pain in the ass."

There are many reasons for that, among them the obvious fact that the Gang of 71 doesn't control all that much money. Why should the mutual fund industry give them special breaks? Worse, the fund companies feel betrayed. The funds' No. 1 complaint is that these advisers aren't what they say they are—that they're not buy-and-hold investors but traders. At the meeting the fund companies presented data showing that advisers actually trade in and out of funds far more than the average individual investor. That so-called hot money makes it harder and more expensive to manage a fund. The Gang of 71's response: "It's them, not us. Other advisers may yank money in and out, but we don't."

LOOKING FORWARD

Evensky even began using the phrase "wealth manager" to distinguish himself and his cohort from the rest of the industry. Whatever they choose to call themselves, the fact is that some smaller, hungrier companies such as Montgomery Asset Management, Thornburg Funds, and Undiscovered Managers have begun catering to advisers, offering special funds with higher minimum requirements and lower fees. Evensky is optimistic that trend will continue: "We think much of what we're barking about today will be a given tomorrow."

The question is, Will Evensky and his kind be around to see tomorrow? These new planners may represent nothing more than a transitional species between the old school and the equally monolithic and corporate new school—a temporary fluke while the big boys adapt to the changing climate. If the big brokerage firms with national brand names begin offering the same customized planning and objective advice as the little guys, those smaller firms may find it hard to compete. "They're fighting the good fight, and I'd hate to see them lose, but they may be the kind of people who get trampled in the rough-and-tumble world of big business," says Phillips. And for the consumer, the omnipresent danger, of course, is that the personalized, in-depth advice that independent planners offer will become a one-size-fits-all proposition.

So, are these newfangled planners something we really need? Let's begin by remembering that these people are running businesses, and that for all their touchie-feelie populism, many of them serve a very exclusive client base: According to a recent survey of CFPs, just 2% of their clients had a net worth of less than $100,000; Evensky Brown Katz & Levitt requires a minimum of $2 million. Many firms work on a referral-only basis. And though Katz says she and others at her level worry about their upper-crust focus, you don't see anyone working pro bono.

Still, most of us could benefit from a good financial plan. With safety nets like Social Security getting more threadbare by the day, a savvy plan may make all the difference. Even if you know what fiscally smart behavior is, having someone tell you what to do may make you more inclined to do it. And hiring an adviser may ease the worry that something is slipping through the cracks.

Remember, nothing comes free, so it is important to consider how much you're willing to pay and how you want to structure that payment. If you want constant attention—and you've got the minimum assets—it probably makes sense to find a planner who charges an annual fee. If you simply want to get started on the right foot or you don't have much of a nest egg, you'll have to pay an hourly fee, a flat fee, or a commission. But even a commission-based plan can make sense, provided you know exactly what you're buying. And that way you know you'll carry the plan through: You'll have to—your adviser will be there to make sure of it.

TAX ADVICE FROM FORTUNE'S MONEY MANAGER

• ● •

FORTUNE's CAROLYN T. GEER *discusses*
confidentiality, summertime deductions,
inheritance payments, munis,
and life insurance trusts.

• ● •

HOW MUCH CAN YOU TELL YOUR ACCOUNTANT?

———————————————— ● ————————————————

When tax season comes around, you grab your shoebox full of receipts, W-2s, and stray chewing-gum wrappers and scurry on over to your accountant for a checkup. You've probably got some questions, or perhaps you'd like to fess up about some income that you "forgot" to report every year for the past ten years.

Accountant-client privilege: The good news is that the 1998 tax act extended the common-law attorney-client confidentiality privilege to certain communications between CPAs and their clients. That means it is now easier for your accountant to shield information about you from the IRS. The bad news is that the new law is both limited and vague. Some things clearly are not protected (confessions to your accountant about crimes you've committed, for example). Others fall into a vast gray area, creating a minefield for unsuspecting taxpayers. "People are going around saying this is the greatest thing since the invention of the wheel," says New York attorney Edward Schlesinger. "They are going to have mud on their faces when they find out this wheel isn't all that round."

Exactly how the law will be interpreted won't be known until cases go to court or the IRS issues regulations. Until then, how can you protect yourself (short of doing your own return)? Here's a guide:

The accountant-client privilege extends only to tax advice given by someone authorized to practice before the IRS, such as a CPA. Unlike the attorney-client privilege, the CPA version does not apply to general business advice, such as whether to buy or lease a building.

A fuzzy definition: The definition of "tax advice" is fuzzy, but in general it appears to include written and spoken analyses and opinions about specific tax situations—say, whether a transaction produced income or capital gains, whether certain income is reportable this year or next, or whether a certain expense is deductible or not.

CPA Thomas Ochsenschlager, a partner in Grant Thornton's Washington, D.C., office, provides an example: Say the back porch of your termite-infested house falls off, and you want to take a casualty loss. Your CPA writes you a memo detailing relevant court cases and assessing whether you're likely to win an IRS challenge. That memo would seem to be privileged. In the past it would have been protected only if produced by an attorney.

Still vulnerable: Once you decide to take the deduction, however, your calculations of the loss, including documents showing what you paid for the porch, definitely are—and always have been—reachable by the IRS. Otherwise, the feds couldn't enforce the tax laws. In fact, the new CPA-client privilege does not apply to any documents intended for third parties such as the SEC or the IRS—for instance, your tax return itself. Nor does it apply to work papers your accountant uses to prepare the return. (This is true of the attorney-client privilege too.) In other words, most of what's in your shoebox is vulnerable to an IRS subpoena.

Note, too, that the accountant-client privilege pertains only to federal tax issues. It doesn't shield your financial information from other regulatory bodies, such as the SEC or the EPA, or from state or local tax authorities (although more than a dozen states have their own CPA-client confidentiality statutes, and others are expected to adopt versions of the federal law). Nor does it apply in civil disputes that don't involve the IRS. Your accountant still could be forced to divulge your assets in a divorce proceeding or malpractice case, for example.

Not surprisingly, the new law shows no mercy to people engaging in corporate tax shelters. It specifically denies protection for any written communications regarding such schemes—a huge limitation, considering the expansive definition of "tax shelter."

As for illegal acts: And here's the biggest loophole: The CPA-client privilege doesn't cover illegal acts, as the attorney–client privilege does. But exactly when something becomes a criminal matter isn't always clear. Forgetting to report some income for one year probably is not a crime. Doing so several years in a row very well could be. One fear is that the IRS will start classifying more cases as criminal investigations to get around the new privilege: "You won't talk. Your client won't talk. Fine, we think this is a criminal matter." If so, no one is sure whether the privilege could be revoked retroactively, requiring the accountant to cough up years of records. Information given to a lawyer would have been protected all along.

MAKE YOUR SUMMER TAX-DEDUCTIBLE

Summer brings more than just school breaks. It can bring valuable tax breaks too. With a little planning, you just might be able to get Uncle Sam to help pay for some of your fun in the sun. Here are a few commonly overlooked summertime tax-saving opportunities:

Travel: If you combine business with pleasure on a domestic trip, you may be able to deduct all your travel costs, plus your hotel costs and half of the meal and entertainment expenses attributable to the days you work. To qualify, the trip must be primarily for business, says Mark Watson, a CPA with KPMG in Washington, D.C. A single week of work plus five vacation weeks won't cut it. One freebie: If you work on Friday and Monday, you can deduct your weekend lodging and meal costs.

Your employer gets the tax deduction, not you, if the employer reimburses you; all that you can deduct are unreimbursed business expenses, subject to IRS limits on itemized deductions. If you are in business for yourself, however, you can deduct all the expenses without limit on schedule C of your tax return.

Taking along the spouse and kids? Unless they are your employees and accompanying you for business reasons, their expenses generally are not deductible.

In any case, keep your receipts and a diary or other proof that you were working. Ed Slott, a CPA in Rockville Centre, N.Y., tells of a doctor who had taken deductions for attending a pharmaceuticals convention in Florida. When the IRS demanded proof that he deserved the deductions, the doctor produced photos of himself that had been shot at the convention, greatly helping his case.

Entertainment: Ralph Anderson, a CPA with Richard A. Eisner & Co. in Florham Park, N.J., has a client who throws a $100,000 party at his beach house every summer. For years, before he met Anderson, the client didn't deduct any of the costs of the party. Then Anderson informed him that he could deduct a goodly chunk because three-quarters of the guests are business associates. Counting food (50% deductible) and other (fully deductible) expenses, the client was able to rack up $62,000 in deductions this year for the affair. (There is no minimum percentage of guests that must be business-related, but the event should be primarily for business purposes, says CPA Watson.)

Again, meticulous records are key. The client got off easy when he was audited because he was able to produce not just receipts and a guest list, but also photocopies of the envelopes in which the invitations had been mailed.

Vacation homes: Perhaps you rent out your summer house— or yacht, motor home, or anything else with sleeping, cooking, and bathroom facilities that qualifies as a second home. You can do this for up to 14 days per year without owing tax on the rental income, though you cannot deduct any of the rental expenses. If you rent out your second home for more than 14 days and also use it yourself for more than 14 days or more than 10% of the number of days it is rented (whichever is greater), the rental income is taxable. However, you can deduct rental expenses up to the amount of the income generated. (Losses can be carried forward to years when the property shows a profit.)

Summer camp: Here's one tax break you can qualify for no matter what your income, provided you and your spouse both work and have a child under age 13—the child-care credit. Known mostly as a way to help defray the cost of a baby-sitter, the credit also applies to fees for day camp (though not sleepover camp). This is a dollar-for-dollar credit off your tax bill. For most people it amounts to 20% of expenses up to $2,400 for one child or $4,800 for two or more kids, for a maximum credit of $960 per year. To claim the credit, you will need the camp's tax identification number. Get it now. If you wait till next April when you're doing your taxes, the camp may be closed.

Summer jobs: If you'd rather put your kids to work, employing them in the family business is a great way to shift income out of your estate. The money you pay them is tax-deductible to your business and possibly tax-free to them. Children claimed as dependents on your tax return can earn up to $4,300 (the standard deduction for single filers) free of federal income tax.

No matter who employs them, your kids could funnel their paychecks into Roth IRAs. They spent all their earnings at the mall? You still could give each kid up to $2,000 to fund the IRAs, thereby shifting more income, free of gift taxes. (The $2,000 maximum IRA contribution is well below the $10,000 limit on tax-free gifts.) The law says only that you need earned income to open an IRA, says CPA Slott, who is also editor of *Ed Slott's IRA Advisor.* It doesn't matter where the money for the contribution comes from.

INHERITING TAX HEADACHES

Aging baby-boomers starting to come into inheritances are now being thrust into an even more complex world, the parallel universe of estate- and gift-tax law. This is foreign territory for most, complete with its own rules, tax forms, and traps for the unwary. Questions from readers follow:

Inheritances:

This year my wife received $5,000 [cash] from her grandmother's [estate]. Is this income we need to claim when filing our taxes? What category would it come under? How should we claim it?

D.H., Phoenix

I am happy to report that this is one bit of income you won't have to pay taxes on. In general, inheritances are free money: No income tax is owed by the recipients. (This is different from the federal estate tax, which hits estates of over $650,000—$1.3 million for a couple—and is paid out of the estate.) This fact surprises a lot of people used to paying tax on all they make.

The big exceptions are inherited IRAs and company retirement accounts, such as 401(k)s, in which the decedent's pretax contributions have grown tax-deferred. Here, the income is taxable to you, the beneficiary, at your ordinary income tax rate as you take distributions. If the dearly departed's estate was large enough to be whacked by the federal estate tax, you can take an income tax deduction for any estate tax that was paid on these retirement accounts—and the deduction needn't exceed 2% of your income, as is the case with most miscellaneous itemized deductions. Many beneficiaries end up overpaying their taxes because they don't know about this deduction, says CPA Slott, who has also written *Your Tax Questions Answered.*

Another exception: If money or property you inherit earns some income while the estate is being settled, that income must be reported either by you or by the estate. Usually the estate reports the income, but the estate executor might shift the tax burden to you if you have already received your share of the assets.

On filing 1041s:

As beneficiary [of] an estate, closed in 1998, I'm due K-1 and 1041 info regarding income produced by the estate and my tax liability for same. I have not received this info from the estate attorney, despite repeated requests. Is there anything in IRS regs to give me leverage in getting this info?

J.G., Daytona Beach Shores, Fla.

Estates file their tax returns on form 1041 (U.S. Income Tax Return for Estates and Trusts). Your share of the income is reported to you on schedule K-1 (Beneficiary's share of income, deductions, credits, etc.) of form 1041. Unfortunately for you, the estate executor doesn't have to provide you with the K-1 until the estate's tax return is due. When is that? you ask.

If the estate is on a calendar year, its return is due April 15 (or July 15 if the executor gets an automatic extension, or Oct. 15 if the executor gets a second extension). That may force you to file an extension of your own. Alternatively, you can file your return, estimating the taxes you owe, and file an amended return later, after you get the K-1. If the income is likely to be "material," go for the extension, advises Arthur Andersen partner Stephen Corrick.

If the estate is on a fiscal year (estates are among the few entities that can be), the return—and therefore the K-1—is due $3^1/2$ months after the close of the fiscal year. The executor can choose a fiscal year ending anywhere up to 12 months after the decedent died. Say your father passed away in July 1998, and the executor elected a fiscal year ending June 1999: The estate's return isn't due until October 1999, not including extensions. Thus, if you received any taxable income as part of your inheritance, you won't have to declare it until you file your tax return for 1999, in the year 2000—even if you actually had the income in hand in 1998. This is one reason executors choose fiscal years over calendar years: to allow beneficiaries to defer the taxes on their inheritances for an extended period.

If you don't get your K-1 on time, you can file form 8082 with your next tax return. Or contact your local IRS office. Uncle Sam can slap your executor with a fine of up to $100 or 10% of the amount required to be reported, whichever is greater. Reminding your executor about this penalty before the deadline passes might help dislodge the information.

MUNIS MAKE BALANCED FUNDS LESS TAXING

When equity investors get nervous in volatile or down markets, they move money into fixed-income investments. With balanced funds, which invest in both stocks and bonds, bond income can cushion the blows of a volatile stock market. A recent study in *Journal of Investing* suggests that, for taxable accounts, a balanced portfolio of stocks and munis beats the traditional balanced-fund mix of stocks and taxable bonds. The study's authors: Donald Peters and Mary Miller, co-managers of the T. Rowe Price Tax-Efficient Balanced fund, a blend of growth stocks and muni bonds. No coincidence, that. Following are some highlights from their study:

Returns: Using data from Morningstar, Peters and Miller studied the returns, tax efficiency, and risk characteristics of four types of funds over ten and 20 years: growth, growth and income, muni bond, and taxable bond. For anyone at or above the 28% tax bracket, growth funds had higher pretax and after-tax returns than growth and income funds, the typical equity component of a traditional balanced fund. Muni bond funds had lower pretax returns but higher after-tax returns than taxable bond funds.

Tax-efficiency: Of all the portfolios, muni funds and growth funds had the highest "tax-efficiency," or after-tax return as a percentage of pretax return. They also were more volatile than their counterparts, however, meaning that their returns ranged more widely year to year. This makes sense: Growth funds lack the ballast of income-producing stocks, the very trait that keeps their taxes down; munis have longer maturities than taxable bonds, on average, so their prices are more sensitive to interest rate swings.

Next, Peters and Miller married the growth and muni bond portfolios fifty-fifty and compared the results with the traditional balanced-fund mix of 60% growth and income stocks, 40% taxable bonds. (By law the growth-muni combo must maintain at least 50% of its assets in munis for investors to reap the tax benefits.)

The smaller equity stake in the growth-muni mix hurt the fifty-fifty combo's pretax performance. Its average annual pretax return for the 20 years through 1997 was 11.9%, vs. 12.8% for the traditional mix, for investors in the top tax bracket. After taxes, though, the growth-muni blend pulled ahead, 10.1% to 8.8%. Thus, a traditional balanced fund remains the better choice for tax-deferred accounts, such as IRAs, but a mix of growth stocks and munis is better for taxable accounts.

WHY MUNIS AREN'T
ALWAYS TAX-FREE

• ● •

Want to build a portfolio of municipal bonds yourself? Watch out. Tax-free munis sometimes pack a tax punch for high-net-worth investors. You're probably aware that although munis are exempt from federal taxes, most states tax interest on out-of-state bonds. But did you know that Illinois, Kansas, Iowa, Oklahoma, and Wisconsin tax interest on their own municipal bonds?

You probably also know that there is no capital gain or loss on a muni bought at par, or face value, and held to maturity, and that bonds sold before maturity can generate gains and losses. But are you aware that munis bought at a premium to face value do not generate deductible losses when they mature or are called, and that, conversely, bonds bought at a discount may generate gains that are taxed at ordinary income tax rates? "Most people get thrown by that," says Robert Harrison, a tax partner at accountants Richard A. Eisner & Co. This latter wrinkle, known as the "market discount rule," tends to hit intermediate-term bonds particularly hard and is "one of the real uglies in the muni market," says T. Rowe's Miller.

Otherwise tax-exempt interest from certain "private activity" munis, such as those issued to build airports, may be subject to the dreaded alternative minimum tax. Muni-related investment expenses—custody fees, investment advisory fees—are not deductible (except where bond interest is state-taxable, in which case the expenses are deductible on your state return). Nor is interest on money you borrow to purchase muni bonds.

When you die, of course, the value of any municipal bonds you held is included in your estate for estate tax purposes. "Tax-exempt means income-tax-exempt, not estate-tax-exempt," lectures Harrison. "There are still people around who think otherwise."

Volatility: The growth-muni mix was more volatile than the traditional balanced blend but not as volatile as the stand-alone growth and muni portfolios. For example, the growth-muni portfolio achieved 77% of the growth portfolio's after-tax return, but with only 70% of the volatility. One reason: Munis and stocks perform fairly independently, so losses from one can offset gains from the other—a valuable tool in any taxable account. In marketspeak, the "correlation" between the two over the past five years was just 0.39. (A 1.00 would imply that the two move in lockstep.)

You could build your own tax-efficient balanced fund by splitting your money between a good muni-bond fund and a good growth-stock fund. If you prefer a ready-made fund, there are a handful of no-loads to choose from. Most use growth stocks of some kind on the equity side.

THE PROFITS, AND PERILS, OF LIFE INSURANCE TRUSTS

Life insurance trusts, in fact, have become so alluring that there is now an estimated $300 billion of insurance sloshing around in them. The reason life insurance trusts are hot is that they can be a nifty way to save taxes and make sure your insurance proceeds get where you want them to go. But these legal devices are also complex and can easily go awry, leaving you and your heirs with a big mess. As their popularity grows, so too do the problems.

Consider: Consultants Towers Perrin recently audited one bank trust department and unearthed 16 insurance policies underwritten by Executive Life, an insurer that went broke in 1991. In a survey, Custom Administration Services Co. (CASCO), a trust administrator, found that up to 85% of trust-held life insurance policies could be restructured to provide more value— at least 40% more death benefit for the same premium or the same death benefit for at least a 40% lower premium.

Consider first: So before you jump on the life insurance trust bandwagon, first ask yourself, Do I really need one of these things? Assuming you need life insurance at all, you could own the policy yourself and make your estate the beneficiary. Downside: The proceeds would be subject to probate, creditors' claims, and federal estate taxes, which kick in on assets over $625,000—an amount slated to rise to $1 million by 2006.

If you are married, you could leave everything to your spouse tax-free, thanks to the unlimited marital deduction. Of course, any assets left at your spouse's death would get whacked, and if your spouse died before you did, the marital deduction would be lost.

If you have a child who is both old enough and wise enough, you could make him the owner and beneficiary of your policy, but then the money would be vulnerable to his creditors and ex-spouses.

A trust solves all these problems. An experienced lawyer should be able to draw one up for a few thousand dollars. You name the trust owner and beneficiary of the policy. At your death, the trustee distributes the proceeds—providing cash to pay estate taxes, for example.

Don't expect much help: Unfortunately, many banks and lawyers are reluctant to serve as trustees of life insurance trusts, figuring it isn't worth the hassle—or potential liability. Generally, you, as the "grantor," can't be the trustee of a trust you set up for your heirs. That leaves the task to a responsible trust beneficiary or to an uncle, priest, or rabbi—none of whom know any more than you do about trusts or life insurance. "Grantor, trustee, and beneficiary form a triangle of ignorance," says William Arnold, a principal at Towers Perrin.

Don't expect the insurance agent who sold the policy to be much help either. CASCO found that 95% of trust-held policies had no agent servicing the business. The reason: Agents get most of their commission up front, so there is little incentive for them to stick around. A $1 million policy covering a husband and wife, both age 60 and in good health, might cost $20,000 per year. Of that, the agent pockets at least $10,000 the first year but only $1,000 or less in future years.

Bottom line: You are on your own, so do your homework. Here are some pointers: If you already own a policy, you can

GOT A VARIABLE-LIFE POLICY? BETTER CHECK IT!

• ● •

Attention, variable life insurance fans: When and if the stock market falls, your policy may be in jeopardy. Variable life catches fire in a bull market because it allows you to invest your premiums in mutual-fund-like accounts. In the recent bull market, insurance salesmen were allowed to project annual returns of up to 12%, and many policyholders expected returns far higher than that. Traditional whole-life policies looked downright dowdy in comparison. These earn fixed returns tied to an insurer's bond-laden general account, but they do have one thing going for them: As long as you pay your premiums, the policy is guaranteed never to lapse. Not so with variable life.

Example: A healthy 45-year-old man who doesn't smoke can buy a $1 million variable policy for $11,500 a year for ten years. This assumes his premiums can earn 12% each year. If he suffers a big loss in just one year, eventually the money in his policy will fail to cover the cost of the death benefit and other contract expenses, and the policy could expire before he does. At that point, the only way to keep it alive would be to dump more money in, but by then the premiums will be prohibitive because the policyholder will be older.

While it's true that if the account in our example does better than 12% in some years the policy could be saved, the point is that variable-life policyholders need to check. Ask your agent or insurance company for an "in-force illustration" to see whether your policy is performing as expected.

assign it to a trust, but you may owe gift tax on the transfer, and you will have to live another three years, or the policy will be swept back into your taxable estate. Make sure you sign away all your ownership interests in the policy, including the rights to borrow the cash value, cancel the policy, and pledge it as collateral for a loan. And don't forget to change the beneficiary—a common oversight, says New York estate lawyer Jonathan Blattmachr.

A lot to think about: If you are healthy, consider having the trust buy a new policy on your life. That would avoid the three-year problem and probably lower your premiums. But don't be rash. If the trust buys the policy, you need to give it cash to pay the premiums. John Scroggin, a trust lawyer in Roswell, Ga., suggests contributing slightly more than that to avoid the appearance that the trustee is doing your bidding. "The IRS hates life insurance trusts," he warns, and looks for any reason to attack them.

You can contribute up to $10,000 per year per beneficiary without owing gift tax if certain conditions are met; for example, the beneficiaries must receive written notice every time a deposit is made, and ample opportunity—30 days, say—to withdraw the money.

The insurance policy should be reviewed periodically. Is it the right kind of policy for your needs? Is it providing good value? If not, can it be improved or replaced? Pay close attention to variable-life policies (see box).

Most trustees aren't up to this analysis. One resource: the Consumer Federation of America (202-387-0087). For $40, an actuary will measure the real return on your cash-value life insurance policy. Also, check out insurance adviser Glenn Daily's Website (www.glenndaily.com). It has a policy review checklist and, if you want to keep your agent in the loop, a sample of a service contract you might have him sign outlining his duties during the life of the policy.

YOU NEED AN ESTATE PLAN

BY CAROLYN T. GEER

● ● ●

*Boomers need an estate plan
just as much as their parents.*

● ● ●

Think you're too young to worry about estate planning? One fortysomething executive at a New York investment firm recently asked financial adviser Bill Knox to hammer out an estate plan for him and his wife in just four days. Why the rush? The two were about to fly to Europe without their kids, and "they didn't want to be sitting on that plane saying, 'What if ...?' " says Knox, of Bugen Stuart Korn & Cordaro in Chatham, N.J.

It may take an impending transatlantic flight to remind young, successful people that they aren't immortal, but baby-boomers need estate plans just as much as their Eisenhower-generation parents do. After all, Uncle Sam doesn't discriminate when it comes to levying estate taxes. No matter how old you are when you die, you risk losing a good chunk of your assets to the tax-man unless you plan ahead.

A LESS CERTAIN FUTURE

●

Trouble is, the boilerplate documents used by estate lawyers are typically written for 65-year-olds with adult children, a litter of grandchildren, and big, stable bond portfolios. Boomers face a different set of issues—their kids are younger, their spouses are more likely to remarry if widowed, and their wealth is more likely to be tied up in some volatile Internet company. Bottom line: Their future is less certain than that of their parents, so their estate plans must be more flexible.

For example, a primary function of any estate plan is to take full advantage of the federal estate-tax exemption, currently $650,000 per person. Planners typically accomplish this by dividing the marital assets so that each spouse has at least $650,000. This strategy presents a problem for young families, however. The younger you are when you die, the greater the chance that your spouse will remarry and, perhaps, have children with the new mate. In that case, any assets you shifted to your spouse before you died might never end up in your own children's hands as you probably intended.

One solution is to put the assets in an irrevocable qualified terminable interest property (QTIP) trust. Such a trust specifies that your spouse gets income from the trust for life but that when he or she dies, the assets must be distributed to your children. If your children are very young when the trust is created, it often makes sense to give your spouse some flexibility—for instance, the choice of distributing the assets outright after death or keeping them protected in trust. Who knows whether your kids will grow up to be model citizens or deadbeats?

GIVE NOW

Another way to ensure your children's inheritances—and shrink your estate-tax bill—is to give away assets while you are still alive. Everyone is allowed to give up to $10,000 per year to each of his or her children—or to anyone, for that matter—without owing gift taxes. (A husband and wife together can give $20,000 per child.) You also can hand over larger gifts, which eat away at your $650,000 estate-tax exemption. If your kids are minors, you could place these gifts in an irrevocable trust for them.

There are two potential problems with making direct gifts, both easily addressed. For one thing, the children could die prematurely (heaven forbid), leaving no heirs. The solution is to have the trust revert to your spouse, but not so that it gets counted in the spouse's estate. The spouse gets limited rights to the trust assets during his or her life (generally, income and, at the trustee's discretion, principal) and limited rights to direct where the property goes at death. "This gives you a second bite of the apple," says attorney Stephen Ziobrowski, of Boston's Peabody & Arnold, "but you won't find it in standard trust documents."

The second problem: Assets you give today might crater in value tomorrow. In contrast with their parents, who built their fortunes slowly and steadily in the family widget factory, boomers are placing bets on tech companies and the like, "things that shoot up to the sky and go poof," says Ziobrowski. Say you give your children stock that you expect to explode in value down the road, using up part of your estate-tax credit in the process. If the stock falls to zero, your credit is wasted.

The answer, again, is to have a plan B. By law, the children can "disclaim" the gift up to nine months after it is made. The catch: They must not have "accepted" it yet—easier said than done. For this reason, Ziobrowski likes to put these gifts into "family limited partnerships" instead of trusts. Such partnerships limit your heirs' rights in certain ways, making it harder for the IRS to claim they accepted the gift.

So you have lots to do before kissing your kids good-bye and boarding that plane. Get your estate plan in order. And have a safe trip.

WHEN THERE ARE NO DEPENDENTS

Single boomers with no dependents tend to find it hard to figure out where their money should go after they leave this earth. "There isn't an obvious choice that presents itself," says Michael Puzo, an estate lawyer with Boston's Hemenway & Barnes. Happily married people with children often leave everything to the spouse and kids. Married couples and singles without children often pick their extended family. But not always. "With the bull market, more people are becoming very concerned about huge amounts of wealth passing to children who are already being benefited," says attorney Joanne E. Johnson, an estate and tax planner at J.P. Morgan in New York.

Here are a few estate-planning techniques worth considering:

Tuition payments. You can pay for anyone's education without owing gift taxes, as long as the payments are made directly to the school and are used to cover tuition and books, not room and board. (This is in addition to the $10,000 per year you can give to any number of people free of gift taxes.) Puzo has a bachelor client who has educated several friends' children this way. He likes the fact that the money is targeted for a specific purpose, not just adding to the children's already ample resources.

Also, don't forget the new tax-favored college savings accounts offered by some states. You can use your $10,000 tax-free gifts to open accounts for anyone. The money grows tax-deferred until it is tapped for tuition, books, and sometimes room and board. Then the earnings are taxed at the student's rate.

Grantor retained income trusts. A GRIT lets you transfer assets to heirs during your life and minimize the gift tax. Congress has outlawed its use for lineal relatives (spouses, children, siblings), but it can still be used to benefit nonrelatives or collateral relatives (nieces, nephews, cousins). Consider this example from Johnson: A 50-year-old man contributes $1 million to a GRIT for his nephew. During the term of the trust—say, ten years—the uncle is required to receive the income generated. For federal gift-tax purposes, the value of the $1 million gift to the nephew would be reduced by the present value of the uncle's future income stream, which is figured using an IRS-mandated discount rate that changes monthly and reflects Treasury bond yields. Based on a discount rate of, say, 7%, the gift would be valued at $465,000, well under this year's $650,000 unified credit for estate and gift taxes, so no gift tax would be owed. If the trust earned 8.4%, the nephew would get $1.5 million at the end of the term—about $1 million more than the uncle had been assessed for giving. If the assets continued to earn 8.4% until the uncle died, say, 19 years later, the nephew would end up with $3.4 million. That's $1.2 million more than he would have gotten had the $1 million accumulated at the same rate outside the trust, where it would have been subject to estate taxes at the uncle's death at a 37% rate. (Note: If the uncle terminates before the trust does, the assets get pulled back into his taxable estate.)

Private foundations. Richard Morawetz, 54, a neurosurgeon, and his wife, Mary Jean, 53, a speech pathologist and landscape designer, expect to amass assets of $10 million to $15 million by the time they die. With no children of their own, they are already paying the private-school tuition of one of Richard Morawetz's two teenaged nieces and will probably pay for both girls' college and graduate school too. Assuming the Morawetzes live at least seven more years, when the estate tax exemption reaches $1 million per spouse, they could then bequeath $2 million to the nieces in trust, estate tax–free, to be distributed when the girls are older.

They are contemplating leaving the balance of their estate to a private foundation, also estate tax–free, to benefit local charities in their hometown of Birmingham, Ala. The nieces could be trustees, drawing a "reasonable" salary and distributing the money. "A big unsung advantage of the foundation is that it helps build the character of the trustees," says Stewart Welch III, a financial planner in Birmingham. The trustees could name their kids as successor trustees, he adds, "so you could build a legacy of character."

Due to the heavy setup and maintenance fees, plus reporting requirements, it usually doesn't make sense to create a foundation unless you're giving at least a few million dollars. Morawetz, for one, worries about saddling his nieces with a chore for which they may not have the time or inclination.

For these reasons, consider establishing your foundation while you are still alive, leaving yourself some wiggle room. (You would get a limited charitable income-tax deduction.) Then you can change trustees or dissolve the foundation by paying out all the money. Meanwhile, you will have had a chance to enjoy the fruits of your giving.

●•●•●

USING THE WEB
TO MAKE THE MOST OF YOUR MONEY

● ● ●

Websites offer a wealth
of information and opportunity.

● ● ●

When it comes to making money, timing is everything. Whether it's the richer benefits that compound interest brings to an IRA started at age 20 rather than 35 or the split-second a favorable spread lasts on a Nasdaq stock, financial opportunity is for those who seize the moment. The tools necessary to make such choices were once the province of a select class of financial professionals. But the Web, with its easy and immediate access to information and its unique interactive technologies, has given ordinary citizens the power to succeed—or to fail—as their own financial planners.

Advances on the Web have made it possible for events to move at a new speed: real time. Checking how a stock is trading no longer requires settling for the 15-minute delay offered previously on the Web, much less for something as quaint as checking the tables in the next day's paper. Real-time quotes are the standard for serious players, and sites such as Charles Schwab, Quote.com, and Fidelity Investments offer them free. News headlines that move markets are pushed to your desktop in a constant stream, or flash across the top of any number of Websites, from portals like Yahoo to news sites like CNN. Snap decisions can be made, reversed, and made again, all within a moment's surf.

Long-term decisions, too, are made easier on the Web. Planning your finances for distant events—kids' tuition, retirement, even death—is aided by the wealth of information available there. Calculators like those offered by Discover Brokerage or bankrate.com help you make choices on when to sell mutual funds or what kind of retirement account to open. Such recommendations, based on specific goals and circumstances, employ the same formulas that a paid financial adviser uses. While some situations certainly require a more expert opinion, helping you get started early and on the right track is where the Web's interactive tools excel.

PERSONAL FINANCE

The true power of the Web comes when real-time information is combined with interactivity. Traditional financial software offers some of the features found online, but where the Web wins is in the real-time data it feeds to the applications. This puts heavy-duty analysis in the hands of individuals and enables them to make sophisticated financial decisions that just weren't possible before.

Perhaps the best example of this confluence of technologies is The Map of the Market featured on the SmartMoney Interactive site. It is an essential tool for trend-seeking market watchers. The editors of *SmartMoney* have chosen the 500 or so most important stocks, represented them as colored boxes, and grouped them by sector. By dragging your cursor across the screen to the areas of green (good) or red (bad) recent performers, the names and most recent price of individual stocks pop out. Further clicking will bring charts, company news, or more specific sector analysis. It's a dynamic view of the markets that static charts and tables can't provide on their own.

Useful, too, are sites that collect information on investing goals, risk tolerance, and available assets, and return personalized recommendations. Personal Wealth, operated by Standard & Poor's, a licensed investment adviser, bases its advice on 40 different model portfolios. Microsoft's MoneyCentral features an investment finder that rates stocks and funds based on over 500 criteria. The SEC has even unveiled a mutual funds costs calculator, which evaluates the front-end and yearly expenses of any fund to determine the real cost of ownership.

Most of these applications employ Java technology, which enables small calculation programs to run in the user's Web browser. For older versions of some browsers, Java can be a problem. But for individuals who want to reap the full benefits of the

Web for their personal finances, the investment in an updated browser is one that's sure to pay off.

RETIREMENT AND ESTATE PLANNING

Most online investors—apart from the day traders, who ride the markets up and down, living one session at a time—are working toward events on an extended time horizon. The big one is retirement—the time when you can live off the fruits of your electronic labors. Most financial sites encourage this kind of thinking, if only because it keeps you coming back today.

Standard & Poor's and T. Rowe Price, among others, have created Websites with interactive and customized retirement planners. The FinanCenter site features 15 retirement calculators in which users enter a profusion of personal financial information to receive answers to such questions as "What will my expenses be after I retire?" and "Am I saving enough?" As the baby-boom generation approaches its computer-literate retirement, these questions—and the number of people looking for the answers online—should only increase.

Another event on the horizon that requires planning, at least from a financial perspective, is death. Increasing numbers of people are looking to the Web for information on estate planning. Although the perception that wills are just for rich people has kept the number of estate-planning Websites comparatively low, this will change as the ranks of retirees, and potential heirs, swell.

Yahoo Seniors Guide recently added estate-planning advice to its retirement Website. "It has drawn plenty of attention," says site producer Rob McHugh. Other heavy hitters among the retirement sites, such as Standard & Poor's Personal Wealth, will offer estate-planning pages. One much visited site, Nolo.com, created by Nolo Press, contains an introduction to making a will and basic pointers on drawing up a "no-frills will." It's a fertile market; as Nolo points out, about 70% of Americans don't yet have a will.

Among the first to offer an estate-planning Website was Robert Clofine, a lawyer in York, Pa. Since 1996 his estate-planning site has been widely regarded as a model of clarity. The most popular topic on his site is living trusts, which are set up to avoid probate, the legal process of judging the validity of a will. Probate and inheritance law are complex, so it's advisable to use online information only as a supplement to consultation with a good lawyer. Says Clofine: "People would be foolish to rely entirely on the Web in any area of the law, but it doesn't hurt to educate yourself."

ONLINE BROKERS

The array of financial planning materials available on the Web can help you choose from the pool of stocks, bonds, funds, and IRAs available. But with the burgeoning ranks of online brokers doing business on the Web, it can be just as daunting deciding where to buy them.

Online brokerages are a balance of two concerns: service and price. The online broker wars have driven commission prices down to just a few dollars a trade at firms like Datek and Web Street Securities. Other firms, including Schwab and Fidelity, have kept commissions closer to $30 per 1,000 shares but offer a mix of services, such as real-time quotes, research tools, and investment analysis. In what might be called the super-services category, Wall Street titan Merrill Lynch recently launched an online operation, Unlimited Advantage, which will cater to its high-net-worth clientele.

For most investors, some amount of services will be worth the price. If you can get most of the tools you want at one site, it might be worth a few extra dollars' commission not to have to surf around every time you want to make a deal. Whichever broker you choose, make sure trades are executed promptly. Waiting around while the price falls can eat up online commission savings in a hurry.

Even the best online broker isn't much help if the site goes down and you can't connect. Perhaps the wisest decision when trading online is to keep a broker's phone number close by.

Following is a list of Websites that offer information about investing, estate planning, wills, loans, credit cards, retirement plans, legal issues, and more.

SEEING THE SITES

● **bankrate.com**   www.bankrate.com

Bankrate.com is a useful compendium of independent financial information. As its name suggests, the site features data on auto loan, credit card, mortgage, and other rates, as well as tips on how to get the best ones. You can also subscribe to an e-mail service that notifies you of rate changes. The site's calculators help determine the costs of everything from relocation to your next car lease.

● **Charles Schwab**   www.schwab.com

The discount brokerage pioneer continues to sit at the top of the online trading heap despite its relatively high commissions. The Schwab name is certainly a draw, but the well-designed site gives investors their money's worth with easy access to real-time quotes, research, and, of course, securities trading. For high-net-worth or very active clients, Schwab's Signature Services provide an extra bit of pampering.

● **Robert Clofine's Estate Planning Page**
www.estateattorney.com

Attorney Robert Clofine from York, Pa., started this site in 1996 to provide information on how to transfer retirement wealth to the next generation with the least amount of trouble. Clofine's site offers clear, concise explanations of subjects such as protecting a spouse's income while paying for nursing care. Clofine says the pages that get the most visits are those on living trusts, which are for avoiding probate.

● **Crash Course in Wills & Trusts**   www.mtpalermo.com

Learning how to make your own will via the Web seems ripe for exploitation, particularly since the majority of Americans don't have one. Here's a concise and practical guide to the law of wills and trusts, the work of Lexington, Ky., lawyer Michael Palermo. The site is based, says Palermo, on questions, concerns, and issues encountered over many years by people at all economic levels.

● Discover Brokerage   www.discoverbrokerage.com

Consistently ranked among the top online brokers, Discover Brokerage offers a good mix of mid-range commission trades and additional services, including investment research, an IPO center, and real-time quotes. Discover has also led the way with some innovative investment packages, like the Blue Chip Basket in which customers invest in the ten top Dow stocks for one moderately priced commission.

● E*Trade   www.etrade.com

One of the biggest providers of online trading, E*Trade offers a complete range of investment features. Its commissions are relatively inexpensive, but even if you don't trade, E*Trade provides free real-time quotes as long as you register for membership. The site offers its own S&P index fund, designed for online investors. There are research reports, investor chat, and selective access to IPOs.

● Fidelity   www.fidelity.com

Fidelity offers a full-service personal finance site with retirement planning, tax assistance, and annuity information as well as online investing. Fidelity made its name in mutual funds, and its Website, in addition to featuring prominent pictures of Peter Lynch, lives up to its reputation, with data on more than 3,300 funds. But even for do-it-yourselfers, Fidelity recommends seeking professional advice.

● Fortune investor   www.fortuneinvestor.com

Fortune's own investment site offers financial news, detailed market information, investing tools, and portfolio tracking. Notable is the Quick Search feature, which enables users to screen stocks by clicking easy terms like "high growth" or "undervalued" rather than more complicated criteria like EPS and P/E ratios. Three levels of paid subscription provide extra benefits, but there's plenty that's free.

● FinanCenter   www.financenter.com

FinanCenter is the home of personal-finance calculators on the Web. There are more than 100 here on topics including auto loans, mortgages, insurance, credit cards, retirement, and investing. Technical terms are defined, and there is other useful information to supplement your calculations. You can follow FinanCenter's links to sites where you can apply for a car loan or credit card.

● The Legal Survival Network   www.friran.com
This site from Friedman & Ranzenhofer provides excellent information on estate planning. It presents informative articles on tax law and recent court cases, and you can download, free, forms for making lists for wills and a health-care proxy. The estate-planning checklists are very complete, and there is even one for trustees' duties. The site's FAQs on executors and wills are worth a visit too.

● LifeNet   www.lifenet.com
A general financial site, LifeNet covers everything from homebuying, life insurance, and estate taxes to tips on avoiding the hassle of probate for heirs. LifeNet features a calculator for estimating estate tax and probate costs. You fill in the blanks, and it provides the sum of what you can't take with you. The rest of the estate-planning section is clear and concise, useful for a quick overview.

● Money   www.money.com
A member of Time Warner's network of sites, Money's online version offers a good selection of financial information. The site's free advice is sound. There are research tools and calculators, a financial newswire, and links to articles in *Money* magazine as well as other Time Warner publications, including FORTUNE.

● MSN MoneyCentral   moneycentral.msn.com
MoneyCentral is a revamped version of the old Microsoft Investor site. It has been significantly expanded to include not only investment information, but also retirement and estate planning, real estate, insurance, banking, taxes, and family finances. The site is full of research wizards that help personalize the information, as well as reference guides that cover the basics of each topic.

● National Association of Financial and Estate Planning
www.nafep.com
A big site published by the representative association of financial and estate planners. Although it is a little dense and earnest in pre-

sentation, the site, which is free, does offer good information on general estate planning and asset protection. It serves as a useful reminder: Consider trying to get such a large and detailed amount of information this quickly without the Web.

● Nolo.com Self-Help Law Center   www.nolo.com

Mention any popular legal subject, and Nolo Press is sure to be there. Its site includes advice on wills and estate planning. As is usual with Nolo, the information is clear and direct. The wills section has hard-to-find information, particularly on the "no-frills will." There is also information on probate and executors, living trusts, estate and gift taxes, and funeral planning (well, someone has to mention it).

● Quicken.com   www.quicken.com

Quicken's site builds on its reputation as a top provider of financial software with a site that offers a range of personal finance services. In addition to tracking the market and your investment portfolio, you can find mortgage information, get answers to tax questions, and compare insurance quotes. There are also sections devoted to retirement planning and small business finances.

● S&P Personal Wealth   www.personalwealth.com

Standard & Poor's trend-setting site is Web service at its best, combining analysis of portfolios and retirement plans with recommendations for investments. (S&P is a registered investment adviser.) The actual planning is done by S&P's policy committee, which puts together the 40 model portfolios on which the recommendations are based. S&P says asset allocations should be reconsidered every six months.

● Mutual Funds Cost Calculator   www.sec.gov/mfcc/mfcc-int.htm

The Securities and Exchange Commission is doing its part to help the individual investor. In addition to the regulatory filings posted on its EDGAR site, the SEC's site offers a calculator to evaluate the true cost of mutual fund fees. Comparing load and no-load funds with varying yearly expenses is complicated, and this application helps. But as the SEC warns, fees are just one aspect to consider when choosing a fund.

● SmartMoney Interactive   www.smartmoney.com

SmartMoney's site is one of the best financial information resources on the Web. Its interactive Map of the Market is a unique tool for investors. To help investors spot winners and losers as the market moves, the color-coded map charts the performance of 500 stocks, grouped by industry for easy analysis. The site contains loads of other useful information, including advice on estate and retirement planning.

● T. Rowe Price   www.troweprice.com

Every retiree or every person facing retirement should probably visit this site for its sensible economic and financial advice. Its section on retirement plans presents a clear overview of the economy and succinct paragraphs on equities, bonds, and overseas markets. There is also the usual access to analyzers, financial calculators, and account information.

● Yahoo Finance   finance.yahoo.com

As you might expect, the leading Internet portal contains a wealth of financial and investment information. The Finance site is a good place to start research on any subject related to your net worth, and the chat room is lively.

● Yahoo Seniors' Guide   seniors.yahoo.com

This section on estate planning, recently added to Yahoo's financial offerings, is geared toward the over-65 set.

● ● ●

CHAPTER FIVE

●●●

PLANNING FOR A SECURE RETIREMENT

BLUEPRINT FOR BUILDING A WEALTHY FUTURE

BY CAROLYN T. GEER

— ● ● ● —

Constructing a dream retirement is likely to cost more than you ever imagined. But don't worry: You can get there. All you need is a simple plan.

— ● ● ● —

In many respects we are a nation of planners. We delight in planning our vacation, our wedding, our dream house. And why not? All these things involve spending money, America's favorite pastime. But when it comes to our retirement, let's face it: Most of us just wing it. After all, planning for retirement involves saving money and, well, where's the fun in that? Consider: Only 44% of workers surveyed in 1999 by John Hancock Financial Services have a specific plan for the way they invest the money in their 401(k)s. Even among those who say they are aiming for a certain mix of assets—so much in stocks, so much in bonds, for example—fewer than 25% are hitting their target. "People have set their retirement plans on autopilot," says Wayne Gates, an economist at John Hancock, "and they don't know if their instruments are properly calibrated."

You might ask whether that's really such a tragedy. Visit Florida, Arizona, or any graybeard mecca, and you'll find it teeming with prosperous seniors who never dreamed of constructing the kind of retirement plan envisioned by the worrywarts at John Hancock. If you're 40 and shunting 6% of every paycheck into your 401(k), you're probably doing more than your parents ever did to prepare for retirement. Why not leave it at that?

The answer is simple: This is not your father's retirement scene. The G.I. Generation and their younger siblings in the Silent Generation reached retirement armed with old-fashioned corporate pensions (the kind that pay a fixed monthly income for life), houses that had appreciated like Internet stocks, and a Social Security system that seemed to get more generous with each new act of Congress. Those days are over.

Today, if you don't plan for your retirement dreams, you risk waking up at age 55 to find they are simply unattainable. According to a study by the Employee Benefits Research Institute (EBRI), people who have taken the trouble to figure out how much money they will need for their golden years have accumulated nearly five times as much as those who never tried to do so. Why? Probably because the analysis opened their eyes to how much more they should be saving. Unfortunately, barely half of American workers have even made a stab at determining a price tag for the kind of retirement they want to have.

That may be the main reason they remain so confident they will have enough to live comfortably throughout their retirement. According to the John Hancock study, nearly two-thirds of workers expect to retire before age 65 and are, at most, only somewhat concerned about their finances thereafter.

They may be in for a shock.

NOT A CLUE

"Most people don't have a clue about how much money it takes to retire," observes Ron Roge, a financial planner in Bohemia, N.Y. And how much is that? Roge calculates that wage earners not covered by an old-fashioned, employer-funded pension plan will need investments of at least $1.5 million in 1999 dollars (excluding home equity) to supplement Social Security beginning at age 62. And that's just for a modest retirement, with expenses of perhaps $50,000 a year.

Roge's calculation is miles above the couple of hundred thousand dollars many people think they'll need to save. But then most people forget to factor in taxes, inflation, and increased life expectancy, says Roge, all of which put an extra burden on your nest egg. Remember, you don't really own all that money in your 401(k) or traditional IRA. You can't lay your hands on those accounts without paying income taxes on them at your maximum tax rate. That knocks at least 30% or so right off the top. Then there's inflation, which guarantees that your retirement income will have to rise yearly just to keep you in the same place. And that income will have to keep rising longer than you might expect. It's not inconceivable that you could spend one-third or more of your life retired.

SIMPLE IS GOOD

The good news is that imposing as all this sounds, a prosperous retirement is well within reach—if you have a plan. And the key to a successful plan? Simplicity. That's right. The dirty little secret of the investing world is that the best strategies are also the simplest. Too often we get caught up in the day-to-day numbers. From one week to the next, some investments will be winners and some not, but over the 20 or 30 years you will be investing, it should all wash out.

In his book *Common Sense on Mutual Funds*, John Bogle, founder of the Vanguard Group and a 50-year veteran of the investing business, calls simplicity "the master key to financial success." He is convinced that investors complicate things needlessly by recklessly chasing unrealistic performance. "Follow a simple plan," he writes, "and let the cycles of the market take their course."

In the same spirit of simplicity, we offer you our six-step program for retiring rich. It begins with an intelligent calculation of your retirement's price tag and continues with five investing guidelines that can ensure you'll have the money to pay the bill.

1. Find Out How Big Is Big Enough

How large does my nest egg have to be before I can call it quits? This question goes to the heart of your entire plan, but few people even ask it, let alone try to answer it. Like much else in retirement planning, answering the riddle is simpler than it seems. The way to start is by deciding how well you want to live once you leave work.

For most people the goal is to live at least as well in retirement as during their peak earning years. Because in retirement you no longer have to pay commuting costs and other work-related expenses—and because once you're in your golden years you can finally stop saving for them—you can maintain your current

THE INCOME YOU'LL NEED

• ● •

Once you retire, you can generally expect to maintain your preretirement standard of living on 65% to 85% of your salary today. The so-called replacement ratio is lowest for middle-income folks, since a bigger share of their working income is absorbed by work-related expenses and taxes that shrink in retirement.

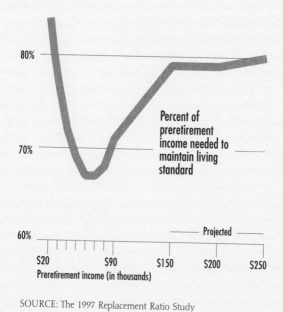

Percent of preretirement income needed to maintain living standard

Projected

Preretirement income (in thousands)

SOURCE: The 1997 Replacement Ratio Study

standard of living in retirement with less than your current income. Researchers at Georgia State University and Aon Consulting have found that a married couple need roughly 65% to 85% of their preretirement gross to keep up their lifestyle.

This so-called replacement ratio starts out high but drops quickly for those with middling incomes. It then rises again for those approaching the six-figure bracket. For example, a worker now making $60,000 could retire without breaking stride on about

67% of his current wages. His boss, making $150,000, would need about 80%. The main reason: taxes. A rich retiree needs more pre-tax dollars than others to keep the IRS happy and maintain a pre-retirement standard of living.

Use those numbers as a starting point, then factor in the retirement life you want to live. You may decide you need 100% of your preretirement income, at least for the years right after you quit working. Sure, you'll spend less on power ties and commuting, but you may spend more on restaurants and vacations.

Don't expect Social Security to shoulder much of the burden. It already accounts for less than 25% of retirement income for someone whose preretirement wage was $90,000, vs. 40% for the average retiree. Only 12% of workers now expect Social Security to be their most important source of income when they retire, according to the EBRI study. Half of workers, compared with 18% of retirees, say their most important source will be personal savings, either through a plan at work, such as a 401(k), or other investments.

Just how big will that pot of savings have to be to meet your income goal? Well, there are plenty of software programs and Websites (not to mention eager financial consultants) that can help you make that nest egg calculation, but be careful here. The standard formula yields seemingly precise but dangerously misleading answers. For example, if you're 40 and want a retirement income that starts out at $50,000 and lasts 40 years, you might be told that you need to amass $1.1 million in savings and will need to save $24,200 a year from now until you're 60. What you might not be told is that this number will be wrong fully half the time. That is, there is a 50% chance that $24,200 a year won't build you a nest egg of $1.1 million. Even if it does, there's a 50% chance that $1.1 million won't suffice to produce the income you want for as long as you need it.

The reason, of course, is that your exact investment return is unknowable—both before your retirement and during it. For example, your money may average 8% a year in the long run, but it won't earn 8% every year. Since you will be continually putting money in and taking it out over your lifetime, the real growth of your account depends on the sequence of returns over time. If

THE ASSETS YOU'LL NEED

● ⬤ ●

Since your investment returns after retirement are unknowable, the best you can do is calculate the probability that any sum you acquire will provide the income you'll need for as long as you need it. If you figure you'll spend $50,000 a year (rising annually with inflation) for 40 years, then a $1.1 million nest egg gives you a 50% chance of not outliving your money. A $1.6 million stash has a 90% chance of never running out.

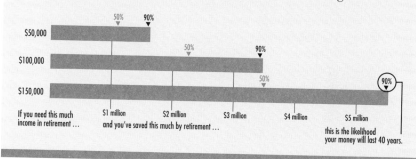

high returns come when your assets are peaking, you're in luck; if low returns strike at that time, you'll have less.

What you really need to find out, then, is this: Given the uncertainty of any investment projection, what must you do to have a reasonable chance of reaching your goal? To illustrate a realistic approach to the question, financial planner Christopher Cordaro of Bugen Stuart Korn & Cordaro in Chatham, N.J., produced two sets of numbers. The first gives a range of probabilities that your money will last as long as you want. For example, say you think you'll need $100,000 annually for 40 years of retirement. With a $2.3 million nest egg, there is a 50% chance your assets will last at least 40 years. That is the savings target that the standard calculation methods would churn out. If you want to be 90% certain you won't outlive your money, however, you'll need to accumulate $3.5 million.

The second set of numbers shows how much you must save each year to have a reasonable chance of accumulating your retirement stash by your target age. Say you are 20 years from

WHAT TO SAVE

● ● ●

How much you need to save each year depends on three things: how big a nest egg you have to build, how certain you want to be of reaching your goal, and how much time remains until you retire.

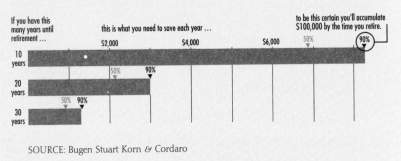

If you have this many years until retirement ...

this is what you need to save each year ...

to be this certain you'll accumulate $100,000 by the time you retire.

SOURCE: Bugen Stuart Korn & Cordaro

quitting time and need a sum of $1 million by then. You'll have a 50% chance of getting there if you save $22,000 a year. If you're willing to salt away $30,000 a year, your chances improve to 90%.

Cordaro assumed a typical investment mix of 60% stocks and 40% bonds for an 8% average annual return. A computer then generated thousands of scenarios for each year's results, factoring in the historical variation in returns for that kind of portfolio. A few other planning firms use the same kind of analysis, known as the Monte Carlo method. One of them, an online investment advisory firm known as Financial Engines, will let you test-drive free. Simply log on to financialengines.com, plug in data as requested, and you'll get back an analysis detailing the probability that your strategy will put your retirement dreams within reach.

The beauty of the Monte Carlo simulation is that it acknowledges the uncertainty inherent in any financial projection. As a result, it affords a more honest and ultimately a simpler way of sizing up your retirement-planning needs: Decide how much uncertainty you can live with, and adjust your plan accordingly. Which brings us to step two.

2. Save

While we would all take blistering returns on our investments, the truth is, we don't need them. It is much easier simply to save enough to begin with and let the power of compounding work its proverbial magic. Time is your greatest ally in this respect. A few decades can transform even a little periodic savings into a tremendous amount. But if you have only a little time before retirement, you need to save a lot.

Consider this example, prepared for us by Financial Engines. A man wants to retire at age 65 with an inflation-adjusted retirement income of $100,000. To do that, he contributes $10,000 a year to his 401(k) plan, the maximum allowed by law, allocating all the money to an S&P 500 index fund. If he starts contributing to the plan at age 30, he will have a 35% chance of reaching his goal with his 401(k) contributions alone. (Add in Social Security and a typical employer's matching contribution, and his chances of reaching $100,000 rise to 55%.)

Now look what happens if he doesn't start contributing until he is 40. In that case he will have less than a 5% chance of reaching his $100,000 goal. To have the same 35% chance of hitting the mark that he had at age 30, he'll have to more than double his savings, to $21,000 per year. But since he's already maxing out his 401(k) contributions, the additional money will have to be invested in an after-tax account. Assuming he's in the 30% tax bracket, that would mean he'd actually need to come up with a total of $25,700 to be able to invest the whole $21,000.

The moral is obvious: It's much easier to get an early start.

3. Go for Growth

As anyone who hasn't been living in a cave already knows, stocks have outperformed every other major financial asset class over the long haul. It follows that any long-term investor should make a serious commitment to stocks, and indeed, most retirement investors have got the message. Three-quarters of the respondents to the John Hancock survey said they invested at least part of their 401(k) in equities, more than double the proportion invested in any other investment option and up from 42% in 1992. Trouble is, again, investors appear to have no real plan here.

START SAVING EARLY

● ● ●

Suppose you want to retire at 65 with $100,000 a year. If you start saving $10,000 a year at age 30, you have a 35% chance of success. (As the chart on the left shows, you also have a 5% chance of retiring on $240,000.) If you wait until 40 (chart at right), your chances drop below 5%.

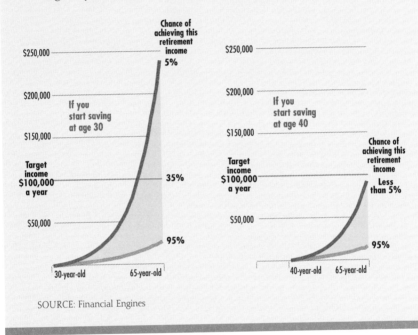

SOURCE: Financial Engines

For one thing, they may be getting too much of a good thing. On average they think 47% of one's portfolio should be in equities, yet 57% admit they invest more than that. "This suggests people aren't thinking about having a target mix and sticking with it," says Hancock's Gates. "It's a let-it-ride philosophy. They're leaving their stock gains on the table." At the same time, investors seem too ready to bail. In the wake of a market decline of 10% or more, most say they would transfer money out of the stock market or allocate less of their future contributions to stocks. "If they had a plan, they'd be doing the opposite or sitting tight," notes Gates.

Financial planners say you should keep at least half your portfolio invested in stocks at all times. The classic "balanced" mix of assets is 60% stocks, 40% bonds. But a daredevil twentysomething investor just starting to accumulate assets might plunge 100% in stocks, while a nervous Nellie retiree with plenty of assets already on hand might scale back to only 30%—but never less than that.

4. Diversify

In their book *Getting Rich in America*, economists Dwight R. Lee and Richard B. McKenzie advocate taking what they call "prudent risks," meaning only those risks that have real potential to increase your return. Loading up on one kind of equity (like, say, Internet stocks) or a single issue—say, all that employer stock in your 401(k)—is an example of risk taking that doesn't sufficiently increase your expected return. The results from such concentrated gambles range from moonshot gains to total wipeout, depending on wholly unforeseeable events.

On the other hand, diversifying your stock holdings—owning a mix of large, small, and foreign stocks—is a way of converting the market's unpredictability into a prudent risk. Sure, the market as a whole can still go through rough patches. But because random good luck in one stock can offset the opposite in another, a carefully diversified portfolio ensures a performance that roughly tracks the market as a whole and eliminates the possibility of truly disastrous returns.

If you have the money and the inclination, you can try your hand at assembling a portfolio of individual stocks. But bear in mind that you'll need to spread your money among at least 15 stocks to be fully diversified.

A simpler alternative is to buy index funds. Remember, you're not trying to beat the market here. You need only to buy in, and index funds basically guarantee you 98% of the market's return. These days, thanks to the surge of interest in indexing, it is easy to cobble together a portfolio of market-tracking funds. You might put three-quarters of the money in a fund that tracks the Wilshire 5000 index, which is composed of nearly all publicly traded U.S. stocks, and the remaining quarter in a broad-based international-

KEEP AN EYE ON COSTS

• • •

If a 30-year-old does his investing in a low-cost fund with 0.19% annual fees, he has a 35% chance of reaching his goal (left chart). Investing the same sum in a fund with 1.35% expenses, the chance of success drops to 20% (right chart).

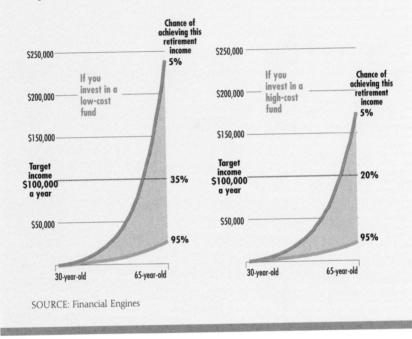

SOURCE: Financial Engines

stock index fund. Schwab and Vanguard sell both kinds. Meanwhile, Fidelity has rolled out a fund of index funds that invests 55% in a fund that seeks to match the S&P 500 index and 15% each in an international-stock index fund, a U.S.-bond index fund, and a fund that reflects the performance of small and mid-sized company stocks.

Index funds may seem boring, but they do allow you to have a life. If you're the type who thinks stock picking is fun and you're just dying to try your hand at day trading, you could divide your money into two accounts: a serious money account and a play money account. Stash the index funds in your serious money account; think of it as insurance for your retirement. Then, with your other account, go ahead and "play" the market. At least you'll be playing with money you can afford to lose.

5. Keep Costs Down

Every dollar you pay in sales commissions, investment management fees, trading costs, and taxes is a dollar not working for you. The long holding periods involved in retirement investing can magnify even slight differences in cost. Let's return to our 401(k) investor whose goal is to retire on $100,000 a year. Remember that by contributing $10,000 a year beginning at age 30 and allocating those contributions to an S&P 500 index fund, the investor has a 35% chance of reaching his goal. The index fund has low annual expenses, equal to 0.19% of assets.

Look what happens to a colleague who matches this investor in every respect except that he puts his savings in a typical equity fund, in which operating expenses consume 1.35% of assets each year. The chances of his reaching his $100,000 goal drop to 20% To achieve his more frugal colleague's 35% chance of hitting his target, the second investor would have to increase his savings some 30%, to around $13,000. Again, he would have to invest the additional $3,000 after taxes, which would siphon $4,300 out of his income.

Bottom line: The lower-cost fund allows our investor to earn higher returns and—here's the beauty part—to do so without taking on any added risk.

6. Be Patient

Even the best plan will amount to nothing if you don't give it time to work. That means having the discipline to continue saving even when you are tempted to splurge on that 12th pair of Guccis. It means having the stomach to stay invested even when the market is in a tailspin. It means having the fortitude to maintain a diversified portfolio even when it looks as if Internet stocks are a sure thing. And it means keeping an eye on costs even in good times, when costs don't seem to matter. Adopt a simple plan. Set the wheels in motion. Then, go live your life.

WHY 100% STOCKS IS 80% WRONG

BY WALTER UPDEGRAVE

• ● •

*In this heady market, some retirement
investors don't see why they need to own
anything but stocks. Here's why.*

• ● •

It's amazing how a few selective facts can make investing for
retirement seem like a no-brainer. Let's see, by mid-1999 the
stock market had more than doubled in value over the past three
years, tripled over the past five, and returned an annualized 20%
since the beginning of the bull market in August 1982. And that's
just the lumbering large caps in the Standard & Poor 500. If
you've invested where the real action is—in Net stocks—you
might have achieved comparable gains in a matter of weeks. The
obvious conclusion: If you want your retirement nest egg to grow
at warp speed, stocks are the place to be. The only place.

Listen to James Glassman, a former financial columnist at the
Washington Post, and co-author of *Dow 36,000* (Times Books). He
tells us in his books that after 17 years of a bull market, stocks still
remain severely undervalued. He predicts that equities will triple or
quadruple during the next few years until they hit a price/earnings
ratio that he considers reasonable. That P/E: about 100.

REALITY CHECK

●

We now interrupt this New Paradigm fantasy to bring you a
reality check. The chance that stocks will deliver uninter-
rupted double-digit gains from now until you're ready to leave it
all to the kids is close to zero. Stocks have lost money for considerable lengths of time in the past and could do so again. The market's P/E was 27 in the summer of 1999, off the scale by historical standards. In the past such a valuation, far from being a
springboard to a quadrupling of the Dow, has actually heralded
long stretches of single-digit returns.

The past few years notwithstanding, the stock market remains a risky place. Sure, today's portfolio strategy seems self-evident: Just stash 100% of your money in equities, then sit back and savor the gains. But at some point between now and the time you retire, that approach will make a great many people very unhappy. As a long-term investor, you would be wiser to embrace the retro notion of diversification and devote a portion of your portfolio to bonds.

Let's start by looking at the stock market's record. Yes, over very long stretches the average return on stocks has roughly doubled that of bonds. And yes, that makes a compelling argument for including equities in any long-term portfolio. Problem is, we forget that long-term averages are just that—averages. The oft-quoted calculation from the Chicago research firm Ibbotson Associates—that stocks averaged 11.2% a year from 1926 through 1998—represents the return you would have earned had you invested money at the beginning of the period and let it ride. But most of us don't keep our money invested for 73 years. Nor do we invest all at once. In effect, we get different returns on each little bundle of money we invest, depending on when we buy and sell. So the Ibbotson numbers are not, in fact, a notarized guarantee of double-digit gains. Over the 54 overlapping 20-year calendar periods since 1926, stocks have returned less than 10% a year nearly 40% of the time. And that's before transaction costs.

No less an authority than Nobel laureate economist Paul Samuelson summarily rejects the idea that stocks are preordained to beat bonds. What you buy in either security is the promise of a future stream of cash. And what matters is how much you pay for it. The giddier people become about stocks, the less likely they are to collect the returns they now consider a birthright.

In fact, research by the Leuthold Group, a Minneapolis investment firm, shows that buying stocks when they are most expensive can lock you into a below-average return for a very long time. If you invested in stocks when P/Es were between 14 and 16—the average for the market for most of this century—you typically earned a return of 11.8% over the following ten years, close to Ibbotson's long-term figure. But look what happened if you bought stocks when P/E ratios were 22 or higher. The typical

HIGH P/Es MEAN
LOW RETURNS TO COME

● ● ●

If you think the gains of the '90s are a gimme for the future, think again. Whenever the market's P/E has been more than 22 (it's 27 now), the median return over the next decade was just 5% a year. Moral: You can pay too much for stocks.

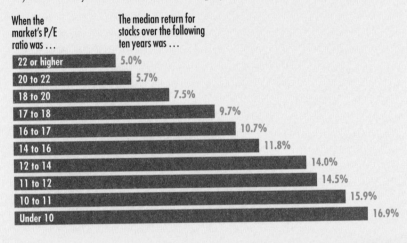

When the market's P/E ratio was ...	The median return for stocks over the following ten years was ...
22 or higher	5.0%
20 to 22	5.7%
18 to 20	7.5%
17 to 18	9.7%
16 to 17	10.7%
14 to 16	11.8%
12 to 14	14.0%
11 to 12	14.5%
10 to 11	15.9%
Under 10	16.9%

return over the following ten years was just 5%, or less than half the rate we've come to think of as money in the bank.

This relationship holds for tech stocks just as much as it does for Ford or Bethlehem Steel. The prevailing wisdom these days is that it's virtually impossible to overpay for Amazon, eBay, and AOL; as long as the Internet is really big in the future, companies like them are bound to be winners. But that logic is dangerous. "Think back to the auto industry from 1918 to 1930," says Michael Murphy, editor of the *California Technology Stock Letter*. "That was a time when the automobile went from an exotic curiosity to a mainstream product, yet the number of auto suppliers went from 4,500 to 20. Some went bankrupt, some collapsed, some were bought for peanuts." Even if Net companies do survive and live up to their potential, they may be lousy investments at today's inflated prices.

The flip side to expecting irrational returns is feeling immune to market downturns. This is crucial. You need an accurate fix on how willing you are to stomach volatility, because to earn equities' lucrative long-term returns you have to be willing to hang on through some periods where stocks can tumble 25% or more.

EXCESSIVE CONFIDENCE, ILLUSIONS

Behavioral economists—the good professors who analyze our psychological and emotional reactions to market forces—know that investors tend to extrapolate from recent experience to make projections. In a market like today's, that leads to the illusion that we, not the markets, are in control.

For a real test of your ability to tough out a bear market, imagine yourself in the market of 1973-74, when the S&P 500 suffered a 43% hit over a period of ten months. In inflation-adjusted terms, it took the market ten years to get back to even. "Those kinds of numbers can haunt your investment performance for a very long time," says Roger Gibson of Pittsburgh's Gibson Capital Management. He points out that for the five, ten, and 15 years ending in 1974, the S&P 500 with reinvested dividends lagged behind both intermediate government bonds and Treasury bills.

No one knows for sure whether we'll see a 1973–74 Armageddon-style market anytime soon (or ever again, for that matter). But if you're 15 or 20 years from retirement and expect to live off your investments for 20 or 30 years after that, well, that's an awfully long time to expect the current market nirvana to continue.

Some market observers think the possibility of something going seriously wrong has been amplified by the online revolution. We've got Net IPOs soaring to huge gains and an estimated three million households trading online. So far this combination of instant gratification and positive reinforcement has helped propel the market upward. But what if the reinforcement turns negative in the wake of a market downturn?

Hersh Shefrin, a finance professor at Santa Clara University and author of *Beyond Greed and Fear: Understanding Behavioral Finance and the Psychology of Investing* (Harvard Business Books), thinks the process of projecting yesterday's gains into the future could kick into reverse. "If things start to look bad, people may extrapolate the other way, and we'll see the flip side of what's happening today," says Shefrin. "That's when the panic sets in."

THE BRAVE DO CAVE

Not you, of course. You are a true long-term investor, willing to look beyond the shadowy valleys to the shining peaks of future returns. Still, when everyone around you is bailing out and you are actually watching your portfolio shrink before your eyes online, it's not going to feel as though the panic will end. Which is why in a bear market even many of the brave eventually cave.

A bear market can be especially dangerous once you've begun to depend on your investment portfolio to provide retirement income. This is basic arithmetic: It's much harder to rebound when you're drawing on your portfolio at the same time it's being ravaged by a market meltdown. "Think of it this way," says Joseph Healy, director of retirement marketing at T. Rowe Price. "A bear market compresses the value per share of your holdings, so you have to consume more shares to get the same amount of income. When the rebound comes, that makes it harder to regenerate the capital you've consumed."

Let's say that you had retired at age 60 at the end of 1968 with $500,000 in a tax-deferred retirement account invested in an S&P 500 index fund. And let's further assume that you had also figured on making annual withdrawals starting at $30,000 with yearly cost-of-living increases of 3%. Had the market returned a steady annual 10%, you should have had no trouble pulling off that plan. But there's the little matter of the 1973–74 bear market, which puts a major dent in the portfolio early on. As a result, if you had stuck to your scheduled withdrawals, you would have run out of money in 1993. But had you instead put 75% of your money in the S&P 500 and 25% in intermediate U.S. bonds, you would have had more than $300,000 left in 1993. And your portfolio would still be going strong, with a balance of more than $200,000 at the beginning of this year.

Ironically, the annualized return on the S&P 500 was actually higher than that for a 75–25 mix of the S&P 500 and intermediate government bonds over the 30 years covered in the above example—12.7% vs. 11.9%. But because the bear market occurred relatively early in retirement in this case, the all-stock portfolio never had a chance to bounce back. In the blended portfolio, on the other hand, the bonds provided some breathing room during the 1973–74 compression.

THE OLD PARADIGM

Which brings us back to that Old Paradigm notion of diversification: Put together a portfolio with a variety of assets that don't all move in sync, so you get a bit of shelter during market storms. This won't get you the highest possible gain, unless all investments earn exactly the same return. But diversifying can give you much of stocks' upside while making it more likely you'll stick with the stocks you do own during market routs.

For example, had you stuck all your money in large-cap stocks in 1973 and let it ride through the end of 1998, you would have earned a 13.6% return, according to the Frank Russell Co. Impressive, although you would have suffered through a 12-month loss of nearly 40% during the 1973–74 bear market. Had you baked your all-stock pie with a 25% position in intermediate government bonds, you would have earned 12.7%—or 93% of large stocks' returns—and never had a 12-month loss worse than 30%.

So what's the best course? If you're depending on your investments for retirement income, you can afford to forget about diversification only if your portfolio is so huge or if you have so many other sources of income that a big downturn in stock prices won't pinch your lifestyle. If you're still building your retirement nest egg, you can skip diversifying if you're absolutely sure you won't panic and sell out during a steep and prolonged bear market. Like Roger Gibson and Hersh Shefrin, I think that's a very big "if." Ultimately, though, you have to do your own gut check of your appetite for risk and build your portfolio accordingly.

A PORTFOLIO FOR A GOOD NIGHT'S SLEEP

BY AMY KOVER

●◉●

You will always need something safe in your portfolio.

●◉●

As stocks have rallied by an amazing annual average of 29.5% over the past three years, the world seems to have forgotten all about income-oriented investing. Traditionally people have put their money largely in stocks as they build toward retirement, then moved more assets into fixed income once they retired. But now financial planners are telling clients to continue holding as much as 70% in equities even after they've stopped working.

Why? One of the greatest risks future retirees face today is that they will outlive their savings. After all, from 1977 to 1997, the average U.S. life expectancy increased by more than three years, to 77. And the longer you live, the more time inflation has to eat into your money's value. Since a bond's interest payments and face value are fixed, bonds have notoriously failed to hold up under inflationary pressure. Hence, stocks are the answer.

All that's true enough. There's just one catch: Even the most brilliant stock portfolio won't save you in a bear market. But an income investment can protect part or all of your money in nearly any noninflationary panic.

For one thing, almost all income-oriented vehicles regularly pay either dividends or interest—so except in the most *outré* versions, you get some return no matter what. Even more important, income investments provide you with much needed diversification. The best way to reduce a stock-heavy portfolio's volatility is to add some investments that have negative correlation with the stock market—meaning that they have historically yinged whenever stocks yanged. You don't get that kind of protection if your whole portfolio moves in sync with the drumbeat of quarterly earnings projections. While this stock-smitten market makes it seem as though there's little to choose from in the income arena, here are several great ideas.

Dividend-paying stocks. If you don't want to veer too far from the stock market, go ahead and buy more stocks. Dividend-paying stocks, that is. While the S&P 500 pays a mere 1.2% dividend yield, stocks in utilities, financials, energy, and consumer staples sometimes produce as much as four times that. So you get the security of a steady dividend plus a little price-appreciation kick. Even more important, dividends can cut down on your portfolio's volatility. "Though many of these companies might grow at slower rates, they do tend to be more conservative and stable," says John Carey, who manages Pioneer Equity Income.

Comfortable. Stable. Sounds like a definition of the electric utility stocks of years past. Fat-cat utility companies historically operated as huge regional monopolies that could easily crank out consistent revenues and pay investors around 4% in dividend yields each year. All that has changed now that deregulation has made the industry more competitive. Today many companies are cutting their dividend payments to make performance-enhancing capital investments instead. "Dividend safety is a much smaller universe these days," explains Morgan Stanley utility analyst Kit Konolige. He suggests looking for businesses that specialize in distribution, an area still heavily regulated.

Another intriguing, albeit a bit riskier, option is financial stocks, which have traditionally thrown off slightly above average dividend yields. The main appeal here, though, is appreciation: Consolidation in areas like regional banking and insurance should continue to pump up the stock price. To stay on the safe side, James Ellman, who was recruited by Merrill Lynch in 1999 to run its Global Financial Service fund, suggests looking for financial companies that depend on fee-based businesses rather than unpredictable capital market trading.

Real estate investment trusts. For the ultimate diversification, you could move away from stocks and bonds entirely and try a little real estate. The easiest way to do that would be through real estate investment trusts (REITs), the stocks of corporations that hold pools of properties such as apartment buildings, hotels, or malls. REITs hand out very generous dividend yields—an average of 7.39% as of the end of June 1999—and their land holdings offer the promise of some capital appreciation. Best of all, REITs tend to move in the opposite direction from large-cap growth stocks. A study by Keith Pauley and Todd Canter of LaSalle Investment Management indicates that REITs have very high negative correlations with large-cap stocks in both technology and communications. That can smooth out periodic jolts in your portfolio. In fact, the LaSalle study shows that a portfolio with five-year annualized returns of 30% cut its standard deviation (the recognized statistical measure of volatility) by nearly 15% simply by adding REITs.

Just one warning: REITs should be used for income, not growth. Many people forgot this back in 1996 and 1997, when the trusts' value rallied by 56.3%. "We were the dot.coms of the year," jokes Skip Aylesworth, portfolio manager of FBR Realty Growth. But price chasers suffered the consequences in 1998, when REITs crashed by 18%. Had you simply ignored the growth and focused on your income instead, none of that would have mattered much to you. That's why it pays to stick with properties that can generate steady earnings from rental fees, like office space, apartment buildings, and warehouses.

Convertible bonds. You really want to limit risk? How about an investment that has weathered the only full-fledged bear in a major market in recent history?

Convertible bonds are low-yielding corporate bonds that can be swapped for a specified number of common shares in the issuing company. As a result, a convert's price will rise more or less with that of the underlying common, but below a certain point it will take on a bond's downside protection. So while a convertible may capture only, say, 80% of its underlying stock's upside, it will suffer a mere 40% of any slide. According to a study from Ibbotson Associates, from 1973 to 1992—a period that included several bear markets—U.S. convertibles beat U.S. common stocks by almost half a point a year. Nick Calamos, who co-manages $3.9 billion for Calamos Asset Management, found that in the Japanese market between 1978 and 1996—a period that included a barnburning rally and, since 1990, an ongoing vicious bear—convertibles returned an annual average of 9.03%, vs. just 7.66% for the Nikkei stock index. In fact, Calamos points out, "the Japanese convertible market today is 40% to 45% above its 1989 peak." The Nikkei? Off 53%.

Of course, convertibles are not risk-free. Smaller and sometimes shakier companies tend to issue them because they're one of the cheapest kinds of debt. Furthermore, many convertibles are available only to institutional investors. That's why it makes sense simply to buy a good fund.

Fixed income. That brings us to actual bonds. No matter how much people like to knock them, bonds are the only investments that aim to return your principal intact while also promising a particular return. And even the most stock-obsessed financial advisers suggest that after you retire—or maybe even before—you should keep at least 30% of your portfolio in bonds. As legendary manager Bill Gross of the PIMCO Total Return fund puts it in the wake of this decade's incredible stock market rally: "Good Lord, let's protect some principal!"

What's more, while bonds and stocks have typically mirrored each other's performance over the past 44 years, a study by Oppenheimer Funds indicates that this trend has begun to change. Since 1998, weekly returns of the S&P 500 and ten-year Treasury bonds have parted ways. The last time that happened in a big way was also the last time we had a spell of such low inflation: the 1960s. Oppenheimer analyst Robert Robis expects the recent trend to go on as inflation fears continue to abate.

Of all debt, Treasury bonds offer the most foolproof protection. They're not only incredibly liquid—after all, they're part of a $3.25 trillion market—but they're also backed by the full faith and credit of the federal government. So unless the U.S. suddenly collapses, you'll get your money back (though inflation will have eaten into part of its real value).

The safest method of investing in Treasuries is to build a laddered portfolio—a series of bonds with staggered maturities. For instance, buy a basket of Treasuries and put equal amounts in securities ranging from one- to ten-year maturities. When the one-year bill comes due, reinvest it in a new ten-year. That way, if rates rise, you capture the higher yield. (Many bond types actually would argue that you're better off taking a little risk in areas with sexier yields, like high-grade corporate debt or even junk bonds.)

Worried about taxes? Load up on municipal bonds, which are exempt from federal taxes and most applicable state and local taxes. Though you lose on the yield, the tax protection can more than make up for it for anyone living in tax hells like New York. Let's say you're in the 33% combined federal and state tax bracket: You would need to get at least 7.13% on a taxable bond to pocket as much after taxes as you would with a muni yielding 4.78%. You may decide to avoid buying mutual funds altogether and purchase your bonds individually. The advantage of buying bonds outright is that (barring an unlikely default) you'll get your full principal and interest payment at maturity. Not so with a bond fund. But watch out. Buying individual municipals or corporates can be incredibly complicated. For one thing, it's expensive: A round lot costs at least $10,000, and in order to properly diversify you'll need close to $1 million. By contrast, you can get into a bond fund for only $2,000 or so. What's more, brokers make their money by adding hidden markups to individual bonds. Costs get steeper if the bonds are riskier or less liquid or if you're buying fewer of them. True, you have to pay annual expenses for a fund, but at least you'll know how much you're shelling out.

Maybe the best way to think of income investing is as a fallout shelter that protects at least a portion of your money from any unforeseen disaster. And the rest of your savings? Throw it into stocks.

WHAT YOU DON'T KNOW ABOUT YOUR 401(K)

BY HENRY WEIL

• ● •

*Can you get a loan? How much
should you put in? The answers
may surprise you.*

• ● •

By now, just about every good corporate employee can recite
by heart the many splendors of the 401(k) plan. It's one of the
few ways to shelter your savings from taxes. It operates by con-
venient payroll deduction. If your company matches your contributions, you even get "free" money in the bargain.

It stands to reason, then, that you should always contribute
the maximum percentage of income your company allows. Don't
worry about needing cash: You can always get a loan or pull
some money out to cover certain approved "hardship" expenses.
Then when you retire, the remaining money is yours immediately. Truly, this is a splendid benefit.

The problem is, none of the statements in the previous paragraph are necessarily true—although plenty of people seem to
think so. While we're not about to deny that 401(k)s are a great
invention, very little about them is written in stone (or the law).
Most of the particulars depend on how an employer chooses to
set up the plan. So, depending on where you work, your company may legally be able to hold on to your money for more than
a year after you retire. Nowhere in the law do you have a right to
a hardship withdrawal or a loan. And in some plans you might
actually be better off curtailing your contribution rate.

In short, you may know less than you should about your
401(k)—and some of what you think you know may get you into
trouble if you act on it. To get the most out of your plan, you
should be aware of some of the more intriguing 401(k) twists,
good and bad, that we've ferreted out. Just remember the first rule
of 401(k)s: Before you do anything, check your own plan's rules
with your benefits administrator or with the plan's summary plan

CAN YOU HAVE TOO MANY 401(K) CHOICES?
• ● •

BY MATT SIEGEL

Back in 1994, the average worker with a 401(k) plan had just 4.6 investment choices—typically, a money-market fund or guaranteed investment contract, a government bond fund, perhaps a couple of equity funds, and the company stock. By 1998 the average number had grown to 8.4, according to Spectrem Group. (Among the most popular additions: aggressive growth, international, and asset allocation.) Some companies are still adding choices. Could it be that we're getting too much of a good thing?

Some experts think so. "You get to a point where it's overkill," says Robert Liberto of Segal Advisors, a 401(k)-consulting firm. Consider the plight of Ford employees, who have to plow through 60 investment options, or workers at American Stores, with a staggering 182 choices. Do they really want that many?

J.P. Morgan has conducted a rigorous series of surveys in this area. From 1993 to 1997, Morgan asked more than 2,000 investors to make explicit tradeoffs among desirable 401(k) characteristics—for instance, would they prefer a large

description (the rule book that employers are required to distribute to participants).

Time your contributions. Why wouldn't you want to contribute as large a share of your salary as you're allowed? Because if you're at a high salary, you might just blow some of your employer's matching contributions. That's free money down the drain.

Larry Heller, a director of PricewaterhouseCoopers Kwasha in Fort Lee, N.J., sketches one scenario: Let's say your base pay is $100,000, and the plan allows you to save 15% of your salary in employer contribution with few investment options or a small employer contribution with numerous options? Respondents didn't place much value on a large number of options. "Once you get above 11 or 12 options, you really start to get confusion at the participant level," says Robert Birnbaum, who ran Morgan's 401(k) business (before moving to Credit Suisse Asset Management).

MCI (now part of MCI WorldCom) learned the too-much-of-a-good-thing lesson the hard way in 1994 when it quadrupled its 401(k) list from four to 16. Despite an extensive employee-education program, says MCI WorldCom spokesperson Jamie DePeau, virtually no money went into the 12 new funds. The company blamed the disappointing response on employee confusion. MCI later scaled back to seven choices.

But MCI is an exception, says Gregory Metzger, director of defined-contribution consulting at Watson Wyatt. Once a company adds a new option, it rarely drops the fund, fearing employee backlash. For the worker/investor, the best solution, the experts say, is to have a multiplicity of options that are organized in tiers based on the employees' financial sophistication. Typical plans have three tiers. One offers seven to 11 core funds. A second tier, for less savvy workers, has three to five premixed portfolios, organized by risk tolerance. And for the truly adventurous, there's a top tier with a wide range of riskier or more sophisticated options.

the 401(k). The company kicks in a 50% matching contribution on the first 6% that you contribute from each paycheck.

At a 15% contribution rate, you would reach the tax-deductible limit of $10,000 per year by the end of August. At that point your contributions would cease. But once your contributions stop, so does the company match. In this case, you would forfeit $1,000 that your employer would have been more than happy to give you.

What should you do instead? Dial back your contribution rate. Had you contributed only 10% of your salary from the start, you wouldn't have bumped up against the tax-deductible ceiling until the end of December. The company would continue its match that whole time, ultimately giving you a total of $3,000.

Learn to love company stock. Nearly all experts say you should spread your investment risks and not keep more than 10% of your assets in any single security. But what if your company makes its matching contribution in its own stock, as most do? If it's the typical 50% match, you're automatically stuck with one-third of your 401(k) assets in one security (or more, if the stock performs better over time than other assets in your plan).

A few employers let workers switch out of company stock at any time, but usually you must hold on to your shares at least until age 59^1/2—and in many cases until you retire. The good news is, there is a loophole. If the employer classifies the plan with the Department of Labor as an employee stock ownership plan, workers are entitled to put half their company shares into other investments within the 401(k) when they turn 55. The bad news is, many plans don't qualify as ESOPs.

But don't get fed up yet. Even if you're stuck with the shares longer than you want, you may get a tax break when you take them out of the plan. How? Anytime after you retire, close out your entire account and withdraw the shares as a stock certificate. (You can roll over the rest of the assets into an IRA.) You'll owe ordinary income taxes (maximum rate: 39.6%) on the stock immediately, but only on the value of the shares at the time they went into your account. You won't owe any taxes on their subsequent appreciation until you sell them. And if you wait at least a year to sell, you'll owe just long-term capital gains taxes of no more than 20% on your profit. By contrast, all other withdrawals from a 401(k) are taxed at the higher, ordinary income tax rate.

One consideration: If you never sell those shares, your heirs wind up owing capital gains taxes on the appreciation going back all the way to their value when they originally came into your possession. That's a lot more than they'll owe on other stocks they inherit, which are taxed only on the appreciation since your death. If you have a choice, then, sell your company stock to meet retirement expenses and leave other assets to the kids.

Make money by borrowing. No, we're not going to tell you that you should never borrow from your retirement stash. If you need a loan, your 401(k) can be an efficient resource. In fact, you might even come out with a larger 401(k) than you would have otherwise! That can happen because you have to pay the loan back, with interest, and the most common lending rate charged by 401(k) plans is one percentage point above prime. You may, then, set a higher rate of return than you'd get from some conservative 401(k) investment options or, for that matter, from equity funds during a bear market.

Not that we're recommending borrowing from your 401(k) as an investment strategy. A 401(k) loan has serious costs—in particular, the opportunity cost of not having the amount of the loan in a high-returning 401(k) option.

Also, if you change jobs or if the company is sold or spun off and the 401(k) plan terminated, you might have to repay the loan sooner than you expected. You'll typically have just 60 days to pay back everything. If you don't, the IRS will consider the outstanding balance to be a premature withdrawal, on which you'll owe ordinary income tax, plus a 10% penalty if you're younger than 59 1/2. Some plans will allow you a longer payback period, which the IRS will honor. Or you may be able to roll over the loan (along with the balance of your old account) into a new employer's 401(k). But don't count on either lifesaver.

Cash out when you're still young. According to David Wray, president of the Profit Sharing/401(k) Council, a few plans give their employees the same early-withdrawal break IRA holders enjoy. You have to follow a strict formula: Divide the number of years you can expect to live (as projected by IRS actuarial tables) into your 401(k) balance. Then you must withdraw that amount every year for five years or until you turn 59 1/2, whichever comes later.

Hop jobs without spoiling your 401(k). If you go to a new job, should you take your 401(k) with you? The question could be moot if the new company doesn't have a 401(k) or doesn't allow rollovers. But assuming you have the choice, what's the best way to go?

The problem with leaving the 401(k) at the old place is that you may have fewer investment options as an ex-employee or fewer opportunities to change your asset allocation than you had when you worked there. You might also lose some loan or hardship-withdrawal privileges. On the other hand, if you plan to keep working after age $59^1/2$, it can be easier to tap a 401(k) account at a different company.

If you do leave your 401(k) with your old plan, stay in touch, warns Martha Priddy Patterson, a consultant for KPMG's compensation and benefits practice in Washington, D.C. Once you retire, the IRS requires you to start taking money out (based on a complex formula) as soon as you turn $70^1/2$. If your ex-boss can't find you, the appropriate amount will be put into an escrow account. Then, if you fail to claim the money after three, five, or seven years—depending on the laws of the state where your old company is based—the state may appropriate it.

Now wait for the payout. Okay, you've finally retired. Don't assume you'll get your money right away.

Federal rules permit a company to hold your funds for up to 60 days after the assets in its 401(k) are valued. Roughly 55% of large companies calculate 401(k) values daily, so you would have to wait no more than two months. But other large companies value assets just monthly, quarterly, or even yearly. Small companies are even more likely to run the numbers only once a year. If you just missed the annual valuation, you could be stuck waiting another whole year, plus the federally allowed 60 days—in all, 14 months.

One final piece of advice: It may be up to your company to set the rules for its 401(k) plan. But it's up to you to take full advantage of those rules.

FINANCING YOUR RETIREMENT HOME

BY CAROLYN T. GEER

*Because you can afford to forgo a
mortgage doesn't mean you should.*

Homebuyers emerge like crocuses in the spring, the busiest moving season of the year. Nowadays that includes lots of retirees and near-retirees looking for that perfect retirement home at the end of the rainbow, either trading down to a smaller house or purchasing a second home in places like South Carolina and Florida.

Unlike most homebuyers, many of these folks, having built up sizable nest eggs, can afford to forgo a mortgage and pay cash. And many do just that. After all, who wants to take on more debt, especially if you've just finished paying off the mortgage on your old house?

In many cases, however, taking out a mortgage is precisely what you should do. "The less you need a mortgage, the more you should have one," says Tim Kochis of Kochis Fitz, a San Francisco-based financial-planning and advisory firm that deals with high-net-worth individuals.

Home-mortgage interest, remember, is fully income-tax deductible (subject to the overall limit on itemized deductions, which for 1998 hit couples whose adjusted gross income exceeded $124,500). That, combined with recent relatively low mortgage rates, drives the "cost" of a mortgage way, way down. The higher your tax rate, the "cheaper" the mortgage.

Many retirees are surprised to find that despite their lack of earned income, they're still forced to pay high taxes simply as a result of their Social Security, pension, and investment income. There is a good chance that a mortgage would cost them less than they could earn, after taxes, investing the money they otherwise would spend on a house.

Say you are in the 28% tax bracket: A 7% mortgage would really cost you only 5.04% after tax (7% x 28% = 1.96%, the deductible portion of the mortgage; subtract that 1.96%, and you've got 5.04%, the real after-tax cost). That means you'd need an after-tax investment return of just 5.04% for the mortgage to be worthwhile. That is much less than stocks have returned on average over the long haul.

If you are in the 39.6% tax bracket, the hurdle is even lower. The same 7% mortgage would translate to an after-tax cost of 4.2%, meaning you'd need an investment return of only 4.2% after tax. Ted Bovard, an investment adviser at Fort Pitt Capital Group, an investment-management company in Pittsburgh, recently helped a client decide whether to take out a $100,000 mortgage or withdraw $100,000 from his IRA to buy a retirement house. Bovard assumed the client could secure a 15-year mortgage with a fixed 7% interest rate, that he would earn 8% on his IRA assets before tax, and that he would remain in the 28% tax bracket or higher for the duration of the mortgage.

His conclusion: In addition to the house, the client would end up with $11,200 more in his IRA at the end of 15 years if he went with the mortgage, even after making the annual mortgage payments with IRA assets. Of course, if the investment return was higher and the mortgage rate lower, the client would end up even further ahead. Even if the client got tired of carrying the debt and paid off the mortgage in six years—the point at which principal payments eclipse deductible interest payments—he still would have accumulated an additional $4,500 in his retirement account.

An added benefit of the mortgage, notes Bovard, is that the client can maintain control of his investments and liquidate them as needed. If he sinks his equity into the house, he will have to endure the delay and hassle of opening a home-equity line of credit before he can get at his money.

It is possible, of course, to get too much of a good thing. Although the law allows you to deduct a total of $1 million of home-mortgage interest on two different residences, you might not feel comfortable carrying that much debt during retirement unless you are in the very highest tax bracket.

CHAPTER SIX

● ● ●

TIMELY TECH TIPS

BUILD YOUR DREAM HOME PAGE
page 170

HOW TO JUDGE IF A WEBSITE
DESERVES YOUR BUSINESS
page 178

HIGH TECH FOR THE
HOME OFFICE OR SMALL BUSINESS
page 181

BEST BOOKMARKS
page 188

BUILD YOUR DREAM HOME PAGE

* ● ●

It's easy now to design your own Website

● ● ●

You haven't learned to create your own Web pages? You haven't built your own Website? Okay, so creating Web pages isn't for everyone. It's not a skill you must have to get a better job, make new friends, or otherwise participate in the world.

But these days nearly anyone can learn to design and construct Web pages. All you need is the right Web-authoring software and a half-decent PC or Macintosh computer to create pages with text, photos, and animated graphics. Newcomers and pros alike can take advantage of the visual design tools and templates such programs offer.

Since the World Wide Web came into being back in 1993, Web-publishing tools have advanced rapidly in sophistication and ease of use. Originally, creating pages meant mucking around, line by line, with a programming language called HTML. Today, long strings of HTML "tags" and instructions still give Web pages their visual appearance—the text fonts, the background colors, the placement of photos, and even the invisible, mouse-activated hyperlinks that connect pages with one another around the world—but instead of writing HTML code by hand, it's now possible for computer programs to automatically generate that code.

Building Web pages has become just another form of desktop publishing: You visually arrange items on the screen until your page looks the way you want it to. The operative phrase for most authoring tools these days is "what you see is what you get," or WYSIWYG (pronounced "wizzy-wig") for short. And it takes only another mouse click or two—and minimal investment—to have your pages put on a Web server, enabling the world to browse your digital handiwork.

Which Web-authoring tool to choose? Your options depend on whether you're going to work with a Macintosh or a PC. Due to its great popularity among graphic designers, the Mac happens to run several of the most functional and sophisticated Web-authoring tools on the market—NetObjects' Fusion and GoLive's CyberStudio, for instance. The Mac also runs some less functional tools that are more than adequate for nonprofessionals. Because HTML is well standardized, it makes little difference whether you've created your pages on a Mac or on a PC. Your audience of surfers, with browsers running on virtually every brand of computer, will pretty much see just what you intended them to.

Of course, it's no surprise that PC owners enjoy a wider selection of high- and low-end authoring programs. The most sophisticated are Macromedia's Dreamweaver and SoftQuad's HoTMetaL Pro. All do a good job of aiding visual placement of text, graphics, and other elements, such as pushbuttons and text boxes. However, the programs differ in how well they help with such advanced features as creating animated graphics or connecting pages to other computer systems that handle credit-card transactions. For most people who aren't making their living authoring Web pages, any of these programs offers a surfeit of functions and features.

Almost all of the Web-publishing programs, for both Mac and PC, come with rich libraries of clip art, page templates, and style sheets, which you can use as is or modify. Several include image-editing tools for adding certain special effects to photos and graphics. And the programs generally make changing the graphic style of a complete Website a snap—from the highest-level home page to the lowest branch of a site's treelike hierarchy. Just pick a new style from the appropriate menu, and *voilà*: Every page's background color, button style, and text font are updated immediately. Think of this as a graphic equivalent of the "search and replace" command in word-processing programs.

Using any of these visual page editors makes the job of assembling elements into pages and stitching the pages into full sites a lot like playing with Tinkertoys. You can try one option, replace it with another, and arrange your site's pages over and over again. Behind the scenes, the authoring program does most of the tedious housekeeping, making sure pages stay linked correctly and keeping track of photos and other items that will eventually be delivered electronically to your chosen Web server.

A note of caution is in order: Don't expect to be able to crank out Web pages containing all the coolest features and razzle-dazzle

WEB HOSTING:
WHERE TO SET UP
A SITE OF ONE'S OWN

● ● ●

Once you've created your own Website, what do you do with it? Unless you want to worry about it 24 hours a day and hire your own technicians, your best option may be to have someone else host the site for you. Most Internet service providers (ISPs) will take care of everything for you, or you can turn to one of the 4,000 "Web hosting" companies. The kinds of sites that professionals and small businesses might require can cost from nothing (see below for the catch) to $100 per month.

In general, the more you pay, the larger your Website, the easier it will be for others to find it and the faster the pages will show up on screen. You can always start with a simple site and move it when you outgrow a particular hosting setup.

For most individuals, the easiest way to get started is with your current Internet service provider. Most ISPs, including America Online, offer as part of their monthly service enough storage space to host a relatively simple Website—usually about 5 MB, or maybe 50 simple pages' worth. The trouble with such a setup is that your Web address will be unwieldy—

that you may see on the Web today. The best animations and eye-popping features are often created with specialized programming and, more often than not, hand-coded HTML. Though authoring programs' scope and function improve with every new release, it's not possible to prepackage or quickly recreate in a software tool every new bit of magic and entertainment that sweeps the Web.

But if you want to try to create some magic of your own, HTML is one of the simplest computer languages to learn. In just a few days, most computer-literate people can grasp the basics, which is enough to build well-organized and useful Web pages. The main benefit of working in HTML itself is the precise control something like www.ISPcompany.com/members/mywebsite/home.html. And, because ISPs often skimp on computing resources for members' Websites, your audience may wait up to a minute to see your page.

So, pay up. First, you'll want to register a unique Internet domain name, a task that most ISPs and Web-hosting specialists will handle for a one-time fee of about $150. Then, starting at about $25 a month (plus a setup fee of $50), an ISP or hosting firm will serve as much as 100 MB worth of pages under that name. The big advantage of hosting firms such as Hiway Technologies and Digiweb is that they've tuned their servers for extra-fast delivery of Web pages. Plus, they offer add-ons such as pre-programmed guestbooks, text chat, and search engines, which you can add to your pages for little or no extra charge. For $50 a month, your pages can even process credit-card transactions so you can sell goods or services on your site. A good place to start your search for Web-hosting specialists is HostSearch, at www.hostsearch.com.

There is another alternative, good primarily for individuals who want to display personal, no-commercial sites. Several dozen companies, including Tripod, GeoCities, NetHosting, and Angelfire, now offer "free" Web hosting. The catch is that the hosting company sells ad space; these ads must appear on or near members' pages.

you gain over the placement and appearance of all elements on a Web page.

Where to begin? Numerous HTML guides are available, all full of helpful examples. These include *HTML for Dummies*, by Ed Tittel et al. (IDG Books, 1998), and *HTML: The Complete Reference*, by Thomas A. Powell (Osborne McGraw-Hill, 1997). There is also a variety of editing tools such as Allaire's HomeSite that will automatically track certain details and check for mistakes in your code. Don't overlook the Web itself, where you will find any number of free tutorial programs such as WebMonkey (www.hotwired.com/webmonkey), which will guide you through the process of creating a Web page and keep you up to date on new design trends and style tricks.

And once you learn the basic premises of HTML, the entire Web can be your textbook. With any mainstream browser program such as Netscape Navigator, you can inspect the actual HTML "source code" that defines any Web page you find appealing. Just pull down the View menu and select "Source." There's nothing to stop you from dissecting that code, learning what makes it tick, and even reusing certain pieces of it in your own pages. That's the Web's founding ethic, after all: Share and share alike.

Following is a list of products to help you set up your home page.

SOME WEB AUTHORING PRODUCTS

● Allaire HomeSite 4.0
$99 on CD; $89 Net download   888-939-2545   www.allaire.com
For-down-and dirty coding in HTML, probably nothing beats Allaire's HomeSite editing tool. It's designed to help authors gain maximum control over the visual layout and programmed behavior of their Web pages. HTML's not difficult to learn, but using the language involves keeping track of many details, and that's where HomeSite helps out. It checks every line of HTML, looking for spelling and syntactical errors, and helps weave other programming languages—such as JavaScript and Perl—into a Web page, too.

A new feature called Design View makes it easier to build prototypes of a page or a full Website rapidly and to make small changes to existing pages.

● FileMaker Home Page 3.0
$99   800-544-8554   www.filemaker.com
Designed for all levels of Web-page experience, Home Page 3.0 is an all-visual tool for designing pages and building complete sites. It requires no knowledge of HTML, even when creating sophisticated pages with content driven by a relational database—namely FileMaker Pro. Available for Macintosh and Windows computers, this pair of programs makes it easy to create a site that displays a

product catalog, for instance, and captures orders or other information from visitors.

Home Page works like a word processor, enabling you to drag and drop text and graphics. It even wraps text around graphics and other elements automatically. Home Page comes with 45 page and site templates and more than 2,500 clip-art images.

● **GoLive Systems CyberStudio 3.1 Pro and Personal editions**
$549; $99   650-463-1580   www.golive.com

CyberStudio 3.1 Pro is one of the most powerful and flexible Web-authoring tools on the market, with facilities for managing the design and structure of single pages and entire Websites. Aimed at Web professionals, CyberStudio 3.1 handles many of the Web's latest functions and technologies, including Dynamic HTML and cascading style sheets.You can align and group objects for easier handling and drag and drop text and graphics. To add audio and virtual-reality panoramas, there's an editor for Apple Computer's QuickTime 3.0 multimedia scheme. The program allows easy previewing of new pages to test for compatibility with different browser programs. For consumers, GoLive offers CyberStudio Personal Edition, which offers strong visual page-design and site-management tools that create only "clean," standardized HTML code.

ADDITIONAL PRODUCTS

● **Adobe Systems ImageStyler**
408-536-6000   www.adobe.com $99
Operating systems: Windows 95/98 and Mac

This new tool helps creative business people and other non-design pros create jazzy graphics for Websites. It works well with any HTML authoring tool listed here, particularly Adobe's Photoshop and Illustrator programs. Among its features, ImageStyler eliminates the JavaScript programming normally required to make graphics change shape or color when touched by a surfer's mouse. Dozens of professionally styled, color-coordinated sets of graphical buttons and other page elements are included.

- **Adobe Systems PageMill 3.0**

  408-536-6000   www.adobe.com $129

  Operating systems: Windows 95/98 and Mac

  PageMill 3.0 is designed to help small-business owners and others create and maintain stylish Websites without having to hire outside help. As with a good word processor, it lets you enter and position text, graphics, pushbuttons, and even multimedia elements using the keyboard and mouse. You can preview your page or site to check its layout and page links. PageMill includes a "lite" version of Adobe's Photoshop software, for editing images.

- **Macromedia Dreamweaver 2.0**

  415-252-2000   www.macromedia.com

  $299 (If you already have an earlier version, the upgrade costs $129.)

  Operating systems: Windows 95/98/NT and Mac

  Dreamweaver is one of the more powerful Web-authoring and site-management tools. It works well with Macromedia's Fireworks, Flash, and Director products, which can add animated graphics to Websites. Dreamweaver lets you build pages and manage full sites visually but also lets you get your hands onto raw HTML code with ease.

- **Microsoft FrontPage 98**

  425-882-8080   www.microsoft.com $149

  Operating systems: Windows 95/98/NT and Mac

  FrontPage 98 is a full-function, visually oriented Web-page authoring and site-management tool. It incorporates most of the Web's latest technologies—Dynamic HTML, cascading style sheets, and so-called channels, for automatically "pushing" information to remote browsers. A built-in image-editing tool produces animated graphics. FrontPage oversees changes to all hyperlinks, content, and structure, so that pages can be repositioned with just a drag and a drop. A less functional version is available for Mac.

- **Netscape Communications Netscape Publishing Suite**

  650-254-1900   www.netscape.com $40 after $80

  Operating systems: Windows 95/NT

  Best known for its Navigator Web browser, Netscape has come out with a suite of Web-publishing tools. It includes Navigator, an e-mail package, an Internet news reader, and all the other Internet programs that Netscape offers in its Communicator product bundle. But to help build Websites, there's also a "lite" version of NetObjects' Fusion (listed above). It allows visual construction of individual pages and complete sites, and supports most of the Web's latest layout standards, such as frames and tables.

● **Symantec Visual Page 2.0**
408-253-9600   www.symantec.com $99.95
Operating systems: Windows 95/98/NT
Visual Page is a great all-around tool for creating stylish, content-rich Websites without working in pure HTML. The program takes care of tedious chores, such as making sure page links are valid and updating any that may be affected by a change in underlying file names. Cascading style sheets help give a site a uniform look and feel. The tool also provides several different views of the site and its pages, showing its physical and logical structure. For Mac users, version 1.11 is still available.

● **Viewpoint DataLabs LiveArt 98**
801-229-3000   www.viewpoint.com $49.99
Operating systems: Windows 95/98
You can't even draw a straight line? Here's an art studio in a box, able to produce illustrations of some 4,000 objects in nearly any style. Pick an object—a seagull, say—and it appears on your screen as a lifelike 3-D object, which you can rotate or zoom in on for the perfect angle. The program redraws the object in the style you've chosen—pen and ink, for instance, or watercolor. Then you can export the work to your Web-authoring program. LiveArt works as a stand-alone product or inside Office 97 applications.

———————————— ● ● ● ————————————

HOW TO JUDGE IF A WEBSITE DESERVES YOUR BUSINESS

BY STEWART ALSOP

● ● ●

Which Web companies
deserve your attention?

● ● ●

How many dot.com companies can you establish a viable relationship with? And what are you as a Web customer worth to investors on Wall Street? Judging by Wall Street valuations, there are two kinds of online companies: portals (like Yahoo) and e-commerce businesses (like Amazon). Portal customers are currently worth about $1,000 each; e-commerce customers, about $2,500. Customers of online companies that combine those properties (like AOL) and customers who actually pay enough so that a Web company can profit from their transactions (like Schwab or eBay) are worth a major premium, closer to $5,000 each.

This notion of valuing companies by their customers presumes that customers go along with the game. But speaking personally as a customer, I'm a little tired of it. I'm tired of getting inane e-mail from companies whose Website I looked at once. I'm tired of the phony enthusiasm with which companies welcome me to their site. I'm tired of having to guess whether a company is competent enough to treat me as the valuable customer I know I am, given how much real money I spend. I'm tired of feeling like a duck in a carnival shooting gallery, constantly dinged by BBs fired at me randomly as I surf past everyone's Website.

In fact, I'm thinking about building a portfolio of favored Web vendors—sites that meet my standards for competence and service, that deserve to be one of my bookmarks. (Yes, I still use Netscape Communicator, which calls stored URLs "bookmarks" instead of "favorites," as Microsoft's Explorer does. But that's another story.) If Wall Street can decide that dot.com companies are worth some multiple of my business with them, then I think I can construct an index that shows their value to me.

I already have a bookmarked list of companies whose Websites I visit regularly and with which I have developed a trusted relationship. I use Biztravel.com (an NEA company) to make travel arrangements; Fidelity to manage my retirement portfolio; Wells Fargo for banking; Connected Corp. for online backup; Visto Corp. (an NEA company) for personal information management; and Amazon.com to buy books and videos. I deal as frequently with other companies too, probably between ten and 20. But most of those haven't figured out how to use the Web to enhance their service to me; I don't consider them preferred vendors. Then there is a host of other companies with which I do business infrequently. Some have given me good Web service when I needed it (like the *Wall Street Journal* and PC Connection). Most still think the Web has to do with spiders.

So here's how the Alsop index works: you start with three components, each of which represents an aspect of the experience you've had with a company. You rate each on a scale of one to 100, with 100 being the top.

Component No. 1: Performance. This reflects how often you need a company and the quality of the online experience. I deal with each business on my preferred list at least once a week. I get very teed off if a site isn't available or if the site is designed to satisfy someone's ego more than my needs—for example, if it has lots of self-serving graphics that make it slow, or if I have to remember tricks to get what I want done faster. Functionality and competence in user-interface design count as much as speed.

Component No. 2: Financial risk. How much of my money is at stake? The very first time I made a stock trade at Fidelity's site, I did the stupidest thing you can do. I made an order to buy shares in a company that I didn't know much about without limiting the price I was willing to pay. When I realized my mistake, I went back to the site. But it wasn't available. Fortunately, my trade executed at the price I was expecting. But since then I've wondered how a major financial institution like Fidelity can design a system that isn't available at a crucial period. (Is it a comfort to know that E*Trade, Schwab, and others have had similar problems?) I'm not as demanding of companies that provide a virtual service, such as searching the Web or giving free information.

Component No. 3: Integration. It isn't enough that a Website be well designed and treat my money appropriately. It has to provide actual, real-world service. I want my main vendors to have customer support just like the support you would expect from an airline or a courier service, and I want them to be competent about delivering products to me. That means the Website can't be isolated from other parts of the business. My earliest positive experience in this regard was ordering jeans on the Web from L.L. Bean. This was before the site offered online ordering; when I called the 800 number it listed, the representative knew I was ordering from a Web page and made me feel very confident of her competence.

The formula is (P+F+I)/(4+LTV/1000)=VV. Got that? You rate each component on a one-to-100 scale and add the result. Divide the sum by your lifetime value as a customer (as noted above, but divided by 1,000 to get a reasonable denominator) plus 4 (a fudge factor). The result is vendor value. Any site that scores higher than 25 is a site you'd readily do business with. I rate Yahoo, for instance, at (100+10+40)/(4+1)=30. Wells Fargo gets (80+100+20)/(4+5)=22. I'm not a Schwab customer, but from what I hear, its site approaches perfection in the numerator. It has great performance; it obviously handles important financial transactions; and it is well integrated with a physical delivery and support system (including a network of stores). So Schwab's vendor value would be (100+100+100)/(4+5)=33.

What's great about this approach to grading vendors is that it factors in Wall Street's estimation of the lifetime value of different kinds of customer. If investors value us highly, then our vendors should have to work harder to achieve a high score (that's why Wells Fargo scores lower than Yahoo). And maybe if the vendors respond to this kind of pressure, they'll quit bothering us with so much offline advertising on radio, TVs, and billboards and let things get back to normal.

●◉●

HIGH TECH FOR THE
HOME OFFICE OR SMALL BUSINESS

●◉●

It's finally worth all the trouble.

●◉●

Like thousands of small business owners, Bob Ellis, managing partner at Ellis & Aeschliman in Columbus, Ohio, has little patience for wasting time with irritatingly complex technologies. "I'm a lawyer, not a computer technologist," says Ellis. Fortunately, more companies are starting to make communications and networking products for people like him.

Now that the Internet has become a vital tool, small businesses, branch offices, and home offices need access to equipment and networking gear that is inexpensive and easy to install and operate, yet capable of providing all the functionality of a corporate office. Most small businesses also need to juggle phone lines, faxes, and voice mail, and manage their telecommunications networks without the help of a technical staff.

Just as desktop PCs and peripherals are now tailored to the small-business setting, a new breed of networking and telephony products cater to the small office and home office (SOHO) market. Many are designed for easy setup and maintenance—think "office in a box" kits—and combine a number of functions in a single appliance, whether it's a modem, server, or switchboard.

For many small businesses the first step is moving from stand-alone computers and single-user Internet access to setting up a local area network, or LAN, which connects those computers, printers, and other gear. Most networks rely on so-called Ethernet connections that deliver data at speeds of either ten or 100 megabits per second (Mbps). These typically require equipment to connect the multitude of cables and often a separate computer that will act as a server to store files that will be shared.

There are simpler alternatives that don't involve a tangle of wires. Proxim's wireless Symphony network and WebGear's Aviator system, for example, use radio signals instead of the traditional wire or cable to connect computers. Several new systems use the phone lines in the office or home. Intel's AnyPoint Home Network kit, for example, complies with the new home phone line network standard. The computer traffic runs at a unique frequency so that regular calls aren't disturbed, and installation is as simple as plugging the computer into the phone jack.

Once on a LAN, computers can share a common Internet connection without needing a separate phone line and modem for each PC. Modems designed for the SOHO market usually include telephony features, such as voice messaging, and some provide higher speeds by using two phone lines at once. To enable two PCs to share access to the Net, products such as the relatively basic NovaWeb Technologies' NovaWeb 2001 combine a modem, an Internet gateway (to direct the traffic to the right computer), and a simple networking kit. Businesses with more than a handful of PCs will want more horsepower. For offices that already have a LAN, the WebRamp 410i from Ramp Networks can link as many as 253 computers to the Internet.

Many of the Internet appliances for small businesses handle a wide range of communications chores in one unit. Products such as WindDance Networks' Breeze Thin Server, Encanto's e.go server, or Whistle Communications' InterJet provide easy access to the Web, along with e-mail and other services. Often they can also be used to run an e-commerce site for selling products over the Web.

Most small businesses get by with ordinary dial-up Internet service, but power users will want faster access through one of the cable modem, digital subscriber line (DSL), or ISDN services. ISDN service is commonly available through phone companies; newer cable modem and DSL services can be hard to find. The cable and telephone companies have only begun to offer these services in a few areas around the U.S., at costs ranging from $30 to $200 per month.

After a computing network is set up, even small offices will require some kind of multiline phone system. The traditional corporate setup is a private branch exchange, or PBX, which runs a single main line and numerous in-office extensions. A PBX is usually not an option for small businesses, because installation is complicated, and hardware costs run from $250 to $500 per phone. As voice and data technology converge, these prices should drop; in the meantime, a small business on a tight budget can look for versatile, less expensive systems designed for managing from two to eight phone lines.

Siemens, for example, offers a wireless phone system starting at $399 that allows multiple lines, up to eight cordless phones, and transfers. Somewhat more complex is Bizfon, a complete, low-cost phone system with a digital communications switch, four desktop phones, voice mail, caller ID, conference calling, call greeting, and routing calls, starting at $995.

Slightly larger offices may want to opt for Centrex, a service available from most local phone companies for a monthly fee that starts at about $10 per line. The service mimics a PBX, with call routing, conferencing, and more, but avoids the hardware expense.

Small businesses may also want to take advantage of new services that send faxes via the Internet. Besides the convenience, this strategy can mean a considerable savings in long-distance charges. This is a boon for businesses with frequent overseas correspondence. NetMoves and .comfax, for example, send faxes over the Web from a PC to any fax machine. SoftTek's webfaxit.com Web-based service integrates fax and e-mail capabilities, making it ideal for mass mailings. On a smaller scale, eFax (www.efax.com) is a free service that provides users with a fax number to receive faxes through e-mail.

For people like attorney Ellis, the computer and communications manufacturers' new-found focus on small business is good news. It took him about 30 minutes to remove his WebRamp from the box and set it up as an Internet gateway for 13 PCs. Now everyone in the office has e-mail and the Internet at their fingertips. "It's easily saved us several thousands of bucks a year we'd otherwise be paying in research costs," Ellis says. "By far it's the most dependable piece of equipment we've had." And that means there is more time available for handling clients' work.

Following are lists of the products, including networking tools, web servers, modems, software, and other services that will allow your home office or small business to function like a corporate office.

HIGH TECH FOR HOME AND SMALL OFFICE

NETWORKING TOOLS

● Best Data Products Home PC Link
818-773-9600   www.bestdata.com $149
Speed: 56 Kbps   Connection: Phone

This home LAN and Internet gateway uses two six-foot telephone cables to network two PCs together. You plug your computers, telephone, printers, and other peripherals into phone jacks on one line, and the computers can simultaneously connect to the Internet over the same phone line. The kit comes with two cards and can support as many as 25 PCs.

● Cisco Systems Cisco 1538 Series Micro Hub 10/100
800-553-6387   www.cisco.com $495
Speed:10/100 Mbps   Connection: Ethernet

This inexpensive Fast Ethernet hub can connect as many as eight PCs directly on its eight ports, or as many as 32 devices with a stack of hubs. The hub can automatically switch back and forth between 10BaseT and faster networks for best performance. It offers up to ten times the performance of traditional Ethernet hubs and comes with a lifetime warranty.

● Diamond Multimedia HomeFree Phoneline 8
800-468-5846   www.diamondmm.com $99
Speed: 1 Mbps   Connection: Phone

Diamond paved the way for easy home networking with its HomeFree kit, and its new HomeFree Phoneline promises to be even simpler: Just install the card and plug the cord into a phone jack—the network operates at a different frequency, so it doesn't interfere with regular phone use.

● Intel AnyPoint Home Network
877-649-5817   www.intel.com $189
Speed: 1 Mbps   Connection:Phone

Intel's AnyPoint is exceptionally easy to set up: The network card is in a module that plugs into a PC's parallel port, which then plugs into a phone jack. Software installation is automatic. And the kit is compliant with Home Phoneline Networking Alliance standards, so you can build onto an existing phone network with single connectors ($99).

● **LinkSys HomeLink PhoneLine Network in a Box**
  800-LINKSYS   www.linksys.com $89
  Speed: 1 Mbps   Connection: Phone

This latest kit from LinkSys provides the easy installation of a phone line network, is capable of supporting up to 25 users, and features a 10BaseT Ethernet port to make upgrades to 10 Mbps simple. Included are cables and PCI cards for two machines and software for sharing a modem and Internet connection. For expansion, individual cards cost $49. Ethernet starter kits are also available.

● **NetGear DB104 Network Starter Kit**
  888-638-4327   netgear.baynetworks.com $179
  Speed: 10/100 Mbps   Connection: Ethernet

NetGear provides home offices and small businesses with a wide selection of networking hardware, and its kits are an excellent way to get started. The newest kit features a four-port dual-speed hub that automatically switches between 10 Mbps and 100 Mbps. Two dual-speed cards are included, along with 25-foot cords, clear instructions, a five-year warranty, and 24/7 tech support. Supports Windows, Novell, and Unix.

WEB SERVERS

● **Cobalt Networks Qube 2**
  888-702-6225   www.cobaltnet.com $995 and up
  Speed: 115 Kbps   Connection: Phone, cable modem, ISDN, XDSL, T1

The Qube is a Linux-based Web server that offers an Internet gateway, e-mail, firewall, and Web publishing. Version 2 features enhanced work-group collaboration capabilities such as cross-platform document management and discussion groups. The Qube 2 also comes with a 250MHz processor and two Ethernet ports for connecting directly to the Internet or an ISP without a router.

- ## Encanto Networks e.go
  888-ENCANTO   www.encanto.com $995
  Speed: 56 Kbps   Connection: Phone

The basic e.go offers Web hosting, e-mail, an Internet connection, a firewall, and administration tools. The $1,295 e-commerce model also provides software for creating a product catalog, access to credit-card payment processing, and a four-port Ethernet hub. ISDN models are available.

- ## Whistle Communications InterJet 100
  888-494-4785   www.whistle.com $1,995
  Speed: 33.6 Kbps   Connection: Phone, ISDN

Like OneGate, the Whistle InterJet Web server offers e-mail, Internet access, firewall security, and the ability to publish on the Web for 25 users. It comes with 8 MB of RAM, a 1.2GB IDE disk drive, and a four-port 10BaseT hub for connecting an Ethernet LAN or PCs to the Internet.

MODEMS

- ## Diamond Multimedia SupraExpress 56i Sp V.90 Modem
  800-468-5846   www.diamondmm.com $119
  Speed: 112 Kbps   Connection: Phone

If you have two phone lines and an ISP that supports modem "bonding," you can double your download speed with this unusual modem. The SupraExpress includes one PCI card and two 56K modems that work together to deliver download speeds as fast as 112 Kbps and upload speeds as fast as 66 Kbps. The SupraExpress 56 PC also possesses fax and voice mail capabilities.

- ## Systems MessageSaver MultiTech
  800-328-9717   www.multitech.com $219
  Speed: 56 Kbps   Connection: Phone

MultiTech's MessageSaver may look like a standard 56K modem, but it also serves as a telephone, a fax machine, and a voice mail messaging system—functions that are unaffected when the PC is turned off. An answering machine handles all incoming calls, while a speaker phone lets users conduct conversations or play back digitally recorded voice mail messages.

• Artisoft TeleVantage 2.1

800-914-9985   www.artisoft.com $750

TeleVantage 2.1 enables up to 144 users to manage virtually all aspects of telephone communications. TeleVantage runs on Windows NT, and when networked with desktop PCs, lets PC users handle multiple incoming calls, set up conference calls, and see and hear voice mail messages. Version 2.1 can also forward calls to any phone or pager number, or to multiple phone numbers.

• .comfax .comfax

888-926-6329   www.comfax.com $15 setup fee, $14.99 access fee

With .comfax, users can save time and money by faxing over the Internet. The software enables the user to send faxes from the PC to another fax machine, from any location and with any ISP. The cost of sending faxes ranges from 10 to 14 cents per minute. Subscribers receive unlimited faxes for local area code in box fax numbers. RSA encryption protects your information.

• NetMoves NetMoves One

800-828-7115   www.netmoves.com $4.95 per month

NetMoves One can send faxes via the Internet to any fax machine. The $4.95 price covers domestic faxing and includes 100 inbound and 100 outbound faxes per month. For inbound and outbound faxing beyond 100, each fax is 5 cents per page. NetMoves One connects the user to NetMoves Global Internet Fax Network for point-to-point and broadcast faxing.

• Symantec TalkWorks Pro 2.0

800-568-9501   www.symantec.com $169.95

This full voice and fax messaging package includes voice mail with multiple mailboxes, customizable or professionally recorded greetings, and call tracking. With its fax-on-demand capability, TalkWorks lets customers call 24 hours a day, follow simple instructions, and select the documents they want faxed. TalkWorks can also page or call you to alert you to messages or faxes.

BEST BOOKMARKS

Here are the favorite Websites of a group of innovative and well-rounded business leaders. Some you may know, but many you will be pleased to learn about for the first time.

Meredith Fischer is vice president for corporate marketing at the postal meter and fax company Pitney Bowes in Stamford, Conn. She is one of the authors of a 1999 study on messaging and work conducted by Pitney Bowes and the Institute for the Future. Here's where Fischer hangs out when she's not messaging.

Virtual Vineyards www.virtualvin.com Comprehensive reviews of different kinds of wines—and they're easy to order. Too bad you can't download a wine tasting!

About.com www.miningco.com I like the mediated approach of this portal. The reviews and real-people guides help lead you to the information you want.

Dell www.dell.com Dell does a great job of market segmentation. The site is very approachable, with easy navigation. Definitely a site to watch.

Matt Hyde, a former climbing guide, is vice president of online sales for REI, the outdoor gear and clothing store based in Seattle. Hyde runs the Internet leader in outdoor gear, rei.com, as well as REI's discount and Japanese online ventures.

Qiang Li's Photo Critique Forum www.photocritique.net This site attracts serious photographers from around the world. You can post scanned photographs and get frank critiques. A great Web community.

New York Times www.nytimes.com Two years ago I most often read my *New York Times* on paper. Now I find that 80% of my *Times* reading happens on the Web.

Janet Baker founded Dragon Systems, which makes speech-recognition software, with her husband, Jim, in 1982. Baker, who is CEO of the Newton, Mass., company, has a Ph.D. in computer sciences from Carnegie Mellon and a background in biophysics.

Yahoo Finance **finance.yahoo.com** For up-to-date stock quotes and financial news.

MapQuest **www.mapquest.com** When I toured the Grand Canyon and Las Vegas, MapQuest's driving directions helped me get around.

Massachusetts Institute of Technology **web.mit.edu** With a digest of current projects and links to MIT labs, this is an important source for trends and research.

Nell Minow leads a double life. A shareholder activist, she works in Washington, D.C., as a principal of the Lens investment fund. She's also a movie buff with a new book, *The Movie Mom's Guide to Family Movies*, and a Website of her own, www.moviemom.com.

Internet Movie Database **www.imdb.com** If I could be hooked up to it intravenously, I would. While I was writing my *Movie Mom* book, I almost was.

Hollywood Stock Exchange **www.hsx.com** A great place to combine my interests. I can trade stocks (movies) and bonds (directors and stars). It's wonderfully authentic, with a ticker, commissions, put and call options, and even mutual funds like "chick flicks" or "Miramax."

EDGAR Database **www.sec.gov/edaux/searches.htm** I'm here all the time, using SEC documents to evaluate corporate governance.

Yahoo message boards **messages.yahoo.com/index.html** Employees reveal things here that analysts don't hear about until much later.

Mark Cuban is co-founder, chairman, and president of Dallas-based broadcast.com, the Internet audio and video broadcast site, which was bought by Yahoo.

Newshub **www.newshub.com** A quick way to skim the headlines for relevant news.

TravelWeb **www.travelweb.com** I travel way too much, so I need a comprehensive site like TravelWeb to get flight and hotel information and make reservations.

Los Angeles Times **www.latimes.com** and *Variety* **www.variety.com** The film, entertainment, and Internet businesses are quickly becoming one. I use these sites to get breaking news.

Softseek **www.softseek.com** The shareware and freeware available here are leading indicators of what the most creative programmers are spending their time on.

Rudy Puryear, Andersen Consulting's first global managing partner for e-commerce. Puryear has helped companies such as Harley-Davidson and Motorola get e-savvy.

CEO Express **www.ceoexpress.com** Designed for busy executives, it's the gateway to just about every kind of cool and relevant content.

Cool Site of the Day **www.cool.infi.net** The easiest way to keep up with innovations in Website design.

GolfWeb **www.golfweb.com** A great source for the latest pro tour news, tips on techniques and equipment, plus an online pro shop.

American Memory: Historical Collections for the National Digital Library **memory.loc.gov/ammem/amhome.html** This Library of Congres-sponsored site is an inspiring cyber-tour of American artifacts: daguerreotypes, documents from the Continental Congress and Constitutional Convention, 19th-century baseball cards, and more.

Steve Kirsch is chairman of InfoSeek, the Sunnyvale, Calif., Web portal that is partly owned by Disney. The engineer, a fan of electric vehicles, and his wife run a $25 million foundation.

Rob Galbraith Online **www.robgalbraith.com** Own a high-end digital camera? This site is a must read.

Microsoft Tech Support **support.microsoft.com/support/ search/c.asp?SPR=ALL** When I have questions that my local systems folk can't answer, I go here.

The Hamster Dance **www.hamsterdance.com** My kids love this page. Check it out.

GO Network **www.go.com** InfoSeek is part of the GO network, which I humbly assert is the best for Web searches and stock quotes.

NECX **www.necx.com** My favorite online computer super-store is reliable and delivers quickly.

Peter Neupert, CEO of drugstore.com, launched his new online business in 1999. Before that, he headed Microsoft's efforts to launch MSNBC and the online magazine Slate.

HomeGrocer.com **www.homegrocer.com** I use the Web to save myself and the family time. Once you get your shopping list built, this great service saves time every week by delivering your groceries—and the quality of the food is fantastic.

REI **www.rei.com** When I have free time, I like to hike or bike. REI is my preferred place to get gear or advice. The site can even motivate me to get out more often.

Slate **www.slate.com** I love Chatterbox, the dialogues, and the thoughtful writing that editor Michael Kinsley has pulled together. The quality of debate are so fine that they have raised my insight and capacity for spin detection.

Joe Nacchio, in two years as CEO of Qwest Communications in Denver, transformed it from a tiny telecom outfit to a budding global powerhouse.

Bloomberg **www.bloomberg.com** I use this site as my one-stop comprehensive Web source for global financial-markets information. It keeps me in touch with what the key financial players are saying about the telecom industry.

CBS MarketWatch **www.cbsmarketwatch.com** With com-prehensive analysis and commentary, this site is great at providing up-to-the-minute quantitative and qualitative information.

Red Herring **www.redherring.com** From the applications of e-commerce to a study of the cultural foundation of the technological revolution, this site covers it all.

Andover.net **www.andover.net** Andover.net stands out for its network of tech sites that feature news and all the Internet-related freeware and shareware you could possibly need.

Orit Gadiesh is chairman of the board of Bain & Co., a leading consulting firm in Boston. The Israeli-born Gadiesh, who was trained as a scientist, has helped make Bain a favorite of FORTUNE 500 CEOs.

Map of the Market **www.smartmoney.com/marketmap**
This is a powerful, continually updated graphic depiction of where value is being added and lost in the economy. As your cursor moves over industries represented by blocks of color, company names pop up. One click leads to detailed data on each.

Corbis' Leonardo Files **www.corbis.com/leonardo97**
Corbis' Leonardo da Vinci profile, detailing his intellectual curiosity and ability to integrate ideas across disciplines, always inspires me.

ALibris **www.alibris.com** This site is terrific for finding first-edition, rare, used, and out-of-print books.

Nova **www.pbs.org/nova** Nova lets me explore new ideas and innovations, and join in expeditions as vicarious adventurer.

G.M. O'Connell is CEO of Modem Media Poppe Tyson, an Internet consulting firm in Westport, Conn., whose clients include Citiigroup and John Hancock. A pioneer of interactive advertising, O'Connell logs on from all over the world.

Excite **www.excite.com** My Excite home page gives me the Web info I need, and a decent search engine as well.

The Industry Standard **www.thestandard.com** The best online resource for keeping up with the Internet economy.

When.com **www.when.com** This site tracks events like concerts and trade shows, and lets me add the ones I want to a customized Web-based calendar I can access from anywhere.

Ann Livermore runs Hewlett-Packard's largest division, the $15-billion-a-year enterprise computing solutions organization.

The Global Schoolhouse **www.globalschoolhouse.org** I want to usher my 9-year-old daughter into cyberspace responsibly. This Website features a network of connected educators and classrooms around the world.

Beanie Babies **www.ty.com** Here's where the 9-year-old goes after homework, for the latest pet collections, virtual adoptions, and the Beanie Connection, a virtual forum for Beanie Babies fans.

iGive.com **www.igive.com** Shoppers at this online mall donate a percentage of each purchase to charity.

Chan Suh is CEO of Agency.com, a cutting-edge interactive services firm in New York. Suh left mainstream media four years ago to found the company; now he has 650 employees helping the likes of British Airways and Texaco get e-savvy.

Apple Computer **www.apple.com/powermac** I'm a die-hard Apple fan, and I use a PowerMac at work. When the pundits think it's dead, Apple roars back. User-friendly interfaces still matter more than market share.

Urban Desires **desires.com** The original Web zine is still the top content destination for me. My partner, Kyle Shannon, started it.

biztravel.com **www.biztravel.com** I travel so much that I need to be able to look at all my travel options. The ability to store my itinerary is a great feature here.

Alexander Graham Bell's research notebooks **www.indiana.edu/~ctwardy/AGB** Getting inside one of the greatest minds of this century is a trip I love to take whenever I feel the need for inspiration.

Dave Duffield is CEO of PeopleSoft, a Pleasanton, Calif., software firm that ranks sixth among FORTUNE's 100 Best Companies to Work For.

NASDAQ.com **www.nasdaq.com** This is the best place for detailed, up-to-date financial info.

Animal Rescue Foundation **www.tlr-arf.org** One of my goals is to return the love and affection pets have provided me and my family. Tony LaRussa's ARF promotes companion-animal care and community education.

Parent Soup **www.parentsoup.com** What keeps me up at night? Our five little kids. This site helps.

Bay Area Backroads **www.bayareabackroads.com** Before silicon and software, the Bay Area had nature. Here's a tour guide.

Latest Earthquake Data **sfbay.yahoo.com/external/usgs**

Alex Mandl is CEO of Teligent, a Vienna, Va., telco serving small businesses. A flashy, brilliant telecom veteran, he was once in line to succeed Bob Allen as CEO of AT&T. But he opted for something entrepreneurial. You can check out what Mandl's up to at www.teligent.com.

Wired News **www.wired.com/news** A great site for a survey of technology news and personalities.

Bloomberg Media **www.bloomberg.com** Worth checking out for business news via Web radio and video.

David Kelley is CEO of IDEO, a Palo Alto firm that has designed products for the likes of Pepsi and Apple, and that helps companies like BMW and Samsung become better innovators.

The Trip **www.thetrip.com/usertools/flighttracking** This site shows you the exact location of any flight. I use it to see whether my friends' planes will arrive on time.

How Stuff Works **www.howstuffworks.com** Ever since Mr. Rogers went to the crayon factory, I can't get enough of knowing how ordinary things work.

Eames Collection **www.eamesoffice.com** Eames gets my vote for the most important American design hero.

Panoramic Pictures **lcweb2.loc.gov/ammem/pnhtml/pnhome.html** It just feels good to look at these old photos, mostly landscapes from the turn of the century.

THE 1999
FORTUNE 500 DIRECTORY

●●●

Despite a booming business cycle and a surging stock market, America's largest companies struggled to keep their momentum going in 1998, as revenue growth sank into the low single digits and profits actually dropped for the first time in seven years. Total revenues for the FORTUNE 500 edged up by a decidedly anemic 4.0%, well below 1997's 8.7% rate. And excluding a one-time gain at No. 2 Ford, overall profits fell 1.8%.

That doesn't mean 1998 will be remembered as a down period for the FORTUNE 500. Instead it will probably be considered a watershed, the year when the New Economy fundamentally parted ways with the old and high-tech consolidated its role as the driving force behind the growth of big business. True, ranking America's 500 largest companies in order of revenues produces a list dominated by traditional giants like Mobil, General Motors, and Coca-Cola. But in 1998 such companies spent the year battling their shrinking top and bottom lines. Meanwhile challengers like Microsoft, Dell Computer, Cisco Systems, and Sun Microsystems—with their 400-megahertz rates of revenue growth and their stock-option-rich employees—made it clear that one day the FORTUNE 500 will be theirs.

The force is with the New Economy and the FORTUNE 500 reflects it.

NELSON D. SCHWARTZ

RANK 1998	COMPANY	REVENUES $ millions	PROFITS $ millions	Rank	ASSETS $ millions	Ra
1	GENERAL MOTORS Detroit	161,315.0	2,956.0	29	257,389.0	
2	FORD MOTOR Dearborn, Mich.	144,416.0	22,071.0	1	237,545.0	
3	WAL-MART STORES Bentonville, Ark.[1]	139,208.0	4,430.0	13	49,271.0	
4	EXXON Irving, Texas	100,697.0[E]	6,370.0	4	92,630.0	
5	GENERAL ELECTRIC Fairfield, Conn.[2]	100,469.0	9,296.0	2	355,935.0	
6	INTL. BUSINESS MACHINES Armonk, N.Y.	81,667.0	6,328.0	5	86,100.0	
7	CITIGROUP New York[3]	76,431.0	5,807.0	7	668,641.0	
8	PHILIP MORRIS New York	57,813.0[E]	5,372.0	8	59,920.0	
9	BOEING Seattle	56,154.0	1,120.0	79	36,672.0	
10	AT&T New York[4]	53,588.0	6,398.0	3	59,550.0	
11	BANKAMERICA CORP Charlotte, N.C.[5]	50,777.0	5,165.0	10	617,679.0	
12	STATE FARM INSURANCE COS. Bloomington, Ill.	48,113.9	1,319.7	62	111,376.1	
13	MOBIL Fairfax, Va.	47,678.0[E]	1,704.0	46	42,754.0	
14	HEWLETT-PACKARD Palo Alto[6]	47,061.0	2,945.0	30	33,673.0	
15	SEARS ROEBUCK Hoffman Estates, Ill.	41,322.0	1,048.0	85	37,675.0	
16	E.I. DU PONT DE NEMOURS Wilmington, Del.	39,130.0[E,¶]	4,480.0	12	39,724.0	
17	PROCTER & GAMBLE Cincinnati[7]	37,154.0	3,780.0	16	30,966.0	
18	TIAA-CREF New York	35,889.1	840.4	106	249,714.6	
19	MERRILL LYNCH New York	35,853.0	1,259.0	66	299,804.0	
20	PRUDENTIAL INS. CO. OF AMERICA Newark, N.J.	34,427.0¶	1,106.0	81	279,422.0	
21	KMART Troy, Mich.[1]	33,674.0	568.0	155	14,166.0	
22	AMERICAN INTERNATIONAL GROUP New York[8]	33,296.0	3,765.6	17	194,398.0	
23	CHASE MANHATTAN CORP. New York	32,379.0	3,782.0	15	365,875.0	
24	TEXACO White Plains, N.Y.	31,707.0[E]	578.0	152	28,570.0	
25	BELL ATLANTIC New York	31,565.9	2,965.3	28	55,143.9	

millions	Rank	$ millions	Rank	1998 $	% change from 1997	1988–98 annual growth rate %	Rank	1998 %	Rank	1988–98 annual rate %	Rank
984.0	28	63,839.5	42	4.18	(51.5)	(5.3)	291	21.4	154	10.2	304
409.0	11	70,881.5	38	17.76	216.0	12.5	72	86.8	30	18.6	160
112.0	13	212,850.0	3	1.98	26.9	18.3	35	107.7	21	27.1	54
750.0	4	178,913.3	8	2.58	(23.4)	2.7	214	22.4	146	17.5	174
880.0	7	360,251.5	2	2.80	13.8	11.6	88	41.0	97	28.0	50
433.0	17	165,747.4	11	6.57	9.3	3.0	211	77.5	39	14.9	217
708.0	5	148,885.3	14	2.43	(4.3)	15.0	52	(6.8)	321	31.7	30
97.0	25	93,699.0	25	2.20	(14.7)	10.2	114	22.8	143	25.1	75
16.0	37	33,855.8	65	1.15	—	2.6	215	(32.4)	413	11.3	281
22.0	9	180,156.3	7	3.55	25.0	—		26.2	134	17.7	172
38.0	2	127,145.0	17	2.90	(30.5)	7.2	162	1.3	282	19.9	137
93.9	6	N.A.		N.A.	—	—		—		—	
70.0	19	71,760.3	37	2.10	(47.6)	(1.9)	267	24.3	137	19.1	150
19.0	23	72,643.0	36	2.77	(6.1)	12.7	71	10.7	214	19.0	152
66.0	99	17,759.9	120	2.68	(10.4)	(3.5)	279	(4.4)	311	14.6	220
08.0	30	64,144.9	41	3.90	87.5	9.9	116	(9.7)	337	17.4	176
36.0	38	121,654.2	19	2.56	12.3	13.1	68	15.9	183	26.3	56
23.2	95	N.A.		N.A.	—	—		—		—	
32.0	51	33,117.5	66	3.00	(37.9)	10.8	99	(7.4)	326	30.2	37
95.0	16	N.A.		N.A.	—	—		—		—	
79.0	102	8,539.3	212	1.01	98.0	(6.6)	297	33.2	112	1.9	361
31.0	8	151,844.4	13	3.57	13.2	11.8	84	33.6	111	25.2	73
48.0	10	73,657.5	33	4.24	5.6	(3.4)	278	32.5	116	22.2	112
43.0	41	28,701.6	77	0.99	(79.7)	(9.5)	304	0.5	286	14.3	226
3.3	33	85,145.7	29	1.86	19.2	1.1	236	22.5	145	17.1	181

		REVENUES	PROFITS		ASSETS	
RANK 1998	COMPANY	$ millions	$ millions	Rank	$ millions	Ra
26	FANNIE MAE Washington, D.C.	31,498.8	3,418.1	21	485,013.8	
27	ENRON Houston	31,260.0	703.0	131	29,350.0	
28	COMPAQ COMPUTER Houston[9]	31,169.0	(2,743.0)	497	23,051.0	1
29	MORGAN STANLEY DEAN WITTER New York[10]	31,131.0	3,276.0	24	317,590.0	
30	DAYTON HUDSON Minneapolis[1]	30,951.0	935.0	98	15,666.0	1
31	J.C. PENNEY Plano, Texas[1]	30,678.0	594.0	149	23,638.0	1
32	HOME DEPOT Atlanta[1]	30,219.0	1,614.0	48	13,465.0	1
33	LUCENT TECHNOLOGIES Murray Hill, N.J.[11]	30,147.0	970.0	96	26,720.0	1
34	MOTOROLA Schaumburg, Ill.	29,398.0	(962.0)	494	28,728.0	1
35	SBC COMMUNICATIONS San Antonio[12]	28,777.0	4,023.0	14	45,066.0	
36	KROGER Cincinnati	28,203.3	410.8*	207	6,700.1	:
37	MERCK Whitehouse Station, N.J.	26,898.2	5,248.2	9	31,853.4	
38	CHEVRON San Francisco	26,801.0ᴱ	1,976.0	40	36,535.0	
39	METROPOLITAN LIFE INSURANCE New York	26,735.0	1,343.0	59	215,346.0	
40	INTEL Santa Clara, Calif.	26,273.0	6,068.0	6	31,471.0	
41	LOCKHEED MARTIN Bethesda, Md.	26,266.0	1,001.0	88	28,700.0	
42	ALLSTATE Northbrook, Ill.	25,879.0	3,294.0	23	87,691.0	
43	UNITED TECHNOLOGIES Hartford	25,715.0	1,255.0	67	18,375.0	
44	BANK ONE CORP. Chicago[13]	25,595.0	3,108.0	26	261,496.0	
45	GTE Irving, Texas	25,473.0	2,172.0*	35	43,615.0	
46	UNITED PARCEL SERVICE Atlanta	24,788.0	1,741.0	45	17,067.0	
47	USX Pittsburgh[14]	24,754.0E	674.0	135	21,133.0	
48	SAFEWAY Pleasanton, Calif.[15]	24,484.2	806.7	111	11,389.6	
49	COSTCO Issaquah, Wash.[16]	24,269.9	459.8	184	6,259.8	
50	CONAGRA Omaha[17]	23,840.5	613.2	145	11,702.8	

STOCKHOLDERS' EQUITY		MARKET VALUE 3/15/99		EARNINGS PER SHARE				TOTAL RETURN TO INVESTORS			
				1998 $	% change from 1997	1988–98 annual growth rate %	Rank	1998 %	Rank	1988–98 annual rate %	Rank
millions	Rank	$ millions	Rank								
452.8	27	73,700.6	32	3.23	14.1	19.7	29	31.7	118	35.7	19
048.0	84	22,499.9	95	2.02	531.3	18.0	36	39.9	100	23.7	86
351.0	43	53,337.5	53	(1.71)	(243.7)	—		49.0	81	35.7	20
119.0	31	58,921.8	47	5.33	28.1	—		21.4	152	—	
311.0	125	30,843.2	70	1.98	24.5	13.2	67	62.1	58	25.8	62
169.0	81	9,906.3	189	2.19	4.3	(3.1)	276	(19.5)	385	10.7	295
740.0	65	95,523.1	24	1.06	36.8	30.5	11	108.4	20	44.8	8
534.0	118	139,525.9	15	0.73	73.8	—		175.9	5	—	
222.0	39	40,874.8	59	(1.61)	(183.0)	—		7.7	230	20.3	132
780.0	35	104,211.1	23	2.03	153.8	8.7	138	49.7	78	22.9	100
387.8)	492	17,424.9	124	1.55	(1.3)	29.2	12	64.6	54	29.9	41
401.8	34	198,868.1	4	2.15	15.0	15.5	50	41.3	96	25.5	67
471.0	20	55,099.1	52	3.01	(39.2)	1.5	232	11.0	213	18.4	164
465.0	29	N.A.		N.A.	—	—		—		—	
477.0	12	196,615.5	5	3.45	(10.9)	27.1	16	69.0	49	44.8	7
37.0	98	15,223.0	135	2.63	—	(1.9)	268	(12.5)	350	16.6	189
40.0	21	31,994.6	69	3.94	10.8	—		(13.9)	357	—	
78.0	144	29,116.1	75	5.05	20.0	7.2	162	51.7	73	21.5	119
60.0	15	67,162.6	40	2.61	19.2	7.2	159	6.4	246	20.5	129
66.0	64	60,621.0	44	2.24	(22.8)	2.3	219	28.7	127	16.9	185
73.0	80	N.A.		3.14	92.6	10.4	111	—		—	
05.0	92	9,261.4	198	N.A.	—	—		—		—	
82.1	202	27,700.7	79	1.59	42.0	—		92.7	27	—	
55.9	212	19,938.2	108	2.03	38.1	0.5	242	61.8	60	7.1	331
78.9	226	15,169.4	136	1.33	(0.7)	11.9	80	(2.8)	302	19.7	140

		REVENUES	PROFITS		ASSETS	
RANK 1998	COMPANY	$ millions	$ millions	Rank	$ millions	Rc
51	JOHNSON & JOHNSON New Brunswick, N.J.	23,657.0	3,059.0	27	26,211.0	1
52	BELLSOUTH Atlanta	23,123.0	3,527.0	20	39,410.0	
53	WALT DISNEY Burbank, Calif.[11]	22,976.0	1,850.0	43	41,378.0	
54	PEPSICO Purchase, N.Y.[18]	22,348.0	1,993.0	39	22,660.0	
55	INGRAM MICRO Santa Ana, Calif.	22,034.0	245.2	282	6,733.4	2
56	FIRST UNION CORP. Charlotte, N.C[19]	21,543.0	2,891.0	31	237,363.0	
57	CIGNA Philadelphia	21,437.0	1,292.0	65	114,612.0	
58	CATERPILLAR Peoria, Ill.	20,977.0	1,513.0	52	25,128.0	
59	MCKESSON HBOC San Francisco[20,21]	20,857.3	154.9	328	5,607.5	3
60	LOEWS New York	20,713.0E	464.8	183	70,906.4	
61	AETNA Hartford	20,604.1	848.1	105	105,148.1	
62	WELLS FARGO San Francisco[22]	20,482.0	1,950.0	41	202,475.0	
63	XEROX Stamford, Conn.[23]	20,019.0	395.0	215	30,024.0	
64	SARA LEE Chicago[7]	20,011.0	(523.0)	484	10,989.0	2
65	PG&E CORP. San Francisco	19,942.0	719.0	128	33,234.0	
66	LEHMAN BROTHERS HOLDINGS New York[10]	19,894.0	736.0	124	154,000.0	
67	AMERICAN STORES Salt Lake City[1]	19,866.7	233.7	291	8,885.3	2
68	NEW YORK LIFE INSURANCE New York	19,848.9	752.9	121	90,368.1	
69	RAYTHEON Lexington, Mass.	19,530.0	864.0	101	27,939.0	
70	INTERNATIONAL PAPER Purchase, N.Y.	19,500.0	213.0	301	27,080.024	
71	AMR Fort Worth	19,205.0	1,314.0	63	22,303.0	
72	AMERICAN EXPRESS New York	19,132.0	2,141.0	36	126,933.0	
73	COCA-COLA Atlanta	18,813.0	3,533.0	19	19,145.0	
74	COLUMBIA/HCA HEALTHCARE Nashville	18,681.0	379.0	223	19,429.0	
75	DOW CHEMICAL Midland, Mich.	18,441.0	1,310.0	64	23,830.0	

CKHOLDERS' ITY		MARKET VALUE 3/15/99		EARNINGS PER SHARE				TOTAL RETURN TO INVESTORS			
lions	Rank	$ millions	Rank	1998 $	% change from 1997	1988–98 annual growth rate %	Rank	1998 %	Rank	1988–98 annual rate %	Rank
?0.0	32	122,224.6	18	2.23	(7.5)	12.0	77	29.0	125	25.2	72
?0.0	26	91,162.5	26	1.78	8.5	7.3	157	80.9	34	22.7	104
?8.9	18	73,572.4	34	0.89	(6.6)	10.9	97	(8.6)	333	19.2	148
?1.0	93	57,185.1	49	1.31	(3.7)	10.5	106	14.3	192	22.9	98
?9.3	345	2,555.6	365	1.64	24.2	—		21.5	151	—	
?3.0	22	50,279.6	55	2.95	(1.3)	7.9	150	21.9	150	23.2	94
?7.0	68	16,747.6	126	6.05	24.0	12.3	73	36.9	106	22.6	107
?1.0	128	16,230.2	128	4.11	(5.9)	10.5	107	(3.1)	304	13.2	247
?6.8	343	17,560.1	122	1.59	5.6	3.6	199	47.0	85	31.2	33
?1.2	50	9,259.9	199	4.06	(41.2)	(3.8)	282	(6.4)	320	10.7	296
?8.9	42	11,580.2	165	5.41	(3.4)	(1.4)	262	12.6	202	9.9	307
?9.0	14	63,501.7	43	1.17	(33.1)	7.6	154	5.1	255	29.6	43
?4.0	117	35,603.7	63	0.52	(74.3)	(1.1)	257	62.2	57	24.2	81
?6.0	300	24,111.8	88	(1.14)	(157.9)	—		1.7	278	21.1	125
?6.0	71	12,422.4	154	1.88	7.4	—		7.9	229	12.9	256
?3.0	121	7,216.9	239	5.19	10.0	—		(13.1)	354	—	
?9.2	232	10,081.4	185	0.84	(16.8)	10.2	113	82.3	33	19.8	138
?5.5	116	N.A.		N.A.	—	—		—		—	
?6.3	48	18,499.0	116	2.53	16.1	3.2	209	7.0	240	15.0	216
?9.024	60	13,310.2	149	0.70	—	(14.3)	317	6.2	249	9.6	314
?8.0	87	10,435.8	181	7.52	39.5	6.6	170	(7.6)	328	8.3	322
?8.0	53	56,650.4	50	4.63	11.6	6.7	169	15.9	179	19.1	151
?3.0	66	169,350.2	9	1.42	(13.4)	14.8	56	1.3	281	30.1	38
?1.0	74	11,944.7	157	0.59	—	—		(16.2)	366	—	
?9.0	77	21,363.1	102	5.76	(25.2)	(3.8)	283	(7.0)	322	8.9	318

RANK 1998	COMPANY	$ millions	$ millions	Rank	$ millions	R
76	**J.P. MORGAN & CO.** New York	**18,425.0**	**963.0**	97	**261,067.0**	
77	**BRISTOL-MYERS SQUIBB** New York	**18,283.6**	**3,141.2**	25	**16,272.5**	1
78	**DELL COMPUTER** Round Rock, Texas[1]	**18,243.0**	**1,460.0**	55	**6,877.0**	2
79	**FREDDIE MAC** McLean, Va.[25]	**18,048.0**	**1,700.0**	47	**321,421.0**	
80	**MCI WORLDCOM** Jackson, Miss.[26]	**17,678.0**	**(2,669.0)**	496	**80,193.0**	
81	**DUKE ENERGY** Charlotte, N.C.	**17,610.0**	**1,252.0**	70	**26,806.0**	1
82	**UAL** Elk Grove Township, Ill.	**17,561.0**	**821.0**	108	**18,559.0**	1
83	**REPUBLIC INDUSTRIES** Fort Lauderdale	**17,487.3**	**499.5**	176	**13,925.8**	1
84	**UNITED HEALTHCARE** Minneapolis	**17,355.0**	**(166.0)**	470	**9,701.0**	2
85	**HALLIBURTON** Dallas[27]	**17,353.1**	**(14.7)**	437	**11,112.0**	2
86	**SUPERVALU** Eden Prairie, Minn.[28]	**17,201.4**	**230.8**	295	**4,093.0**	3
87	**AMERITECH** Chicago	**17,154.0**	**3,606.0**	18	**30,299.0**	
88	**SPRINT** Westwood, Kan.	**17,134.3**	**414.5**	204	**33,231.1**	
89	**RJR NABISCO HOLDINGS** New York	**17,037.0**[E]	**(577.0)**	488	**28,892.0**	1
90	**ELECTRONIC DATA SYSTEMS** Plano, Texas	**16,891.0**	**743.4**	122	**11,526.1**	2
91	**ARCHER DANIELS MIDLAND** Decatur, Ill.[7]	**16,108.6**	**403.6**	209	**13,833.5**	1
92	**ALBERTSON'S** Boise[1]	**16,005.1**	**567.2**	156	**6,234.0**	2
93	**CARDINAL HEALTH** Dublin, Ohio[7,29]	**15,918.1**	**247.1**	281	**3,961.1**	3
94	**FDX** Memphis[17]	**15,872.8**	**503.0**	172	**9,686.1**	2
95	**FEDERATED DEPARTMENT STORES** Cincinnati[1,30]	**15,833.0**	**662.0**	139	**13,464.0**	1
96	**ALCOA** Pittsburgh[31,32]	**15,489.4**	**853.0**	102	**17,462.5**	1
97	**SYSCO** Houston[7]	**15,327.5**	**296.8**	256	**3,780.2**	3
98	**WALGREEN** Deerfield, Ill.[16]	**15,307.0**	**511.0**	168	**4,902.0**	3
99	**CVS** Woonsocket, R.I.	**15,273.6**	**396.4**	213	**6,736.2**	2
100	**ALLIEDSIGNAL** Morristown, N.J.	**15,128.0**	**1,331.0**	60	**15,560.0**	1

					1988–98 annual growth rate			1988–98 annual rate	
			1998	% change from			1998			
llions	Rank	$ millions	Rank	$	1997	%	Rank	%	Rank	%	Rank
1.0	44	22,067.2	97	4.71	(34.3)	(1.3)	260	(3.8)	308	16.1	197
75.2	76	129,518.4	16	1.55	(1.3)	8.0	149	43.5	92	23.8	85
21.0	255	111,322.1	21	1.05	64.1	51.3	1	248.5	1	79.7	1
35.0	49	41,754.2	58	2.31	22.9	17.1	38	55.1	66	33.7	26
95.0	3	160,654.0	12	(2.12)	(630.0)	—		137.2	11	—	
59.0	67	21,603.9	100	3.40	36.0	3.3	206	19.9	159	16.3	193
81.0	186	4,227.4	311	6.83	(23.7)	(3.2)	277	(35.5)	418	11.7	273
24.2	120	6,190.9	254	1.06	3.9	—		(36.2)	419	—	
38.0	156	9,966.9	187	(1.12)	(149.6)	—		(13.3)	356	44.1	9
51.2	155	15,757.5	131	(0.03)	(101.7)	—		(42.1)	428	10.9	291
01.9	374	2,701.5	359	3.65	40.9	9.3	126	36.8	107	11.6	276
97.0	46	73,080.8	35	3.25	56.3	11.1	95	61.5	62	23.5	90
48.3	36	56,168.6	51	N.A.	—	—		62.3	56	20.4	131
44.0	72	9,648.7	192	(1.91)	(285.4)	—		(15.0)	362	—	
16.5	106	23,423.4	90	1.50	1.4	—		16.0	176	—	
04.9	90	8,824.6	207	0.68	13.3	2.0	226	(16.2)	365	12.3	263
10.5	223	14,864.7	139	2.30	10.6	14.2	58	36.6	108	22.8	101
25.2	315	21,005.0	103	2.22	31.4	21.0	25	51.7	74	38.7	14
61.2	161	13,936.4	143	3.37	8.0	6.6	172	46.1	87	13.4	241
09.0	110	8,301.4	217	2.96	22.8	—		1.2	283	—	
55.9	100	13,848.4	146	2.42	4.8	(0.1)	248	6.7	243	12.7	258
56.8	349	9,416.2	195	0.86	1.2	13.5	65	22.2	147	20.4	130
49.0	220	30,324.7	72	1.02	15.9	14.5	57	87.8	29	33.4	27
10.6	200	19,559.3	109	0.98	1,300.0	(5.0)	288	72.7	42	15.9	202
97.0	126	25,968.7	84	2.32	14.9	11.6	87	15.9	182	21.7	116

		REVENUES	PROFITS		ASSETS	
RANK 1998	COMPANY	$ millions	$ millions	Rank	$ millions	R
101	**FLEMING** Oklahoma City	**15,069.3**	**(510.6)**	483	**3,491.0**	3
102	**HARTFORD FINANCIAL SERVICES** Hartford	**15,022.0**	**1,015.0**	87	**150,632.0**	
103	**MINNESOTA MINING & MFG** St. Paul	**15,021.0**	**1,175.0**	75	**14,153.0**	1
104	**FRED MEYER** Portland, Ore.[1,33]	**14,878.8**	**(162.8)***	468	**10,151.2**	2
105	**TEXAS UTILITIES** Dallas	**14,736.0**	**740.0**	123	**39,514.0**	
106	**PFIZER** New York	**14,704.0**	**3,351.0**	22	**18,302.0**	1
107	**NORTHWESTERN MUTUAL LIFE INS.** Milwaukee	**14,644.9**	**808.9**	110	**77,995.7**	
108	**TIME WARNER** New York	**14,582.0**	**168.0**	325	**31,640.0**	
109	**MICROSOFT** Redmond, Wash.[7]	**14,484.0**	**4,490.0**	11	**22,357.0**	1
110	**DYNEGY** Houston[34]	**14,258.0**	**108.4**	368	**5,260.0**	3
111	**DELTA AIR LINES** Atlanta[7]	**14,138.0**	**1,001.0**	88	**14,603.0**	1
112	**BERKSHIRE HATHAWAY** Omaha[35]	**13,832.0**	**2,830.0**	32	**122,237.0**	
113	**DEERE** Moline, Ill.[6]	**13,821.5**	**1,021.4**	86	**18,001.5**	1
114	**BERGEN BRUNSWIG** Orange, Calif.[11]	**13,720.0**	**3.1**	429	**3,003.2**	4
115	**WINN-DIXIE STORES** Jacksonville[7]	**13,617.5**	**198.6**	308	**3,068.7**	4
116	**FLUOR** Irvine, Calif.[6]	**13,504.8**	**235.5**	290	**5,019.2**	3
117	**AMERICAN HOME PRODUCTS** Madison, N.J.	**13,462.7**	**2,474.3**	33	**21,079.1**	1
118	**EMERSON ELECTRIC** St. Louis[11]	**13,447.2**	**1,228.6**	72	**12,659.8**	1
119	**COCA-COLA ENTERPRISES** Atlanta	**13,414.0**	**142.0**	337	**21,132.0**	1
120	**MAY DEPARTMENT STORES** St. Louis[1]	**13,413.0**	**849.0**	103	**10,553.0**	2
121	**EASTMAN KODAK** Rochester, N.Y.	**13,406.0**	**1,390.0**	57	**14,733.0**	1
122	**GEORGIA-PACIFIC** Atlanta	**13,223.0**	**98.0***	376	**11,538.0**	2
123	**ATLANTIC RICHFIELD** Los Angeles	**13,195.0**[E,¶]	**452.0**	186	**25,199.0**	1
124	**LIBERTY MUTUAL INSURANCE GROUP** Boston	**13,166.0**	**385.0**	221	**49,317.0**	
125	**NATIONWIDE INS. ENTERPRISE** Columbus, Ohio	**13,105.0**	**1,195.7**	73	**104,624.4**	

lions	Rank	$ millions	Rank	1998 $	% change from 1997	1988–98 annual growth rate %	Rank	1998 %	Rank	1988–98 annual rate %	Rank
0.0	447	298.0	453	(13.48)	(2,111.9)	—		(22.4)	394	(8.8)	376
23.0	91	12,919.2	151	4.30	(22.9)	—		19.2	161	—	
86.0	104	32,028.3	68	2.88	(43.1)	1.2	234	(10.9)	340	12.1	268
4.4	256	10,378.2	182	(1.02)	(700.0)	—		65.6	53	22.3	111
46.0	69	12,175.6	155	2.79	(2.1)	(3.5)	280	18.5	165	13.3	243
0.0	63	182,211.4	6	2.55	50.0	15.8	45	68.9	50	36.0	18
0.8	137	N.A.		N.A.	—	—		—		—	
62.0	62	85,393.0	28	(0.31)	—	—		101.1	24	18.0	167
27.0	24	418,578.8	1	1.67	27.0	39.1	4	114.6	16	57.5	4
8.0	384	1,989.1	388	0.66	—	—		(37.3)	422	—	
3.0	157	9,773.7	190	12.68	15.0	7.2	160	(12.4)	349	8.6	321
3.0	1	114,802.2	20	2,262.00	46.7	20.6	27	52.2	71	31.0	34
9.8	153	7,733.4	230	4.16	11.2	10.8	100	(42.5)	429	10.6	299
9.1	436	2,787.5	356	0.03	(96.3)	(23.9)	328	67.1	52	22.2	113
8.9	348	6,353.9	251	1.33	(2.2)	6.4	176	5.2	254	18.4	163
5.6	326	2,231.7	378	2.97	69.7	15.4	51	15.9	180	7.3	330
4.8	54	88,751.0	27	1.85	19.0	8.8	136	50.0	77	22.7	103
3.3	108	25,586.7	87	2.77	10.8	9.1	131	9.3	220	18.0	168
8.0	248	15,704.9	132	0.35	(18.6)	0.2	244	1.0	284	22.1	114
6.0	163	14,406.0	141	3.46	11.6	6.7	168	17.0	170	17.1	179
8.0	159	21,546.8	101	4.24	42,300.0	(0.2)	249	21.9	149	11.1	288
9.0	191	8,844.5	206	1.08	47.9	(13.8)	316	(1.9)	297	11.2	284
0.0	75	19,519.9	110	1.40	(74.1)	(10.8)	309	(15.1)	363	9.8	308
4.0	86	N.A.		N.A.	—	—		—		—	
1.0	45	N.A.		N.A.	—	—		—		—	

RANK 1998	COMPANY	REVENUES $ millions	PROFITS $ millions	Rank	ASSETS $ millions	R
126	IBP Dakota City, Neb.	12,848.6	190.0	312	3,008.1	
127	DANA Toledo[36]	12,838.7	534.1	165	10,137.5	
128	WASHINGTON MUTUAL Seattle[37]	12,745.6	1,486.9	54	165,493.3	
129	WASTE MANAGEMENT Houston[38]	12,703.5	(770.7)	493	22,715.2	
130	GOODYEAR TIRE & RUBBER Akron	12,648.7	682.3	134	10,589.3	
131	JOHNSON CONTROLS Milwaukee[11]	12,586.8	337.7	241	7,942.1	
132	UTILICORP UNITED Kansas City, Mo.	12,563.4	132.2	348	5,991.5	
133	ABBOTT LABORATORIES Abbott Park, Ill.	12,477.8	2,333.2	34	13,216.2	
134	MCDONALD'S Oak Brook, Ill.	12,421.4	1,550.1	49	19,784.0	
135	US WEST Denver[39]	12,378.0	1,508.0	53	18,407.0	
136	KIMBERLY-CLARK Irving, Texas	12,297.8	1,165.8	77	11,510.3	
137	LOWE'S North Wilkesboro, N.C.[1]	12,244.9	482.4	179	6,344.7	
138	VIACOM New York	12,096.1	(122.4)	462	23,613.0	
139	PUBLIX SUPER MARKETS Lakeland, Fla.	12,067.1	378.3	225	3,617.3	
140	BANKERS TRUST CORP. New York[40]	12,048.0	(73.0)	454	133,115.0	
141	TOSCO Stamford, Conn.	12,021.5[E]	106.2	372	5,842.8	
142	TRW Cleveland	11,886.0	477.0	180	7,169.0	
143	PHILLIPS PETROLEUM Bartlesville, Okla.	11,845.0[E]	237.0	287	14,216.0	
144	TEXTRON Providence	11,549.0[¶]	608.0	146	13,721.0	
145	TECH DATA Clearwater, Fla.[1]	11,529.0	129.0	354	3,842.1	
146	ENTERGY New Orleans	11,494.8	785.6	117	22,848.0	
147	HOUSTON INDUSTRIES Houston	11,488.5	(141.1)	465	19,138.5	
148	SOUTHERN Atlanta	11,403.0	977.0	93	36,192.0	
149	RITE AID Camp Hill, Pa.[28]	11,375.1	316.4	249	7,655.3	
150	ANHEUSER-BUSCH St. Louis	11,245.8E	1,233.3	71	12,484.3	

lions	Rank	$ millions	Rank	1998 $	% change from 1997	1988–98 annual growth rate %	Rank	1998 %	Rank	1988–98 annual rate %	Rank
0.9	344	1,932.8	391	2.03	62.4	11.9	82	39.8	101	16.0	200
9.2	214	6,259.3	253	3.20	(8.3)	4.8	191	(11.8)	345	11.7	275
4.4	57	26,878.0	81	2.56	106.5	12.9	70	(8.0)	331	28.0	51
2.5	145	28,814.7	76	(1.32)	(207.3)	—		18.8	164	34.3	25
5.8	168	8,031.1	221	4.31	22.1	3.5	202	(19.1)	381	9.7	313
1.4	288	5,353.5	278	3.63	16.3	9.9	118	25.8	136	15.8	205
6.3	336	2,239.9	376	1.63	8.2	2.3	218	(0.7)	292	13.6	236
3.7	109	76,845.5	31	1.51	12.7	13.8	60	51.8	72	25.9	60
4.7	55	59,924.7	46	1.10	(3.9)	9.9	117	61.8	59	21.4	122
5.0	420	28,162.6	78	3.02	—	—		—		—	
7.2	162	26,881.4	80	2.11	31.1	6.0	178	12.8	201	17.9	169
6.0	197	22,635.3	93	1.36	32.7	19.5	30	115.4	14	36.0	17
0.0	40	32,602.4	67	(0.42)	(120.3)	—		78.6	37	—	
7.6	254	N.A.		1.74	7.4	15.6	48	—		—	
6.0	138	8,303.2	216	(1.05)	(113.7)	—		(20.8)	389	15.0	214
3.0	290	3,377.5	338	0.67	(51.1)	(11.2)	311	(31.0)	409	19.6	141
8.0	293	5,380.7	276	3.83	—	6.0	179	7.6	232	13.9	231
9.0	149	10,788.6	176	0.91	(74.8)	(10.4)	306	(9.7)	336	12.2	265
7.0	210	12,505.1	153	3.68	11.9	10.7	101	23.5	141	23.7	87
7.7	399	843.1	432	2.47	28.6	21.7	22	3.5	267	28.6	47
7.0	82	6,994.3	244	3.00	191.3	4.1	194	9.6	219	13.1	253
1.9	146	8,102.0	220	(0.50)	(130.1)	—		26.1	135	16.9	186
7.0	52	17,509.4	123	1.40	(1.4)	0.3	243	17.9	169	17.4	177
6.5	216	6,372.1	250	1.22	96.8	3.4	203	71.5	46	22.8	102
6.0	150	35,961.5	62	2.53	7.2	7.5	155	52.3	70	18.1	165

		REVENUES	PROFITS		ASSETS	
RANK 1998	COMPANY	$ millions	$ millions	Rank	$ millions	F
151	TOYS "R" US Paramus, N.J.[1]	11,200.0	(132.0)	463	7,899.0	
152	WEYERHAEUSER Federal Way, Wash.	10,766.0	294.0	258	12,834.0	
153	MASS. MUTUAL LIFE INS. Springfield, Mass.	10,668.1	432.8	196	68,166.0	
154	UNION PACIFIC Dallas	10,553.0	(633.0)	490	29,374.0	
155	WHIRLPOOL Benton Harbor, Mich.	10,323.0	325.0	247	7,935.0	
156	AMERICAN GENERAL Houston	10,251.0	764.0	119	105,107.0	
157	WARNER-LAMBERT Morris Plains, N.J.	10,213.7	1,254.0	69	9,230.6	
158	EDISON INTERNATIONAL Rosemead, Calif.	10,208.0	668.0	137	24,698.0	
159	GILLETTE Boston	10,056.0	1,081.0	83	11,902.0	
160	ELI LILLY Indianapolis	10,051.3	2,097.9	37	12,595.5	
161	FLEET FINANCIAL GROUP Boston	10,002.0	1,532.0	51	104,382.0	
162	CSX Richmond	9,898.0	537.0	162	20,427.0	
163	TENET HEALTHCARE Santa Barbara[17]	9,895.0	261.0*	272	12,833.0	
164	SUN MICROSYSTEMS Palo Alto[7]	9,790.8	762.9	120	5,711.1	
165	HUMANA Louisville	9,781.0	129.0	353	5,217.0	
166	NIKE Beaverton, Ore.[17]	9,553.1	399.6	211	5,397.4	
167	PACIFICARE HEALTH SYSTEMS Santa Ana, Calif.	9,521.5	202.4	305	4,630.9	
168	PACIFICORP Portland, Ore.[41]	9,442.5¶	312.0	251	13,198.6	
169	LIMITED Columbus, Ohio[1]	9,346.9	2,053.6	38	4,549.7	
170	H.J. HEINZ Pittsburgh[42]	9,209.3	801.6	112	8,023.4	
171	ST. PAUL COS. St. Paul[43]	9,108.4	89.3	383	38,322.7	
172	CBS New York	9,061.0¶	(21.0)	440	20,139.0	
173	LEAR Southfield, Mich.	9,059.4	115.5	364	5,677.3	
174	GAP San Francisco[1]	9,054.5	824.5	107	3,963.9	
175	NORTHWEST AIRLINES St. Paul	9,044.8	(285.5)	475	10,280.8	

STOCKHOLDERS' EQUITY		MARKET VALUE 3/15/99		EARNINGS PER SHARE				TOTAL RETURN TO INVESTORS			
				1998 $	% change from 1997	1988–98 annual growth rate %	Rank	1998 %	Rank	1988–98 annual rate %	Rank
$ millions	Rank	$ millions	Rank								
24.0	171	4,455.7	305	(0.50)	(129.4)	—		(46.1)	434	0.3	367
26.0	140	11,604.7	164	1.47	(14.0)	(5.8)	295	7.2	237	11.3	283
88.8	194	N.A.		N.A.	—	—		—		—	
93.0	78	12,991.1	150	(2.57)	(247.7)	—		(26.6)	402	10.6	298
01.0	282	3,729.4	331	4.25	—	12.1	76	3.1	268	11.5	280
71.0	61	19,152.9	112	2.96	35.2	5.6	182	47.6	83	23.1	97
2.2	172	60,526.9	45	1.48	42.8	13.5	64	83.4	32	30.9	35
9.0	131	9,048.7	203	1.84	6.4	0.5	241	6.4	247	12.1	267
43.0	139	67,982.5	39	0.95	(23.7)	12.0	78	(3.8)	307	29.5	44
9.6	143	105,871.6	22	1.87	—	10.9	98	29.1	124	27.0	55
9.0	56	24,029.0	89	2.52	6.3	5.1	190	22.0	148	18.0	166
0.0	107	8,549.1	211	2.51	(30.7)	18.4	33	(21.1)	391	13.1	249
8.0	174	5,970.2	256	0.84	—	(1.7)	265	(20.8)	388	11.5	279
3.6	177	42,186.5	57	1.93	(1.5)	24.0	20	114.7	15	35.3	21
0.0	307	3,121.4	344	0.77	(26.7)	(6.7)	299	(14.2)	359	13.7	234
1.6	188	15,824.9	130	1.35	(49.6)	14.9	55	5.0	257	29.9	39
8.1	261	3,408.2	337	4.40	—	31.5	9	44.8	89	37.3	15
0.6	154	5,203.4	281	0.98	(27.4)	(5.5)	294	(19.0)	380	8.2	324
3.3	262	8,482.3	213	8.32	953.2	28.5	13	18.4	166	9.8	309
5.5	264	18,818.3	114	2.15	165.4	8.3	144	14.0	194	17.2	178
6.4	88	7,772.9	229	0.32	(91.6)	(16.1)	319	(13.0)	353	16.2	195
4.0	59	25,817.2	86	(0.03)	(103.6)	—		11.6	208	4.9	347
0.0	365	2,342.3	371	1.70	(44.1)	—		(18.9)	378	—	
3.7	320	39,644.9	60	1.37	58.1	28.2	14	138.4	10	39.0	13
5.7)	493	2,259.3	374	(3.48)	(166.8)	—		(46.6)	435	—	

RANK 1998	COMPANY	REVENUES $ millions	PROFITS $ millions	Rank	ASSETS $ millions
176	OFFICE DEPOT Delray Beach, Fla.[44]	8,997.7	233.2	292	4,113.0
177	COLGATE-PALMOLIVE New York	8,971.6	848.6	104	7,685.2
178	BURLINGTON NORTHERN SANTA FE Fort Worth	8,941.0	1,155.0	78	22,690.0
179	JOHN HANCOCK MUTUAL LIFE INS. Boston	8,911.7	627.3	143	67,079.4
180	NORTHROP GRUMMAN Los Angeles	8,902.0	214.0	300	9,564.0
181	FOUNDATION HEALTH SYSTEMS Woodland Hills, Calif.	8,896.1	(165.2)	469	3,929.5
182	CIRCUIT CITY GROUP Richmond[28]	8,870.8	104.3	374	3,231.7
183	MANPOWER Milwaukee	8,814.3	75.7	387	2,381.1
184	FARMLAND INDUSTRIES Kansas City, Mo.[16,45]	8,775.0	N.A.		2,812.8
185	HOUSEHOLD INTERNATIONAL Prospect Heights, Ill.[46]	8,707.6	524.1	166	52,892.7
186	US AIRWAYS GROUP Arlington, Va.	8,688.0	538.0	161	7,870.0
187	MONSANTO St. Louis[47]	8,648.0	(250.0)	474	16,724.0
188	AMERISOURCE HEALTH Malvern, Pa.[11]	8,575.4	50.5	408	1,552.3
189	CHS ELECTRONICS Miami	8,545.8	45.7	412	3,572.1
190	TRICON GLOBAL RESTAURANTS Louisville	8,468.0	445.0	187	4,531.0
191	TEXAS INSTRUMENTS Dallas	8,460.0	407.0	208	11,250.0
192	CISCO SYSTEMS San Jose[48]	8,458.8	1,350.1	58	8,916.7
193	HONEYWELL Minneapolis	8,426.7	572.0	154	7,170.4
194	BESTFOODS Englewood Cliffs, N.J.[49]	8,374.0	624.0	144	6,435.0
195	BEST BUY Eden Prairie, Minn.[28]	8,358.2	94.5	379	2,056.3
196	ULTRAMAR DIAMOND SHAMROCK San Antonio	8,346.5E	(78.1)	456	5,315.0
197	ARROW ELECTRONICS Melville, N.Y.	8,344.7	145.8	334	3,839.9
198	CROWN CORK & SEAL Philadelphia	8,300.0	105.1	373	12,469.0
199	INGERSOLL-RAND Woodcliff Lake, N.J.	8,291.5	509.1	171	8,309.5
200	SCHERING-PLOUGH Madison, N.J.	8,077.0	1,756.0	44	7,840.0

CKHOLDERS' ITY		MARKET VALUE 3/15/99		EARNINGS PER SHARE				TOTAL RETURN TO INVESTORS			
				1998 $	% change from 1997	1988–98 annual growth rate %	Rank	1998 %	Rank	1988–98 annual rate %	Rank
ions	Rank	$ millions	Rank								
8.9	277	8,473.2	214	0.91	(6.2)	28.0	15	54.8	67	31.6	31
5.6	271	26,810.2	82	2.61	15.0	8.4	142	28.0	130	25.9	59
0.0	73	16,231.4	127	2.43	29.3	13.6	63	12.0	203	19.6	142
8.7	182	N.A.		N.A.	—	—		—		—	
8.0	219	4,470.1	304	3.07	(48.7)	3.3	207	(35.1)	417	14.5	222
2.3	422	1,128.3	419	(1.35)	—	—		(46.6)	436	—	
0.0	302	7,178.5	241	1.13	(18.7)	7.2	161	40.9	98	19.4	145
8.9	431	1,914.0	393	0.93	(52.8)	—		(28.0)	404	—	
2.7	404	N.A.		N.A.	—	—		—		—	
5.8	94	21,816.4	98	1.03	(52.5)	(1.0)	254	(5.6)	316	21.3	123
3.0	441	4,637.9	296	5.60	(43.3)	3.9	196	(16.8)	370	4.3	350
5.0	133	30,342.4	71	(0.41)	(153.2)	—		13.4	198	23.5	89
5.3	486	1,812.4	396	2.08	10.1	—		11.6	209	—	
8.0	411	389.3	448	0.82	(37.9)	—		(1.1)	293	—	
3.0)	498	10,545.0	180	2.84	—	—		72.5	43	—	
7.0	89	38,848.2	61	1.02	(77.5)	0.1	246	91.4	28	25.4	69
5.6	83	166,615.6	10	0.84	24.3	—		149.7	8	—	
5.5	225	9,569.5	194	4.48	22.7	—		11.6	210	20.8	128
4.0	395	13,895.0	144	2.09	82.5	8.6	139	7.5	233	18.8	156
7.7	450	10,376.5	183	1.04	5,100.0	33.8	5	232.9	2	46.0	6
4.0	346	1,720.3	399	(0.89)	(147.3)	—		(21.0)	390	—	
7.3	332	1,440.4	408	1.50	(8.5)	6.8	166	(17.7)	372	23.2	95
5.0	211	3,463.7	336	0.71	(66.2)	(4.5)	286	(37.0)	421	7.9	325
7.5	231	8,209.2	218	3.08	33.3	11.9	81	18.3	167	17.7	171
2.0	158	84,658.1	30	1.18	21.6	18.4	32	79.6	36	34.6	23

	REVENUES	PROFITS		ASSETS
RANK 1998 COMPANY	$ millions	$ millions	Rank	$ millions
201 NATIONAL CITY CORP. Cleveland[50]	8,070.8	1,070.7	84	88,245.6
202 ROCKWELL INTERNATIONAL Costa Mesa, Calif.[11,51]	8,025.0¶	(427.0)	480	7,170.0
203 DILLARD'S Little Rock[1,52]	8,012.0	135.0	345	8,178.0
204 BEAR STEARNS New York[7]	7,979.9	660.4	140	154,495.9
205 GUARDIAN LIFE INS. CO. OF AMERICA New York	7,973.8	160.4	326	25,854.2
206 MARRIOTT INTERNATIONAL Bethesda, Md.[53]	7,968.0	390.0	217	6,233.0
207 CONTINENTAL AIRLINES Houston	7,951.0	383.0	222	7,086.0
208 TJX Framingham, Mass.[1]	7,949.1	424.2	199	2,747.8
209 PNC BANK CORP. Pittsburgh	7,936.0	1,115.0	80	77,207.0
210 PACCAR Bellevue, Wash.	7,894.8	416.8	203	6,794.8
211 NAVISTAR INTERNATIONAL Chicago[6]	7,885.0	299.0	254	6,178.0
212 CONSECO Carmel, Ind.[54]	7,716.0	588.1	150	43,599.9
213 PRINCIPAL FINANCIAL Des Moines	7,697.4	693.0	132	73,943.3
214 UNITED SERVICES AUTOMOBILE ASSN. San Antonio	7,687.4	979.5	92	28,830.6
215 U.S. BANCORP Minneapolis	7,664.0	1,327.4	61	76,438.0
216 WILLIAMS Tulsa[55]	7,658.3	127.5	356	18,647.3
217 BINDLEY WESTERN Indianapolis	7,623.1	19.1	424	1,294.4
218 BANKBOSTON CORP. Boston	7,609.0	792.0	116	73,513.0
219 TENNECO Greenwich, Conn.	7,605.0	255.0	275	8,791.0
220 ITT INDUSTRIES White Plains, N.Y.	7,523.1	1,532.5	50	5,024.0
221 PPG INDUSTRIES Pittsburgh	7,510.0	801.0	113	7,837.0
222 CAMPBELL SOUP Camden, N.J.[48]	7,505.0¶	660.0	141	5,633.0
223 GATEWAY 2000 San Diego	7,467.9	346.4	237	2,890.4
224 NEBCO EVANS Greenwich, Conn.[56]	7,421.0	(152.3)	467	1,935.8
225 UNISOURCE Berwyn, Pa.[11]	7,417.3	(231.8)	472	1,966.7

millions	Rank	$ millions	Rank	1998 $	% change from 1997	1988–98 annual growth rate %	Rank	1998 %	Rank	1988–98 annual rate %	Rank
012.9	85	22,842.9	92	3.22	(12.0)	5.3	184	13.4	197	21.1	124
245.0	189	8,812.3	208	(2.16)	(172.7)	—		(5.1)	314	13.6	237
842.0	221	2,732.6	357	1.26	(45.5)	0.7	239	(19.1)	382	7.6	327
291.5	147	7,791.9	227	4.60	9.5	19.3	31	(20.1)	386	23.1	96
555.4	323	N.A.		N.A.	—	—		—		—	
570.0	239	9,310.1	196	1.46	—	—		—		—	
93.0	375	2,484.3	367	5.02	0.6	—		(30.4)	407	—	
220.6	373	10,604.0	179	1.27	46.0	—		69.6	47	25.3	71
43.0	101	17,825.2	119	3.60	9.8	3.5	201	(2.4)	300	15.9	204
64.2	301	3,534.0	334	5.30	20.2	9.5	123	(18.5)	375	13.6	235
69.0	418	2,515.4	366	4.11	149.1	(6.9)	301	14.9	189	(6.1)	374
73.6	127	11,725.7	161	1.77	(33.0)	21.0	24	(32.0)	412	47.0	5
67.2	112	N.A.		N.A.	—	—		—		—	
75.1	79	N.A.		N.A.	—	—		—		—	
70.0	103	25,860.6	85	1.78	59.9	—		(3.1)	303	22.0	115
57.4	148	15,257.2	134	0.28	(65.0)	(4.2)	285	11.6	211	23.9	83
42.3	468	595.6	436	0.84	(29.6)	6.8	167	113.2	17	25.3	70
17.0	136	13,882.1	145	2.64	(6.5)	1.3	233	(14.9)	361	16.6	188
04.0	242	5,220.2	280	1.51	(17.9)	(12.1)	314	(11.0)	341	2.0	360
00.0	365	3,820.7	329	13.55	1,422.5	9.0	132	28.9	126	19.3	146
30.0	218	9,285.4	197	4.48	13.7	7.7	153	4.3	263	14.5	223
74.0	409	18,714.9	115	1.44	(3.4)	10.5	105	0.4	287	24.5	78
44.4	351	10,979.2	171	2.18	211.4	—		56.3	65	—	
33.4)	491	N.A.		N.A.	—	—		—		—	
98.4	427	529.6	441	(3.36)	(486.2)	—		(45.4)	432	—	

RANK 1998	COMPANY	$ millions	$ millions	Rank	$ millions	Ra
226	TYSON FOODS Springdale, Ark.[11]	7,414.1	25.1	418	5,242.5	3
227	SUNTRUST BANKS Atlanta[57]	7,392.1	971.0	95	93,169.9	
228	TELE-COMMUNICATIONS Englewood, Colo.[58]	7,351.0	1,943.0	42	41,851.0	
229	FORT JAMES Deerfield, Va.	7,301.1	497.6	177	7,792.3	2
230	PAINE WEBBER GROUP New York	7,249.6	433.6	194	54,175.9	
231	UNISYS Blue Bell, Pa.	7,208.4	387.0	219	5,577.7	3
232	MARSH & MCLENNAN New York	7,190.0	796.0	114	11,871.0	1
233	UNICOM Chicago	7,151.3	510.2	169	25,707.1	1
234	ORACLE Redwood Shores, Calif.[17]	7,143.9	813.7	109	5,819.0	2
235	COASTAL Houston	7,125.2[E]	444.4	188	12,304.1	1
236	STAPLES Westborough, Mass.[1]	7,123.2	185.4	318	3,179.3	3
237	AFLAC Columbus, Ga.	7,104.2	486.8	178	31,183.4	
238	KEYCORP Cleveland	7,100.0	996.0	91	80,020.0	
239	CONSOLIDATED EDISON New York	7,093.0	729.7	126	14,381.4	1
240	SUNOCO Philadelphia[59]	7,024.0[E]	280.0	265	4,849.0	
241	MEDPARTNERS Birmingham, Ala.	7,003.6[¶]	(1,260.5)	495	1,181.8	4
242	ASHLAND Covington, Ky.[11]	6,933.0	203.0	304	6,082.0	
243	PHARMACIA & UPJOHN Bridgewater, N.J.	6,893.0	691.0	133	10,312.0	
244	SEAGATE TECHNOLOGY Scotts Valley, Calif.[7]	6,819.0	(530.0)	485	5,645.0	
245	SCI SYSTEMS Huntsville, Ala.[7]	6,805.9	145.1	335	1,944.7	
246	KELLOGG Battle Creek, Mich.	6,762.1	502.6	173	5,051.5	
247	SODEXHO MARRIOTT SERVICES Gaithersburg, Md.[60,61]	6,704.0	122.0	360	1,341.0	
248	FPL GROUP Juno Beach, Fla.	6,661.0	664.0	138	12,029.0	
249	AMERICAN STANDARD Piscataway, N.J.	6,653.9	(16.3)*	438	4,107.8	
250	EATON Cleveland	6,625.0	349.0	235	5,665.0	

CKHOLDERS' ITY		MARKET VALUE 3/15/99		EARNINGS PER SHARE		1988–98 annual growth rate		TOTAL RETURN TO INVESTORS 1998		1988–98 annual rate	
lions	Rank	$ millions	Rank	1998 $	% change from 1997	%	Rank	%	Rank	%	Rank
0.4	285	4,745.0	292	0.11	(87.1)	(11.4)	312	4.2	265	14.3	229
8.6	70	22,378.3	96	3.04	(2.9)	9.8	119	8.7	223	25.8	61
8.0	47	N.A.		N.A.	—	—		—		—	
1.4	389	6,601.2	248	2.26	—	(0.4)	250	6.1	250	6.5	338
8.9	247	5,801.8	261	2.72	6.3	31.8	8	13.1	200	26.2	57
7.0	328	7,874.3	225	1.06	—	(11.5)	313	148.2	9	3.1	355
9.0	170	20,022.9	107	2.98	87.0	8.1	145	20.6	155	15.8	206
9.4	130	7,869.7	226	2.34	—	(2.5)	274	31.3	120	8.8	319
7.6	213	43,187.0	56	0.81	0.0	32.6	6	93.3	26	40.4	11
5.8	178	7,384.4	237	2.03	53.8	8.5	140	14.2	193	13.2	246
6.9	310	14,959.7	138	0.41	20.6	—		136.1	12	—	
9.7	166	13,583.1	148	1.76	(15.4)	17.2	37	73.0	41	29.9	40
7.0	97	15,157.1	137	2.23	8.0	7.8	151	(7.0)	324	19.0	155
8.2	96	11,161.5	170	3.04	3.1	2.1	223	34.7	110	15.9	201
4.0	329	2,995.2	348	2.95	9.3	47.6	2	(11.8)	346	6.3	339
4.2)	497	618.1	435	(6.64)	—	—		(76.5)	455	—	
7.0	268	3,149.1	343	2.63	(27.7)	(4.1)	284	(7.9)	330	6.8	334
0.0	114	29,527.5	74	1.31	114.8	0.0	247	58.3	63	14.6	221
7.0	215	7,588.3	234	(2.17)	(182.8)	—		57.1	64	21.5	118
8.0	421	2,234.1	377	2.13	26.0	16.7	41	32.6	115	22.6	105
9.8	408	15,516.5	133	1.23	(6.8)	2.4	217	(29.6)	406	10.4	303
5.0)	494	1,312.2	414	N.A.	—	—		20.0	158	—	
6.0	129	10,121.3	184	3.85	7.8	1.2	235	7.4	235	13.3	242
0.1)	495	2,364.3	370	(0.22)	(117.5)	—		(6.0)	319	—	
7.0	274	4,969.7	288	4.80	(8.4)	5.4	183	(19.0)	379	13.0	254

		REVENUES	PROFITS		ASSETS	
RANK 1998	COMPANY	$ millions	$ millions	Rank	$ millions	R
251	AMERADA HESS New York	6,617.5E	(458.9)	481	7,883.0	
252	GENUINE PARTS Atlanta	6,614.0	355.8	233	3,600.4	
253	COMPUTER SCIENCES El Segundo, Calif.[20]	6,600.8	260.4	274	4,046.8	
254	BAXTER INTERNATIONAL Deerfield, Ill.	6,599.0	315.0	250	10,085.0	
255	OCCIDENTAL PETROLEUM Los Angeles	6,596.0	363.0	231	15,252.0	
256	WELLPOINT HEALTH NETWORKS Thousand Oaks, Calif.	6,573.0	231.3	293	4,225.8	
257	COLUMBIA ENERGY GROUP Herndon, Va.	6,568.2	269.2	269	6,968.7	
258	NCR Dayton	6,505.0	122.0	360	4,892.0	
259	AON Chicago	6,492.9	540.5	159	19,688.0	
260	SAFECO Seattle	6,452.1	351.9	234	30,891.7	
261	TRANSAMERICA San Francisco	6,428.6	707.0	130	58,502.6	
262	ARAMARK Philadelphia[11]	6,377.3	129.2	352	2,741.3	
263	CHUBB Warren, N.J.	6,349.8	707.0	129	20,746.0	
264	AMERICAN ELECTRIC POWER Columbus, Ohio	6,345.9	536.2	163	19,483.2	
265	BAKER HUGHES Houston[62,63]	6,311.9	(297.4)	478	7,810.8	
266	CUMMINS ENGINE Columbus, Ind.	6,266.0	(21.0)	440	4,542.0	
267	SAKS Birmingham, Ala.[1,64]	6,219.9	(0.9)*	431	5,189.0	
268	BOISE CASCADE Boise	6,162.1	(37.0)	446	4,966.7	
269	CASE Racine, Wis.	6,149.0	64.0	395	8,726.0	
270	LINCOLN NATIONAL Fort Wayne	6,087.1	509.8	170	93,836.3	
271	DOMINION RESOURCES Richmond	6,086.2	535.6	164	17,517.0	
272	GENERAL MILLS Minneapolis[17]	6,033.0	421.8	201	3,861.4	
273	APPLE COMPUTER Cupertino, Calif.[11]	5,941.0	309.0	253	4,289.0	
274	PUBLIC SERVICE ENTERPRISE GROUP Newark, N.J.	5,931.0	644.0	142	17,997.0	
275	AVNET Phoenix[7]	5,916.3	151.4	331	2,733.7	

STOCKHOLDERS' EQUITY		MARKET VALUE 3/15/99		EARNINGS PER SHARE				TOTAL RETURN TO INVESTORS			
millions	Rank	$ millions	Rank	1998 $	% change from 1997	1988–98 annual growth rate %	Rank	1998 %	Rank	1988–98 annual rate %	Rank
643.4	236	4,489.6	303	(5.12)	(6,500.0)	—		(8.4)	332	6.0	340
053.3	275	5,374.9	277	1.98	4.2	6.6	171	1.5	280	11.2	285
001.3	281	10,846.1	173	1.64	33.3	13.7	61	53.9	68	23.3	93
839.0	222	21,743.1	99	1.09	2.8	(1.8)	266	30.3	122	19.0	154
363.0	183	5,715.7	263	0.99	—	(2.0)	269	(40.2)	426	1.8	362
315.2	359	4,954.2	290	3.29	0.6	—		105.9	22	—	
005.3	279	4,499.2	302	3.21	(1.7)	—		11.8	206	—	
447.0	335	4,416.8	307	1.20	1,614.3	—		50.1	76	—	
417.0	206	11,498.1	166	3.11	85.1	9.6	121	(3.8)	309	20.0	136
575.8	115	5,655.6	265	2.51	(24.2)	2.0	225	(9.3)	334	17.6	173
705.9	111	9,056.7	202	5.44	(7.7)	9.4	125	10.4	215	17.5	175
(78.9)	488	N.A.		1.06	(3.6)	—		—		—	
444.1	113	9,624.5	193	4.19	(4.6)	7.0	165	(13.0)	352	18.8	157
441.8	134	7,984.4	222	2.81	4.1	(1.4)	261	(4.1)	310	13.2	248
499.4	192	7,145.1	242	(0.92)	—	—		(58.9)	447	4.3	349
472.0	369	1,664.3	401	(0.55)	(110.0)	—		(38.3)	423	3.2	354
407.6	278	4,377.7	308	(0.01)	(101.4)	—		11.0	212	24.8	77
28.4	340	1,845.1	394	(1.00)	—	—		4.5	261	0.1	368
10.0	269	1,587.4	404	0.76	(85.1)	—		(63.7)	450	—	
487.9	122	9,922.0	188	5.02	(44.1)	12.1	75	7.3	236	19.1	149
15.9	124	7,613.0	233	2.75	27.9	(0.9)	253	16.5	172	12.4	261
90.2	478	11,932.7	158	2.60	(5.8)	4.8	192	11.9	205	17.0	183
42.0	312	4,605.0	298	2.10	—	(3.8)	281	211.9	3	1.0	365
98.0	132	8,697.4	210	2.79	15.8	0.8	238	33.1	113	13.1	251
15.9	357	1,340.6	413	3.80	(10.6)	10.0	115	(7.3)	325	12.4	260

		REVENUES	PROFITS		ASSETS	
RANK 1998	COMPANY	$ millions	$ millions	Rank	$ millions	R
276	WACHOVIA CORP. Winston-Salem, N.C.	5,913.8	874.2	99	64,122.8	
277	R.R. DONNELLEY & SONS Chicago	5,899.9¶	294.6	257	3,787.8	
278	ANTHEM INSURANCE Indianapolis	5,878.2	172.4	323	4,374.0	
279	CINERGY Cincinnati	5,876.3	261.0	273	10,298.8	
280	FIRSTENERGY Akron	5,861.3	410.9	206	18,063.5	
281	REYNOLDS METALS Richmond	5,859.0	66.0	392	6,134.0	
282	CENDANT New York	5,832.0	539.6	160	20,216.5	
283	MELLON BANK CORP. Pittsburgh	5,814.0	870.0	100	50,777.0	
284	QUANTUM Milpitas, Calif.[20]	5,805.2	170.8	324	2,438.4	
285	BANK OF NEW YORK CO. New York	5,793.0	1,192.0	74	63,579.0	
286	EL PASO ENERGY Houston	5,782.0	225.0	298	10,069.0	
287	VENATOR New York[1,66]	5,698.0¶	(136.0)	464	2,876.0	
288	UNION CARBIDE Danbury, Conn.	5,659.0	403.0	210	7,291.0	
289	CHAMPION INTERNATIONAL Stamford, Conn.	5,653.0	75.3	388	8,839.9	
290	ILLINOIS TOOL WORKS Glenview, Ill.	5,647.9	672.8	136	6,118.2	
291	IKON OFFICE SOLUTIONS Malvern, Pa.[11]	5,628.7	(83.1)	457	5,748.8	
292	COMCAST Philadelphia	5,590.5	972.1	94	14,817.4	
293	RALSTON PURINA St. Louis[11]	5,577.0¶	1,105.7	82	5,551.7	
294	VALERO ENERGY San Antonio	5,539.3[E]	(47.3)	450	2,725.7	
295	LG&E ENERGY Louisville	5,528.7¶	(95.5)	459	4,800.0	
296	SEMPRA ENERGY San Diego[67]	5,525.0	294.0	258	10,456.0	
297	MICROAGE Tempe, Ariz.[6]	5,520.0	(8.3)	433	1,315.1	
298	U.S. FOODSERVICE Columbia, Md.[7]	5,506.9	(47.0)	449	1,817.8	
299	AMP Harrisburg, Pa.	5,482.0	2.0	430	4,771.0	
300	CENTRAL & SOUTH WEST Dallas	5,482.0	440.0	190	13,744.0	

CKHOLDERS' JITY		MARKET VALUE 3/15/99		EARNINGS PER SHARE				TOTAL RETURN TO INVESTORS			
					% change from 1997	1988–98 annual growth rate		1998		1988–98 annual rate	
llions	Rank	$ millions	Rank	1998 $	1997	%	Rank	%	Rank	%	Rank
38.2	123	18,370.2	117	4.18	42.2	8.7	137	10.3	218	22.6	106
00.9	363	4,548.2	300	2.08	131.1	4.7	193	20.0	157	12.0	271
02.4	306	N.A.		N.A.	—	—		—		—	
41.2	241	4,611.7	297	1.65	3.8	(5.4)	293	(5.4)	315	14.3	226
49.2	142	6,815.7	245	1.82	(6.2)	4.1	195	18.0	168	13.5	239
4.0	267	2,795.8	353	0.94	(48.9)	(20.2)	324	(10.0)	338	2.4	359
35.6	135	14,530.3	140	0.61	—	—		(43.8)	430	29.7	42
21.0	141	19,251.3	111	3.25	12.8	—		15.9	181	28.4	49
72.0	347	3,567.7	333	1.07	2.9	—		5.9	252	30.6	36
76.0	119	30,248.3	73	1.53	12.9	8.1	146	41.7	93	29.2	45
98.0	270	3,856.6	326	1.85	16.4	—		7.0	239	—	
38.0	391	815.4	433	(1.00)	—	—		(68.1)	452	(10.7)	379
49.0	246	5,771.8	262	2.91	(34.0)	(5.0)	290	1.0	285	18.7	159
95.9	201	4,057.8	317	0.78	—	(16.6)	320	(10.2)	339	3.6	353
38.0	184	17,086.9	125	2.67	14.6	14.9	54	(2.7)	301	22.4	109
27.3	341	2,180.9	383	(0.76)	(191.6)	—		(69.2)	453	(0.9)	371
15.3	164	26,764.1	83	2.41	—	—		86.3	31	24.0	82
39.1	387	9,218.9	200	3.38	166.1	—		8.5	226	—	
35.3	388	1,146.7	418	(0.84)	(148.3)	—		(31.5)	411	—	
41.2	371	2,974.5	349	(0.73)	(149.7)	—		19.4	160	16.2	196
43.0	217	5,072.4	285	1.24	(43.6)	(2.5)	273	(0.2)	290	9.7	312
90.5	472	143.5	456	(0.42)	(129.4)	—		2.1	274	13.3	245
34.7	442	2,094.6	384	(1.04)	(203.0)	—		32.7	114	—	
98.0	233	12,017.6	156	0.01	(99.5)	(39.3)	329	27.2	133	11.7	274
00.0	165	5,328.6	279	2.07	187.5	1.9	227	8.1	227	12.7	259

		REVENUES	PROFITS		ASSETS	
RANK 1998	COMPANY	$ millions	$ millions	Rank	$ millions	R
301	VF Greensboro, N.C.	5,478.8	388.3	218	3,836.7	3
302	OWENS-ILLINOIS Toledo	5,449.9	108.0*	369	11,060.7	2
303	3COM Santa Clara, Calif.[17]	5,420.4	30.2	417	4,080.5	3
304	UNOCAL El Segundo, Calif.	5,379.0[E]	130.0	351	7,952.0	2
305	PROGRESSIVE Mayfield Village, Ohio	5,292.4	456.7	185	8,463.1	2
306	SOLECTRON Milpitas, Calif.[16]	5,288.3	198.8	307	2,410.6	4
307	COMPUSA Dallas[7]	5,286.0	31.5	416	1,160.5	4
308	AVON PRODUCTS New York	5,212.7	270.0	268	2,433.5	4
309	PECO ENERGY Philadelphia	5,210.5	512.7	167	12,048.4	1
310	MBNA Wilmington, Del.	5,195.1	776.3	118	25,806.3	1
311	ALLTEL Little Rock[68]	5,194.0	580.3	151	9,374.2	2
312	RYDER SYSTEM Miami	5,188.7	159.1	327	5,708.6	3
313	AIRTOUCH COMMUNICATIONS San Francisco	5,181.0	725.0	127	17,553.0	1
314	CMS ENERGY Dearborn, Mich.	5,141.0	285.0	261	11,310.0	2
315	GANNETT Arlington, Va.	5,121.3	999.9	90	6,979.5	2
316	FIRST DATA Atlanta	5,117.6	465.7*	182	16,587.0	1
317	COOPER INDUSTRIES Houston	5,100.6[¶]	423.0	200	3,779.1	3
318	NORDSTROM Seattle[1]	5,027.9	206.7	302	3,115.4	3
319	OWENS CORNING Toledo	5,009.0	(705.0)	491	5,101.0	3
320	GENERAL DYNAMICS Falls Church, Va.	4,970.0	364.0	229	4,572.0	3
321	CNF TRANSPORTATION Palo Alto	4,941.5	139.0	341	2,689.4	
322	SHERWIN-WILLIAMS Cleveland	4,934.4	272.9	267	4,065.5	3
323	AIR PRODUCTS & CHEMICALS Allentown, Pa.[11]	4,933.8	546.8	158	7,489.6	2
324	DOVER New York	4,876.7[¶]	378.8	224	3,627.3	3
325	QUAKER OATS Chicago	4,842.5	284.5	262	2,510.3	4

STOCKHOLDERS' EQUITY		MARKET VALUE 3/15/99		EARNINGS PER SHARE				TOTAL RETURN TO INVESTORS			
				1998 $	% change from 1997	1988–98 annual growth rate %	Rank	1998 %	Rank	1988–98 annual rate %	Rank
$ millions	Rank	$ millions	Rank								
066.3	273	5,495.4	270	3.10	14.8	9.3	127	2.6	270	15.6	209
472.0	244	4,051.4	318	0.62	(50.0)	—		(19.3)	383	—	
807.5	224	9,215.8	201	0.08	(96.0)	(8.6)	303	28.3	129	23.4	92
202.0	266	7,528.4	236	0.54	(76.6)	(12.5)	315	(23.1)	397	7.1	332
557.1	240	10,063.7	186	6.11	15.1	16.9	40	41.6	95	37.2	16
181.3	378	10,944.4	172	1.65	20.4	—		123.6	13	—	
414.6	460	539.9	440	0.33	(66.7)	—		(57.9)	445	—	
285.1	473	11,900.1	159	1.02	(19.7)	—		46.9	86	29.1	46
194.8	193	9,029.5	204	2.23	—	(0.4)	251	77.9	38	14.7	219
391.0	251	20,245.0	106	0.97	26.5	—		37.8	105	—	
270.9	187	16,064.0	129	2.09	(22.6)	8.0	148	49.5	79	21.4	121
095.6	385	1,924.6	392	2.16	(4.0)	(1.0)	255	(18.9)	377	3.8	352
325.0	58	52,839.7	54	1.07	37.2	—		74.3	40	—	
216.0	265	4,546.6	301	2.62	0.4	(2.3)	272	13.1	199	9.9	306
979.8	160	17,699.1	121	3.50	40.0	12.0	79	5.6	253	16.5	190
755.9	167	18,967.1	113	1.04	31.6	—		9.3	221	—	
563.6	321	4,194.1	313	3.69	13.2	5.3	185	(0.1)	288	9.1	316
316.7	356	5,683.2	264	1.41	17.5	6.4	174	16.0	178	9.7	311
34.0)	496	1,574.7	405	(13.16)	(1,595.5)	—		4.7	259	4.9	346
219.0	263	7,969.7	223	2.86	14.4	2.4	216	38.5	103	25.5	68
76.4	416	2,004.8	387	2.45	11.9	(2.0)	270	(2.0)	298	4.2	351
15.9	304	4,702.8	294	1.57	4.7	10.6	104	7.5	234	18.6	161
67.3	235	7,280.4	238	2.48	29.8	9.8	120	(1.1)	294	16.9	184
10.9	292	7,783.1	228	1.69	(5.6)	11.8	85	2.6	271	20.0	135
72.7	481	7,618.4	232	1.97	—	2.1	224	15.1	186	12.3	264

RANK 1998	COMPANY	$ millions	$ millions	Rank	$ millions	Ran
326	PRAXAIR Danbury, Conn.	4,833.0	425.0	198	8,096.0	24
327	STARWOOD HOTELS & RESORTS White Plains, N.Y.[69]	4,832.0	1,255.0	67	16,101.0	16
328	AUTOMATIC DATA PROCESSING Roseland, N.J.[7]	4,798.1	605.3	148	5,175.4	31
329	FORTUNE BRANDS Old Greenwich, Conn.	4,797.2	263.1*	271	7,359.7	25
330	TANDY Fort Worth	4,787.9	61.3	398	1,993.6	45
331	MATTEL El Segundo, Calif.	4,781.9	332.3	243	4,262.2	35
332	BROWNING-FERRIS INDUSTRIES Houston[11]	4,745.7	338.8	240	4,999.5	32
333	SERVICEMASTER Downers Grove, Ill.	4,724.1	190.0	313	2,914.9	40
334	OXFORD HEALTH PLANS Norwalk, Conn.	4,719.4	(624.5)	489	1,637.8	46
335	COMPUTER ASSOCIATES INTL. Islandia, N.Y.[20]	4,719.0	1,169.0	76	6,706.0	27
336	PARKER HANNIFIN Cleveland[7]	4,633.0	319.6	248	3,524.8	38
337	UNUM Portland, Me.	4,630.8	363.4	230	15,182.9	16
338	OLSTEN Melville, N.Y.	4,602.8	4.4	428	2,058.8	44
339	FOSTER WHEELER Clinton, N.J.	4,597.0	(31.5)	445	3,495.0	38
340	MEAD Dayton	4,579.2¶	119.7	363	5,142.2	32
341	ALLEGIANCE McGaw Park, Ill.[70]	4,574.4	126.4	357	2,831.2	41
342	BLACK & DECKER Towson, Md.	4,559.9	(754.8)	492	3,852.5	36
343	MERISEL El Segundo, Calif.	4,553.0	18.5	425	945.3	49
344	UNION CAMP Wayne, N.J.	4,502.9	19.3	423	5,176.4	31
345	EASTMAN CHEMICAL Kingsport, Tenn.	4,481.0	249.0	277	5,876.0	29
346	BETHLEHEM STEEL Bethlehem, Pa.	4,477.8	120.1*	362	5,621.5	30
347	SCIENCE APPLICATIONS INTL. San Diego[71]	4,476.8	147.6	332	2,567.4	4
348	CORPORATE EXPRESS Broomfield, Colo.[1,72]	4,474.6¶	(73.3)	455	2,467.6	4
349	FEDERAL-MOGUL Southfield, Mich.	4,468.7	53.7*	405	9,940.1	2
350	HERSHEY FOODS Hershey, Pa.	4,435.6	340.9	239	3,404.1	3

illions	Rank	$ millions	Rank	1998 $	% change from 1997	1988–98 annual growth rate %	Rank	1998 %	Rank	1988–98 annual rate %	Rank
32.0	253	5,495.3	271	2.60	5.7	—		(20.7)	387	—	
02.0	151	5,496.0	269	6.47	729.5	30.8	10	(58.8)	446	(0.7)	370
06.5	181	23,295.9	91	1.98	15.8	13.7	62	31.7	117	24.8	76
97.5	152	5,639.2	267	1.49	166.1	(6.5)	296	(12.5)	351	8.7	320
48.2	410	5,651.3	266	0.54	(66.9)	(11.2)	310	7.7	231	9.0	317
20.2	299	6,561.7	249	1.10	18.3	18.3	34	(36.4)	420	25.5	66
13.5	342	5,939.3	257	1.87	43.8	2.2	221	(21.4)	392	2.7	358
56.5	402	5,438.5	274	0.64	17.1	9.2	130	15.0	188	34.4	24
81.1)	490	1,342.6	412	(7.79)	—	—		(4.4)	312	—	
81.0	243	20,429.3	104	2.06	221.9	26.8	17	(19.5)	384	25.1	74
83.5	308	4,013.5	320	2.85	16.8	11.3	90	(27.4)	403	12.9	255
37.7	229	6,736.1	247	2.57	(0.8)	13.2	66	8.6	225	26.1	58
22.5	413	477.5	444	0.05	(95.7)	(20.5)	325	(49.7)	440	0.4	366
72.1	446	514.1	442	(0.77)	—	—		(49.0)	439	1.4	363
52.0	258	3,155.8	342	1.14	(19.1)	(8.2)	302	6.9	242	6.7	336
69.7	398	N.A.		1.06	35.9	—		165.6	6	—	
74.0	444	4,424.1	306	(8.22)	(449.8)	—		44.8	88	11.3	282
54.3	484	120.4	458	0.23	—	(10.5)	307	(45.7)	433	(8.9)	377
43.9	287	4,681.5	295	0.28	(75.9)	(23.8)	327	29.5	123	10.8	292
34.0	289	3,665.9	332	3.13	(13.8)	—		(22.6)	395	—	
89.5	331	1,152.9	417	0.64	(68.5)	(19.1)	323	(3.6)	305	(9.1)	378
80.4	396	N.A.		2.49	85.8	15.9	43	—		—	
44.3	458	579.3	437	(0.64)	—	—		(59.7)	448	—	
86.2	284	2,794.4	354	0.96	(40.4)	(5.4)	292	47.3	84	12.8	257
42.3	390	8,848.3	205	2.34	4.9	7.0	164	1.8	277	19.5	143

		REVENUES	PROFITS		ASSETS	
RANK 1998	COMPANY	$ millions	$ millions	Rank	$ millions	Ran
351	NORFOLK SOUTHERN Norfolk, Va.	4,428.0	734.0	125	18,180.0	15
352	DOLE FOOD Westlake Village, Calif.	4,424.2	12.1	427	2,915.1	40
353	LITTON INDUSTRIES Woodland Hills, Calif.[48]	4,399.9	181.4	322	4,049.8	36
354	KN ENERGY Lakewood, Colo.	4,387.8	60.0	400	9,612.2	22
355	FMC Chicago	4,378.4	106.5	370	4,166.4	35
356	MASCO Taylor, Mich.	4,345.0	476.0	181	5,167.4	31
357	W.W. GRAINGER Lincolnshire, Ill.	4,341.3	238.5	286	2,103.9	44
358	OFFICEMAX Shaker Heights, Ohio[1]	4,337.8	42.6	413	2,231.9	44
359	PITNEY BOWES Stamford, Conn.	4,334.4	576.4	153	7,661.0	25
360	TRUSERV Chicago[45]	4,328.2	N.A.		1,600.8	46
361	UNIVERSAL Richmond[7]	4,287.2	141.3	339	2,056.7	44
362	LTV Cleveland	4,273.0	(27.0)	442	5,324.0	31
363	INACOM Omaha[73]	4,258.4	42.6	414	1,103.5	48
364	GPU Morristown, N.J.	4,248.8	360.1	232	16,288.1	16
365	HARCOURT GENERAL Chestnut Hill, Mass.[6]	4,235.3	141.6	338	4,449.1	34
366	STATE STREET CORP. Boston	4,234.0	436.0	192	47,082.0	
367	GIANT FOOD Landover, Md.[28]	4,230.6	71.2	389	1,521.9	4
368	DTE ENERGY Detroit	4,221.0	443.0	189	12,088.0	1
369	CONSOLIDATED STORES Columbus, Ohio[1]	4,193.7	96.8	377	2,042.5	4
370	ENGELHARD Iselin, N.J.	4,174.6	187.1	316	2,866.3	4
371	SOUTHWEST AIRLINES Dallas	4,164.0	433.4	195	4,716.0	3
372	NASH FINCH Edina, Minn.	4,160.0	(61.6)	451	825.1	4
373	PACIFIC LIFE INSURANCE Newport Beach, Calif.	4,152.9	187.6	315	38,727.1	
374	NUCOR Charlotte, N.C.	4,151.2	263.7	270	3,226.5	3
375	TURNER CORP. New York	4,129.7	19.6	422	1,129.1	4

CKHOLDERS' JITY		MARKET VALUE 3/15/99		EARNINGS PER SHARE				TOTAL RETURN TO INVESTORS			
				1998 $	% change from 1997	1988–98 annual growth rate %	Rank	1998 %	Rank	1988–98 annual rate %	Rank
lions	Rank	$ millions	Rank								
21.0	105	11,311.0	168	1.93	1.6	5.1	187	6.5	244	15.1	212
21.8	438	1,778.8	398	0.20	(92.5)	(20.8)	326	(33.7)	414	3.0	357
37.2	376	2,679.7	360	3.82	12.4	1.9	228	13.6	195	15.4	210
23.8	372	1,432.0	409	0.92	(43.7)	3.3	208	(31.2)	410	15.9	203
29.4	425	1,641.3	402	3.05	(30.8)	(1.6)	264	(16.8)	371	5.8	341
28.6	230	8,801.4	209	1.39	20.9	2.8	213	14.8	190	11.1	287
78.7	368	4,336.3	310	2.44	7.5	9.6	122	(13.3)	355	13.5	240
38.1	383	1,014.6	423	0.39	(45.8)	—		(14.0)	358	—	
48.0	311	17,946.4	118	2.06	14.4	10.3	112	49.5	80	22.9	99
54.7	467	N.A.		N.A.	—	—		—		—	
47.9	451	911.5	430	3.99	39.0	8.4	143	(12.0)	347	12.4	262
28.0	314	561.4	438	(0.29)	(207.4)	—		(40.8)	427	—	
25.1	459	497.7	443	2.26	4.1	7.3	158	(47.0)	437	4.3	348
31.1	175	5,135.8	283	2.83	2.2	1.8	231	10.3	216	15.2	211
25.7	403	3,283.4	339	1.96	—	5.1	188	(1.4)	295	10.6	300
11.0	257	14,157.7	142	2.66	14.7	15.5	49	21.4	153	28.5	48
02.6	406	N.A.		1.18	(16.9)	(0.6)	252	—		—	
98.0	169	6,065.3	255	3.05	5.9	—		30.6	121	17.0	182
81.9	377	2,874.5	350	0.86	11.7	10.4	110	(54.1)	443	17.1	180
01.6	407	2,611.8	363	1.29	290.9	11.9	83	14.6	191	16.8	187
97.9	250	11,339.9	167	1.23	31.8	21.1	23	38.4	104	27.8	52
56.5	483	100.4	459	(5.45)	—	—		(21.5)	393	(1.7)	372
57.4	380	N.A.		N.A.	—	—		—		—	
72.6	272	3,734.3	330	3.00	(10.4)	8.8	135	(9.6)	335	14.4	225
88.8	485	126.1	457	1.50	262.9	10.6	102	4.1	266	7.0	333

RANK 1998	COMPANY	REVENUES $ millions	PROFITS $ millions	Rank	ASSETS $ millions	R
376	RYERSON TULL Chicago[74]	4,092.7	550.9	157	1,343.9	4
377	KELLY SERVICES Troy, Mich.	4,092.3	84.7	385	964.2	4
378	OMNICOM GROUP New York	4,092.0	285.1	260	6,890.0	2
379	MAYTAG Newton, Iowa	4,069.3	280.6	264	2,587.7	4
380	HILTON HOTELS Beverly Hills	4,064.0	297.0	255	3,944.0	3
381	AMERICAN FINANCIAL GROUP Cincinnati	4,050.0	124.4	359	15,845.2	1
382	APPLIED MATERIALS Santa Clara, Calif.[6]	4,041.7	230.9	294	4,929.7	3
383	HEALTHSOUTH Birmingham, Ala.	4,006.1	46.6	411	6,773.0	2
384	AMERICAN FAMILY INS. GROUP Madison, Wis.	4,002.6	39.6	415	8,949.2	2
385	CENTEX Dallas[20]	3,975.5	144.8	336	3,416.2	3
386	EMC Hopkinton, Mass.	3,973.7	793.4	115	4,568.6	3
387	INTERPUBLIC GROUP New York	3,968.7	309.9	252	6,942.8	2
388	B.F. GOODRICH Richfield, Ohio	3,950.8	226.5	297	4,192.6	3
389	BRUNSWICK Lake Forest, Ill.	3,945.2	186.3	317	3,351.5	3
390	HARRIS Melbourne, Fla.[7]	3,939.1	133.0	347	3,784.0	3
391	ALLEGHENY TELEDYNE Pittsburgh	3,923.4	241.2	284	3,175.5	3
392	GENAMERICA St. Louis	3,913.9	113.5	365	28,949.2	
393	PROVIDENT COS. Chattanooga	3,904.0	254.0	276	23,088.1	1
394	THERMO ELECTRON Waltham, Mass.	3,867.6	181.9	321	6,331.6	2
395	SMITHFIELD FOODS Smithfield, Va.[42]	3,867.4	53.4	406	1,083.6	4
396	MARKETSPAN Brooklyn[75,76]	3,836.1	51.3	407	6,900.0	2
397	MERITOR AUTOMOTIVE Troy, Mich.[11]	3,836.0	147.0	333	2,086.0	4
398	NIAGARA MOHAWK POWER Syracuse, N.Y.	3,826.4	(120.8)	461	13,861.2	1
399	MUTUAL OF OMAHA INSURANCE Omaha	3,820.1	91.3	381	13,281.4	1
400	SMURFIT-STONE CONTAINER Chicago[77]	3,794.0	(200.0)	471	11,631.0	2

STOCKHOLDERS' EQUITY		MARKET VALUE 3/15/99		EARNINGS PER SHARE				TOTAL RETURN TO INVESTORS			
				1998 $	% change from 1997	1988–98 annual growth rate %	Rank	1998 %	Rank	1988–98 annual rate %	Rank
$ millions	Rank	$ millions	Rank								
63.6	449	357.6	450	13.04	512.2	5.8	180	(0.6)	291	(7.5)	375
37.8	452	928.7	429	2.23	5.2	3.3	205	8.9	222	5.4	343
90.0	386	11,724.4	162	1.68	22.6	15.6	47	38.9	102	31.8	29
07.6	455	4,828.7	291	2.99	62.5	3.7	197	69.0	48	16.1	198
87.0	479	3,976.8	321	1.12	19.1	5.1	188	(34.8)	416	5.7	342
16.2	303	2,258.2	375	2.00	212.5	3.2	210	11.6	207	10.0	305
20.6	199	22,514.9	94	0.61	(53.8)	14.9	53	41.7	94	40.8	10
23.0	179	4,708.4	293	0.11	(87.9)	1.8	229	(44.4)	431	25.7	64
24.6	190	N.A.		N.A.	—	—		—		—	
91.2	393	2,047.4	385	2.36	31.1	7.4	156	43.8	91	20.9	127
24.1	185	58,578.9	48	1.49	43.3	—		209.8	4	69.0	2
55.1	370	10,630.9	178	2.21	16.3	13.8	59	61.7	61	27.6	53
99.6	318	2,663.2	361	3.02	25.3	(2.0)	271	(11.1)	343	7.6	326
11.3	360	1,841.1	395	1.88	25.3	(1.6)	263	(16.4)	367	6.7	335
09.3	317	2,406.4	369	1.66	(36.9)	2.9	212	(18.4)	373	13.7	233
39.9	353	3,928.0	323	1.22	(26.9)	(2.7)	275	(18.5)	374	10.4	302
00.2	364	N.A.		N.A.	—	—		—		—	
08.5	180	4,961.9	289	1.82	(1.1)	6.4	175	8.6	224	19.3	147
48.1	259	2,218.9	380	1.07	(24.1)	12.1	74	(61.5)	449	10.9	290
51.0	465	1,068.8	421	1.34	14.5	11.2	93	2.7	269	23.9	84
00.0	209	3,850.7	327	0.23	—	(17.9)	321	(11.4)	344	13.3	244
56.0	475	1,010.2	424	2.13	—	—		2.0	276	—	
10.1	173	2,810.5	351	(0.95)	(693.8)	—		53.6	69	5.4	344
31.2	338	N.A.		N.A.	—	—		—		—	
34.0	313	4,111.1	316	(1.61)	(16,200.0)	—		11.9	204	—	

RANK 1998	COMPANY	REVENUES $ millions	PROFITS $ millions	Rank	ASSETS $ millions	R
401	PP&L RESOURCES Allentown, Pa.	3,786.0	(569.0)*	487	9,607.0	
402	NORTHEAST UTILITIES Berlin, Conn.	3,767.7	(146.8)	466	10,387.4	
403	PITTSTON Richmond	3,746.9	66.1	391	2,331.1	
404	GRAYBAR ELECTRIC St. Louis	3,744.1	59.5	401	1,167.8	
405	TEMPLE-INLAND Diboll, Texas	3,740.1	64.5	394	15,990.0	
406	MCGRAW-HILL New York	3,729.1	333.1	242	3,788.1	
407	NEWELL Freeport, Ill.[78]	3,720.0	396.2	214	4,327.9	
408	ROHM & HAAS Philadelphia	3,720.0	440.0	190	3,648.0	
409	SONAT Birmingham, Ala.	3,709.8	(530.5)	486	4,361.1	
410	WILLAMETTE INDUSTRIES Portland, Ore.	3,700.3	89.0	384	4,687.7	
411	CORNING Corning, N.Y.	3,688.9	394.0	216	4,981.9	
412	AVISTA CORP. Spokane[79]	3,684.0	78.1	386	3,253.6	
413	KOHL'S Menomonee Falls, Wis.[1]	3,681.8	192.3	310	1,936.1	
414	CLARK USA St. Louis	3,668.2[E]	(29.7)	444	1,509.7	
415	SUPERMARKETS GENL. HOLDINGS Carteret, N.J.[80]	3,655.2	(46.2)	448	873.6	
416	FLORIDA PROGRESS St. Petersburg	3,620.3	281.7	263	6,160.8	
417	ESTÉE LAUDER New York[7]	3,618.0	236.8	288	2,512.8	
418	NEW CENTURY ENERGIES Denver	3,610.9	342.0	238	7,672.0	
419	U.S. OFFICE PRODUCTS Washington, D.C.[42]	3,604.3¶	67.2	390	2,541.4	
420	CONSOLIDATED NATURAL GAS Pittsburgh	3,553.0¶	238.8	285	6,361.9	
421	BJ'S WHOLESALE CLUB Natick, Mass.[1]	3,552.2	62.5	397	907.6	
422	SHAW INDUSTRIES Dalton, Ga.	3,542.2	20.6	420	2,261.4	
423	WESTERN DIGITAL Irvine, Calif.[7]	3,541.5	(290.2)	477	1,442.7	
424	REPUBLIC NEW YORK CORP. New York	3,522.6	248.0	278	50,424.2	
425	HOST MARRIOTT Bethesda, Md.[81]	3,519.0	47.0*	410	8,268.0	

lions	Rank	$ millions	Rank	1998 $	% change from 1997	1988–98 annual growth rate %	Rank	1998 %	Rank	1988–98 annual rate %	Rank
40.0	298	4,030.8	319	(3.46)	(292.2)	—		24.0	138	12.0	272
47.4	276	1,956.1	390	(1.12)	—	—		35.4	109	5.1	345
36.0	423	1,126.3	420	N.A.	—	—		—		—	
96.8	471	N.A.		11.22	17.6	19.8	28	—		—	
98.0	283	3,523.6	335	1.15	27.8	(10.7)	308	16.1	175	12.0	270
51.8	324	11,168.4	169	1.67	14.8	5.7	181	40.4	99	16.3	194
12.0	291	7,730.1	231	2.38	30.8	15.9	44	(1.5)	296	21.4	120
61.0	322	5,427.5	275	2.45	15.0	7.8	152	(3.6)	306	13.1	250
29.3	355	3,259.6	340	(4.82)	(339.8)	—		(38.9)	425	10.5	301
42.4	280	4,224.2	312	0.80	23.1	(6.6)	298	6.2	248	14.4	224
45.6	330	13,658.5	147	1.67	(9.7)	3.6	198	23.6	140	14.3	226
7.3	419	677.6	434	1.28	(34.7)	0.1	245	(16.7)	369	11.2	286
2.8	379	11,790.5	160	1.18	30.4	—		80.4	35	—	
2.2	487	N.A.		(1.86)	—	—		—		—	
2.8)	499	N.A.		N.A.	—	—		—		—	
2.0	294	3,923.9	324	2.90	417.9	2.1	222	20.0	156	14.0	230
6.4	428	10,769.2	177	1.78	21.1	—		67.2	51	—	
4.8	237	4,586.8	299	3.05	111.8	3.6	200	6.9	241	16.4	191
6.1	333	171.1	454	2.20	(12.0)	—		(94.5)	457	—	
9.6	249	5,109.7	284	2.49	(21.0)	0.6	240	(7.5)	327	7.3	329
5.0	456	1,789.8	397	0.82	(54.7)	—		47.6	82	—	
7.4	415	3,110.3	345	0.16	(27.3)	(5.0)	289	109.9	18	25.6	65
7.8	470	846.5	431	(3.32)	(216.1)	—		(5.9)	318	7.4	328
0.8	196	5,051.5	287	2.07	(47.5)	2.2	220	(18.7)	376	15.0	215
1.0	361	2,594.4	364	0.27	12.5	(17.9)	322	(23.0)	396	11.5	278

		REVENUES	PROFITS		ASSETS	
RANK 1998	COMPANY	$ millions	$ millions	Rank	$ millions	R
426	FLOWERS INDUSTRIES Thomasville, Ga.	3,505.3	48.3	409	2,860.0	
427	FIRSTAR CORP. Milwaukee[82]	3,501.6	430.1	197	38,475.8	
428	AUTOLIV Ogden, Utah	3,488.7	188.3	314	3,668.1	
429	IMC GLOBAL Northbrook, Ill.	3,483.2	(9.0)**	434	6,674.2	
430	AVERY DENNISON Pasadena	3,459.9	223.3	299	2,142.6	
431	HECHINGER Largo, Md.[11]	3,449.2	(92.9)**	458	1,577.2	
432	PHOENIX HOME LIFE MUTUAL INS. Hartford	3,434.7	124.8	358	19,521.2	
433	ALLMERICA FINANCIAL Worcester, Mass.	3,432.5	201.2	306	27,607.9	
434	PETER KIEWIT SONS' Omaha[83]	3,403.0	136.0	344	1,377.0	
435	CHARLES SCHWAB San Francisco	3,388.1	348.5	236	22,264.0	
436	LEGGETT & PLATT Carthage, Mo.	3,370.4	248.0	279	2,535.3	
437	RELIANCE GROUP HOLDINGS New York	3,369.1	326.4	246	12,775.3	
438	U.S. INDUSTRIES Iselin, N.J.[11]	3,362.0	(44.0)*	447	2,812.0	
439	BALTIMORE GAS & ELECTRIC Baltimore	3,358.1	327.7	245	9,195.0	
440	QUALCOMM San Diego[11]	3,347.9	108.5	367	2,566.7	
441	SERVICE MERCHANDISE Brentwood, Tenn.[41]	3,327.3	(10.4)	436	1,779.4	
442	HANNAFORD BROS. Scarborough, Me.	3,323.6	94.6	378	1,284.5	
443	SUIZA FOODS Dallas	3,320.9	131.6**	350	3,021.3	
444	AMEREN St. Louis	3,318.2	386.5	220	8,847.4	
445	HASBRO Pawtucket, R.I.	3,304.5	206.4	303	3,793.8	
446	TIMES MIRROR Los Angeles	3,291.5	1,417.3	56	4,218.3	
447	YORK INTERNATIONAL York, Pa.	3,289.2	136.5	343	2,106.5	
448	DARDEN RESTAURANTS Orlando[17]	3,287.0	101.7	375	1,984.7	
449	DEAN FOODS Franklin Park, Ill.[17]	3,269.1¶	106.3	371	1,607.2	
450	LONGS DRUG STORES Walnut Creek, Calif.[1]	3,266.9	63.4	396	1,025.1	

CKHOLDERS' ITY		MARKET VALUE 3/15/99		EARNINGS PER SHARE				TOTAL RETURN TO INVESTORS			
				1998 $	% change from 1997	1988–98 annual growth rate %	Rank	1998 %	Rank	1988–98 annual rate %	Rank
lions	Rank	$ millions	Rank								
73.0	445	2,412.5	368	0.49	(31.9)	(1.1)	256	18.9	162	14.8	218
29.9	176	20,343.5	105	1.95	(11.0)	11.2	92	64.4	55	35.3	22
16.0	296	3,823.5	328	1.84	—	—		15.1	187	—	
60.4	295	2,214.6	381	(0.08)	(111.9)	—		(33.9)	415	1.2	364
83.3	412	5,443.8	273	2.15	11.4	9.3	128	2.5	272	17.7	170
38.7	477	N.A.		N.A.	—	—		—		—	
03.7	305	N.A.		N.A.	—	—		—		—	
58.6	245	3,098.5	346	3.33	(12.8)	—		16.3	173	—	
91.0	429	N.A.		4.02	—	—		—		—	
29.0	339	35,340.6	64	0.85	28.8	47.2	3	101.8	23	63.4	3
36.8	337	4,188.4	314	1.24	14.8	16.2	42	6.4	245	24.5	79
15.5	358	1,001.2	425	2.72	40.2	23.9	21	(7.0)	323	16.1	199
50.0	400	1,665.5	400	(0.45)	(114.4)	—		(38.4)	424	—	
71.5	195	3,944.6	322	2.06	19.8	(1.2)	258	(4.9)	313	10.7	293
57.6	401	5,862.1	259	1.47	14.8	—		5.0	256	—	
16.4	474	43.9	462	(0.11)	—	—		(86.8)	456	(23.9)	380
53.4	432	1,962.1	389	2.21	57.9	11.1	94	23.6	139	18.5	162
6.1	433	1,287.0	415	3.58	293.4	—		(14.5)	360	—	
56.1	204	5,154.2	282	2.82	15.6	1.0	237	4.9	258	13.1	252
44.8	286	5,492.9	272	1.51	48.0	10.6	103	15.7	184	19.0	153
42.5	352	4,111.6	315	16.06	601.3	—		(7.8)	329	—	
30.8	424	1,404.8	410	3.36	205.5	—		4.4	262	—	
19.8	392	3,020.8	347	0.67	—	—		44.7	90	—	
19.3	439	1,533.9	406	2.57	19.5	9.2	129	(30.5)	408	9.8	310
89.3	435	1,268.2	416	1.64	10.1	1.8	230	18.8	163	10.7	294

RANK 1998	COMPANY	$ millions	$ millions	Rank	$ millions	Ra
451	INTERSTATE BAKERIES Kansas City, Mo.[17]	3,265.8	127.9	355	1,550.0	4(
452	CABLEVISION SYSTEMS Bethpage, N.Y.	3,265.1	(286.6)	476	7,061.1	2(
453	HORMEL FOODS Austin, Minn.[6]	3,261.0	139.3	340	1,555.9	4(
454	TRANS WORLD AIRLINES St. Louis	3,259.1	(120.5)*	460	2,554.6	4
455	COMDISCO Rosemont, Ill.[11]	3,243.0	153.0	330	7,063.0	2
456	AUTOZONE Memphis[16]	3,242.9	227.9	296	2,748.1	4
457	UNITED STATES FILTER Palm Desert, Calif.[20]	3,234.6	(299.8)	479	3,597.8	3
458	REEBOK INTERNATIONAL Stoughton, Mass.	3,224.6	23.9	419	1,740.0	4
459	DOLLAR GENERAL Nashville[1]	3,221.0	182.0	320	1,211.8	4
460	COMERICA Detroit	3,219.9	607.1	147	36,600.8	
461	AID ASSOCIATION FOR LUTHERANS Appleton, Wis.	3,217.9	133.7	346	19,417.7	1
462	RICHFOOD HOLDINGS Glen Allen, Va.[42,84]	3,203.7	54.7	404	908.9	4
463	SUN HEALTHCARE GROUP Albuquerque[41]	3,142.1	(62.5)	452	3,098.5	4
464	VENCOR Louisville[41,85]	3,132.4	(17.7)	439	2,245.2	4
465	CAROLINA POWER & LIGHT Raleigh	3,130.0	399.2	212	8,347.4	2
466	USG Chicago	3,130.0	332.0	244	2,357.0	4
467	ACE HARDWARE Oak Brook, Ill.[45]	3,120.4	N.A.		1,047.7	4
468	BECTON DICKINSON Franklin Lakes, N.J.[11]	3,116.9	236.6	289	3,846.0	3
469	YELLOW Overland Park, Kan.	3,112.1	(28.7)	443	1,105.7	4
470	SILICON GRAPHICS Mountain View, Calif.[7]	3,100.6	(459.6)	482	2,964.7	4
471	GOLDEN WEST FINANCIAL CORP. Oakland	3,100.2	434.6	193	38,468.7	
472	KNIGHT-RIDDER San Jose	3,099.6	365.9	228	4,257.1	
473	ANIXTER INTERNATIONAL Skokie, Ill.	3,083.7¶	65.6	393	1,319.2	
474	OWENS & MINOR Glen Allen, Va.	3,082.1	20.1	421	717.8	
475	AIRBORNE FREIGHT Seattle	3,074.5	137.3	342	1,501.6	

lions	Rank	$ millions	Rank	1998 $	% change from 1997	1988–98 annual growth rate %	Rank	1998 %	Rank	1988–98 annual rate %	Rank
•5.2	448	1,634.9	403	1.71	34.1	—		(28.6)	405	—	
1.7)	500	10,794.0	175	(3.16)	—	—		109.4	19	20.2	133
3.3	414	2,710.1	358	1.85	29.4	9.0	133	2.0	275	13.8	232
●5.2	480	339.0	452	(2.35)	—	—		(51.6)	442	—	
'9.0	397	2,194.0	382	0.93	19.2	26.8	19	1.6	279	15.7	207
●2.1	362	5,071.7	286	1.48	15.6	—		13.6	196	—	
3.4	367	4,369.7	309	(3.13)	(506.5)	—		(23.6)	399	(0.5)	369
4.4	453	970.2	428	0.42	(81.9)	(10.0)	305	(48.4)	438	3.0	356
●5.8	426	7,193.1	240	0.85	26.5	31.8	7	2.3	273	40.4	12
●6.6	205	10,833.7	174	3.72	16.6	9.5	124	15.6	185	25.7	63
●8.0	327	N.A.		N.A.	—	—		—		—	
4.2	469	1,060.9	422	1.15	(8.0)	—		(25.9)	401	23.6	88
2.4	440	67.2	461	(1.00)	(203.1)	—		(66.1)	451	—	
2.6	405	78.5	460	(0.27)	—	—		—		—	
8.7	207	6,261.6	252	2.75	3.4	10.4	109	16.2	174	16.4	192
●8.0	454	2,309.1	373	6.61	118.2	—		4.2	264	—	
1.5	476	N.A.		N.A.	—	—		—		—	
3.8	316	9,717.8	191	0.90	(21.7)	6.0	177	72.2	45	22.5	108
1.3	463	475.2	445	(1.06)	(157.9)	—		(23.9)	400	(2.7)	373
4.5	334	2,793.9	355	(2.47)	(674.4)	—		4.6	260	10.6	297
4.3	198	5,860.2	260	7.52	22.7	13.1	69	(5.7)	317	20.1	134
2.7	309	3,912.3	325	3.73	(8.6)	10.5	108	(0.2)	289	11.1	289
●8.9	461	465.8	446	1.45	52.6	20.8	26	23.1	142	8.3	323
]1.1	482	399.6	447	0.56	(6.7)	6.6	173	10.3	217	15.7	208
9.2	417	1,531.2	407	2.72	11.5	26.8	18	16.7	171	22.3	110

		REVENUES	PROFITS		ASSETS	
RANK **1998**	**COMPANY**	**$ millions**	**$ millions**	**Rank**	**$ millions**	**R**
476	**REGIONS FINANCIAL** Birmingham, Ala.	3,072.5	421.7	202	36,831.9	
477	**CONECTIV** Wilmington, Del.	3,071.6	153.2	329	6,087.7	2
478	**SLM HOLDING** Reston, Va.	3,064.6	501.5	175	37,210.0	
479	**PHELPS DODGE** Phoenix	3,063.4	190.9	311	5,036.5	3
480	**UNITED STATIONERS** Des Plaines, Ill.	3,059.2	58.0*	402	1,167.0	4
481	**FLEETWOOD ENTERPRISES** Riverside, Calif.[42]	3,050.6	108.5	366	1,129.5	4
482	**UNITED AUTO GROUP** New York[41]	3,045.3	(9.4)	435	1,147.0	4
483	**LUTHERAN BROTHERHOOD** Minneapolis	3,026.6	91.2	382	18,239.8	
484	**GOLDEN STATE BANCORP** San Francisco[86]	3,025.8	247.8	280	54,812.3	
485	**WESCO INTERNATIONAL** Pittsburgh	3,025.4	(7.7)*	432	950.5	4
486	**LEXMARK INTERNATIONAL** Lexington, Ky.	3,020.6	243.0	283	1,483.4	
487	**MICRON TECHNOLOGY** Boise[16]	3,011.9	(233.7)	473	4,688.3	
488	**BB&T CORP.** Winston-Salem, N.C.	3,009.2	501.8	174	34,427.2	
489	**BARNES & NOBLE** New York[1]	3,005.6	92.4	380	1,807.6	
490	**SHOPKO STORES** Green Bay, Wis.[1]	2,993.8	55.6	403	1,373.5	
491	**TRIBUNE** Chicago	2,980.9	414.3	205	5,935.6	
492	**INTEGRATED HEALTH SERVICES** Owings Mills, Md.	2,972.6	(68.0)	453	5,381.2	
493	**SOUTHTRUST CORP.** Birmingham, Ala.	2,943.3	368.6	227	38,133.8	
494	**AGCO** Duluth, Ga.	2,941.4	60.6	399	2,750.4	
495	**NEW YORK TIMES** New York	2,936.7	278.9	266	3,465.1	
496	**MERCANTILE BANCORP.** St. Louis	2,934.0	375.3	226	35,800.2	
497	**NIPSCO INDUSTRIES** Merrillville, Ind.	2,932.8	193.9	309	4,986.5	
498	**DANAHER** Washington, D.C.	2,910.0	182.9	319	2,738.7	
499	**WESTVACO** New York[6]	2,904.7	132.0	349	5,008.7	
500	**BALL** Broomfield, Colo.	2,896.4	16.6	426	2,854.8	
	TOTALS	5,740,596.0	334,334.6		14,288,321.2	

CKHOLDERS' JITY		MARKET VALUE 3/15/99		EARNINGS PER SHARE				TOTAL RETURN TO INVESTORS			
				1998 $	% change from 1997	1988–98 annual growth rate %	Rank	1998 %	Rank	1988–98 annual rate %	Rank
llions	Rank	$ millions	Rank								
00.4	208	8,459.9	215	1.88	(12.6)	8.9	134	(2.3)	299	23.4	91
43.2	297	2,326.1	372	1.50	(9.6)	(1.2)	259	16.0	177	11.6	277
53.6	434	7,580.6	235	2.95	6.1	17.1	39	22.5	144	19.7	139
37.4	238	2,797.3	352	3.26	(50.8)	(6.8)	300	(15.3)	364	12.1	269
70.6	464	544.5	439	1.60	6,300.0	15.6	46	8.1	228	18.7	158
76.0	462	1,000.9	426	3.01	(5.6)	11.2	91	(16.6)	368	13.5	238
59.9	466	170.1	455	(0.55)	—	—		(49.8)	441	—	
41.3	382	N.A.		N.A.	—	—		—		—	
31.8	319	2,628.2	362	3.04	—	—		—		—	
42.6)	489	N.A.		(9.93)	—	—		—		—	
78.1	443	5,869.6	258	3.40	71.7	—		164.5	7	—	
93.0	234	12,789.0	152	(1.10)	(171.0)	—		94.9	25	32.2	28
58.5	227	11,617.1	163	1.71	31.5	5.3	186	28.3	128	20.9	126
78.8	430	2,045.6	386	1.29	69.7	—		27.3	132	—	
59.2	457	976.0	427	2.10	22.8	—		51.1	75	—	
56.6	252	7,950.8	224	3.01	7.1	8.0	147	7.1	238	15.1	213
80.1	354	339.5	451	(1.08)	—	—		(54.7)	444	—	
38.3	228	6,774.2	246	2.25	10.8	11.5	89	(11.0)	342	24.5	80
32.1	394	372.1	449	0.99	(63.5)	—		(73.0)	454	—	
41.5	325	5,623.9	268	1.45	9.0	3.4	204	6.1	251	12.2	266
73.8	203	8,204.7	219	2.41	46.1	11.7	86	(23.3)	398	19.5	144
49.7	381	3,224.8	341	1.59	3.9	8.5	141	27.5	131	21.5	117
51.8	350	7,016.8	243	1.32	2.7	11.1	96	72.3	44	31.6	32
46.4	260	2,225.6	379	1.30	(17.7)	(4.5)	287	(12.0)	348	6.6	337
22.3	437	1,349.5	411	0.44	(74.7)	(14.7)	318	31.5	119	9.4	315
45.0		9,907,232.9									

FOOTNOTES TO THE 1999 FORTUNE 500

● ● ●

N.A. Not available.
  E Excise taxes have been deducted.
  * Reflects extraordinary charge of at least 10%.
  ** Reflects an extraordinary credit of at least 10%.
  ¶ Includes revenues of discontinued operations of at least 10%.

● **1–9**

[1] Figures are for fiscal year ended Jan. 31, 1999.
[2] Acquired Tracor Inc. (1997 rank: 876), June 23, 1998.
[3] Name changed from Travelers Group after acquiring Citicorp (1997 rank: 21), Oct. 8, 1998.
[4] Figures do not include Tele-Communications (1998 rank: 228), acquired March 9, 1999.
[5] Name changed from NationsBank Corp. after acquiring BankAmerica Corp. (1997 rank: 47), Sept. 30, 1998.
[6] Figures are for fiscal year ended Oct. 31, 1998.
[7] Figures are for fiscal year ended June 30, 1998.
[8] Acquired TransAtlantic Holdings (1997 rank: 774), July 1, 1998. Figures do not include SunAmerica (1998 rank: 540), acquired Jan. 1, 1999.
[9] Acquired Digital Equipment (1997 rank: 118), June 11, 1998.

● **10–19**

[10] Figures are for fiscal year ended Nov. 30, 1998.
[11] Figures are for fiscal year ended Sept. 30, 1998.
[12] Acquired Southern New England Telecommunications (1997 rank: 614), Oct. 26, 1998.
[13] Name changed from Banc One after acquiring First Chicago NBD Corp. (1997 rank: 154), Oct. 1, 1998.
[14] Consisting of Marathon Group and U.S. Steel Group.
[15] Acquired Dominick's Supermarkets (1997 rank: 518), Nov. 16, 1998.
[16] Figures are for fiscal year ended Aug. 31, 1998.
[17] Figures are for fiscal year ended May 31, 1998.
[18] Spun off Tricon Global Restaurants (1998 rank: 190), Oct. 7, 1997.
[19] Acquired CoreStates Financial Corp. (1997 rank: 340), April 27, 1998.

● **20–29**

[20] Figures are for fiscal year ended March 31, 1998.
[21] Name changed from McKesson after acquiring HBO, Jan. 13, 1999. Figures do not include HBO (1997 rank: 907).
[22] Name changed from Norwest Corp. after acquiring Wells Fargo & Co. (1997 rank: 160), Nov. 2, 1998.
[23] Acquired Intelligent Electronics Inc. (1997 rank: 709), May 20, 1998.
[24] Figure as of Sept. 30, 1998.
[25] Name changed from Federal Home Loan Mortgage Corp., July 1, 1997.
[26] Name changed from WorldCom after acquiring MCI Communications (1997 rank: 62), Sept. 14, 1998.
[27] Acquired Dresser Industries (1997 rank: 206), Sept. 29, 1998.
[28] Figures are for fiscal year ended Feb. 28, 1998.
[29] Figures do not include Allegiance Corp. (1998 rank: 341), acquired Feb. 3, 1999.

● **30–39**

[30] Figures do not include Fingerhut (1998 rank: 680), acquired March 22, 1999.
[31] Acquired Alumax (1997 rank: 478), June 16, 1998.
[32] Name changed from Aluminum Co. of America, Jan. 1, 1999.
[33] Acquired Food 4 Less (1997 rank: 285), March 10, 1998, and Quality Food Centers (1997 rank: 649), March 9, 1998.
[34] Name changed from NGC Corp., July 6, 1998.
[35] Acquired General Re (1997 rank: 189), Dec. 21, 1998.
[36] Acquired Echlin (1997 rank: 408), July 9, 1998.
[37] Acquired H.F. Ahmanson (1997 rank: 391), Oct. 1, 1998.
[38] Name changed from USA Waste Services after acquiring Waste Management (1997 rank: 165), July 16, 1998.
[39] Separated from the former US West, now MediaOne Group (1998 rank: 503), June 12, 1998.

● **40–49**

[40] Name changed from Bankers Trust New York Corp., April 23, 1998.

⁴¹ Figures are for the four quarters ended Sept. 30,1998.

⁴² Figures are for fiscal year ended April 30, 1998.

⁴³ Acquired USF&G Corp. (1997 rank: 422), April 24, 1998.

⁴⁴ Acquired Viking Office Products (1997 rank: 864), Aug. 26, 1998.

⁴⁵ Cooperatives provide only net margin figures, which are not comparable with the profit figures on the list.

⁴⁶ Acquired Beneficial Corp. (1997 rank: 475), July 1, 1998.

⁴⁷ Spun off Solutia (1998 rank: 509), Sept. 1, 1997.

⁴⁸ Figures are for fiscal year ended July 31, 1998.

⁴⁹ Spun off Corn Products International (1998 rank: 858), Dec. 31, 1997.

● **50–59**

⁵⁰ Acquired First of America Bank Corp. (1997 rank: 607), March 31, 1998.

⁵¹ Spun off Meritor Automotive (1998 rank: 397), Sept. 30, 1997.

⁵² Acquired Mercantile Stores (1997 rank: 456), Aug. 18, 1998.

⁵³ Spun off from Sodexho Marriott Services (1998 rank: 247), March 27, 1998.

⁵⁴ Acquired Green Tree Financial Corp. (1997 rank: 973), June 30, 1998.

⁵⁵ Acquired MAPCO (1997 rank: 395), March 27, 1998.

⁵⁶ Acquired ProSource (1997 rank: 376), May 21, 1998.

⁵⁷ Acquired Crestar Financial Corp. (1997 rank: 618), Dec. 31, 1998.

⁵⁸ Acquired by AT&T (1998 rank: 10), March 9, 1999.

⁵⁹ Name changed from Sun Co., Nov. 6, 1998

● **60–69**

⁶⁰ Figures are for 50 weeks ended Aug. 31, 1998, and are unaudited. Company changed fiscal year-end from Dec. 31.

⁶¹ Name changed from Marriott International, March 27, 1998, after spinning off the new Marriott International (1998 rank: 206).

⁶² Acquired Western Atlas (1997 rank: 488), Aug. 10, 1998.

⁶³ Changed fiscal year-end from Sept. 30.

⁶⁴ Name changed from Proffitt's after acquiring Saks Holdings (1997 rank: 583), Sept. 17, 1998.

⁶⁵ Reflects charge from the cumulative effect of change in accounting of at least 10%.

⁶⁶ Name changed from Woolworth, June 12, 1998.

⁶⁷ Name changed from Enova Corp. after acquiring Pacific Enterprises (1997 rank: 497), June 26, 1998.

⁶⁸ Acquired 360° Communication Co. (1997 rank: 836), July 1, 1998.

⁶⁹ Acquired ITT (1997 rank: 242), Feb. 23, 1998.

● **70–79**

⁷⁰ Acquired by Cardinal Health (1998 rank: 93), Feb. 3,1999.

⁷¹ Figures are for the four quarters ended Oct. 31,1998.

⁷² Changed fiscal year-end from Feb. 28.

⁷³ Figures do not include Vanstar (1998 rank: 508), acquired Feb. 17, 1999.

⁷⁴ Name changed from Inland Steel, Feb. 25, 1999.

⁷⁵ Figures are for the 12 months ended Dec. 31 and are unaudited. Company changed fiscal year-end from Sept. 30 to Dec. 31.

⁷⁶ Name changed from KeySpan Energy Corp. after acquiring Long Island Lighting (1997 rank: 454), May 29, 1998.

⁷⁷ Name changed from Jefferson Smurfit after acquiring Stone Container Corp. (1997 rank: 317), Nov. 18, 1998.

⁷⁸ Figures do not include Rubbermaid (1998 rank: 549), acquired March 24, 1999.

⁷⁹ Name changed from Washington Water Power, Jan. 1, 1999.

● **80–86**

⁸⁰ Revenue is for the fiscal year ended Jan. 31, 1999. Net income is for the four quarters ended Oct. 31, 1998, and assets, equity, and employees are as of Oct. 31, 1998.

⁸¹ Real estate investment trusts are not taxed at the corporate level, which means that their profits are not comparable with those of most companies on the list.

⁸² Name changed from Star Banc Corp. after acquiring Firstar Corp. (1997 rank: 647), Nov. 20, 1998.

⁸³ Spun off from Level 3 Communications (formerly Peter Kiewit Sons'; 1997 rank: 464), March 31,1998.

⁸⁴ Figures do not include Dart Group Corp. (1997 rank: 853), acquired May 15, 1998.

⁸⁵ Spun off from Ventas (formerly known as Vencor; 1997 rank: 463), April 30, 1998.

⁸⁶ Name changed from California Federal Bank after acquiring Golden State Bancorp (1997 rank: 930), Sept. 11, 1998.

THE 1999 FORTUNE 500 INDEX

● ● ●

AMERICA'S
MOST ADMIRED
COMPANIES, 1999

● ● ●

FORTUNE's list of America's Most Admired Companies is the definitive report card on corporate reputations. To rank the top ten, we asked Clark Martire & Bartolomeo (CM&B) to survey more than 10,000 executives, directors, and securities analysts. They were told to choose the companies they admire most, regardless of industry. The top ten in ascending order were General Electric, Coca-Cola, Microsoft, Dell Computer, Berkshire Hathaway, Wal-Mart Stores, Southwest Airlines, Intel, Merck, and Walt Disney.

The CEOs of the top ten mostly mind their own business. Five do not serve on the boards of any public company but their own. Those who do tend to have large investments in—or long relationships with—the businesses of which they are directors.

To create the 55 industry lists that follow, FORTUNE relied solely on the insiders. CM&B asked ballot recipients to rank companies in their own industry on eight criteria, ranging from long-term investment value to social responsibility. The result, backed by 17 years of experience, is an industry-by-industry guide to corporate America's shiniest—and dullest—reputations.

MORTGAGE FINANCE

Rank	Last Year	Company	Score
1	•	Fannie Mae	8.00
2	•	Freddie Mac	7.36
3	2	Charter One Financial	7.04
4	3	Washington Mutual	6.98
5	•	Countrywide Credit Industries	6.78
6	1	Golden West Financial	6.58
7	6	Dime Bancorp	6.25
8	4	H.F. Ahmanson	5.84
9	•	First American Financial	5.83
10	8	Golden State Bancorp	5.36

SECURITIES

Rank	Last Year	Company	Score
1	1	Merrill Lynch	7.58
2	6	Morgan Stanley Dean Witter	7.29
3	3	Charles Schwab	7.24
4	7	Travelers Group	6.67
5	•	Equitable	6.43
6	7	Bear Stearns	6.31
7	4	A.G. Edwards	6.29
8	6	Franklin Resources	6.00
9	10	Paine Webber Group	5.77
10	9	Lehman Brothers Holdings	5.67

INSURANCE: PROPERTY AND CASUALTY

Rank	Last Year	Company	Score
1	1	Berkshire Hathaway	7.86
2	2	USAA	7.33
3	3	American International Group	7.18
4	5	State Farm	7.02
5	6	Allstate	6.91
6	•	Chubb	6.71
7	8	Hartford Financial Services Group	6.66
8	9	Nationwide Insurance Enterprise	6.32
9	10	Liberty Mutual Insurance Group	6.23
10	•	St. Paul	6.06

CONSUMER CREDIT

Rank	Last Year	Company	Score
1	1	American Express	7.44
2	2	MBNA	7.36
3	4	Capital One Financial	7.05
4	•	SLM Holdings	6.47
5	5	Household International	6.35

INSURANCE: LIFE, HEALTH

Rank	Last Year	Company	Score
1	1	Northwestern Mutual Life	7.39
2	3	New York Life	6.65
3	2	Principal Financial Group	6.44
4	4	TIAA-CREF	6.31
5	5	Massachusetts Mutual Life	6.08
6	8	Cigna	6.03
7	•	American General	5.84
8	6	Metropolitan Life	5.82
9	9	Aetna	5.43
10	10	Prudential Insurance of America	5.16

MONEY CENTER BANKS

Rank	Last Year	Company	Score
1	2	Citicorp	7.39
2	3	Chase Manhattan	7.26
3	1	J.P. Morgan	7.16
4	5	First Chicago NBD	6.81
5	6	Bank of New York	6.64
6	7	Republic New York	6.44
7	4	Bankers Trust	5.56

SUPERREGIONAL BANKS

Rank	Last Year	Company	Score
1	1	Norwest	7.43
2	4	NationsBank	6.95
3	2	First Union	6.90
4	•	U.S. Bancorp	6.87
5	5	Banc One	6.41
6	7	Fleet Financial Group	6.32
7	3	BankAmerica	6.28
8	6	BankBoston	6.26
9	9	PNC Bank	6.14
10	8	Wells Fargo	6.12

AEROSPACE

Rank	Last Year	Company	Score
1	2	AlliedSignal	7.28
2	4	United Technologies	7.18
3	3	Lockheed Martin	6.92
4	5	Textron	6.67
5	7	Sundstrand	6.59
6	6	General Dynamics	6.59
7	•	Gulfstream Aerospace	6.57
8	1	Boeing	6.42
9	8	B.F. Goodrich	6.33
10	9	Northrop Grumman	6.26

Rank	Last Year	Company	Score
1	1	Norfolk Southern	7.71
2	2	Burlington Northern Santa Fe	6.91
3	3	CSX	6.63
4	•	Kansas City Southern Industries	6.09
5	4	Union Pacific	5.63

MOTOR VEHICLES AND PARTS

Rank	Last Year	Company	Score
1	5	Ford Motor	7.25
2	2	Daimler-Benz N.A.	7.22
3	1	Toyota Motor Sales U.S.A.	7.19
4	3	Chrysler	7.04
5	4	American Honda Motor	6.53
6	6	Johnson Controls	6.40
7	•	Dana	6.17
8	7	TRW	6.04
9	9	General Motors	5.33

AIRLINES

Rank	Last Year	Company	Score
1	1	Southwest Airlines	7.21
2	2	AMR	6.87
3	3	Continental Airlines	6.72
4	4	UAL	6.36
5	6	Alaska Air Group	5.91
6	7	Delta Air Lines	5.91
7	8	US Airways Group	5.83
8	5	Northwest Airlines	4.98
9	9	America West Holdings	4.90
10	10	Trans World Airlines	4.53

INDUSTRIAL AND FARM EQUIPMENT

Rank	Last Year	Company	Score
1	1	Caterpillar	7.50
2	2	Deere	7.12
3	7	Black & Decker	6.64
4	4	Ingersoll-Rand	6.61
5	6	Parker Hannifin	6.38
6	5	Dover	6.19
7	3	Cummins Engine	6.15
8	10	American Standard	6.15
9	8	Case	5.89
10	9	Dresser Industries	5.70

Rank	Last Year	Company	Score
1	2	CNF Transportation	6.53
2	1	Ryder System	6.49
3	3	Yellow	5.97
4	7	USFreightways	5.84
5	5	J.B. Hunt Transport Services	5.83
6	8	Consolidated Freightways	5.65
7	4	Roadway Express	5.53
8	•	Landstar System	5.49
9	9	Arkansas Best	4.95
10	10	Amerco	4.78

MAIL, PACKAGE, AND FREIGHT DELIVERY

Rank	Last Year	Company	Score
1	1	United Parcel Service	8.18
2	2	FDX	7.55
3	4	Air Express International	6.20
4	3	Airborne Freight	5.95
5	•	Fritz	4.94
6	5	Pittston	4.69

HEALTH CARE

Rank	Last Year	Company	Score
1	3	WellPoint Health Networks	6.65
2	1	United HealthCare	6.60
3	2	Tenet Healthcare	6.41
4	4	PacifiCare Health Systems	5.92
5	6	Allegiance	5.83
6	7	Humana	5.63
7	10	Columbia/HCA Healthcare	4.82
8	8	Foundation Health	4.31
9	•	Oxford Health Plans	3.99
10	5	MedPartners	3.61

OUTSOURCING SERVICES

Rank	Last Year	Company	Score
1	•	ServiceMaster	7.10
2	6	Aramark	6.87
3	•	Administaff	6.48
4	•	ABM Industries	6.13
5	•	Wackenhut	6.08
6	•	Borg-Warner Security	5.82
7	4	Ogden	5.66
8	•	Staff Leasing	5.61

TEMPORARY HELP

Rank	Last Year	Company	Score
1	•	Robert Half International	7.23
2	3	Interim Services	6.16
3	1	Manpower	5.34
4	4	Kelly Services	5.32
5	2	Norrell	5.27
6	8	Accustaff	5.19
7	7	CDI	4.89
8	5	Volt Information Sciences	4.56
9	6	Olsten	4.20

APPAREL

Rank	Last Year	Company	Score
1	2	Liz Claiborne	6.82
2	3	VF	6.69
3	1	Nike	6.65
4	4	Jones Apparel Group	6.24
5	7	Kellwood	5.58
6	6	Russell	5.55
7	8	Warnaco Group	5.55
8	5	Reebok International	4.98
9	•	Nine West Group	4.70
10	9	Fruit of the Loom	4.27

BEVERAGES

Rank	Last Year	Company	Score
1	1	Coca-Cola	8.39
2	3	Anheuser-Busch	7.38
3	2	Coca-Cola Enterprises	7.14
4	4	Adolph Coors	6.72
5	2	PepsiCo	6.55
6	5	Brown-Forman	6.28
7	6	Joseph E. Seagram & Sons	6.13
8	8	Canandaigua Brands	5.56
9	7	Whitman	5.22

FOOD

Rank	Last Year	Company	Score
1	1	Nestlé USA	7.37
2	2	Sara Lee	7.20
3	3	Campbell Soup	7.03
4	6	H.J. Heinz	6.71
5	4	ConAgra	6.62
6	5	Bestfoods	6.34
7	7	RJR Nabisco Holdings	6.03
8	8	IBP	5.62
9	9	Farmland Industries	5.51
10	10	Archer Daniels Midland	5.00

TOBACCO			
Rank	Last Year	Company	Score
1	2	Philip Morris	8.51
2	3	UST	6.74
3	4	Universal	6.49
4	6	Standard Commercial	5.91
5	5	DIMON	5.60

FURNITURE			
Rank	Last Year	Company	Score
1	1	Herman Miller	8.09
2	2	Leggett & Platt	7.73
3	3	Hon Industries	7.42
4	4	Furniture Brands International	6.67

SOAPS, COSMETICS			
Rank	Last Year	Company	Score
1	2	Procter & Gamble	8.10
2	1	Gillette	7.75
3	3	Colgate-Palmolive	7.39
4	4	Estée Lauder	7.02
5	6	Clorox	6.97
6	5	Unilever U.S.	6.51
7	8	Avon Products	6.46
8	7	International Flavors & Fragrances	6.38
9	10	Alberto-Culver	5.57
10	9	Revlon	5.55

SPECIALTY RETAILERS			
Rank	Last Year	Company	Score
1	1	Home Depot	8.19
2	3	Costco	6.69
3	5	Lowe's	6.50
4	7	Limited	6.40
5	•	Office Depot	6.29
6	4	Circuit City Group	6.06
7	9	Best Buy	5.95
8	6	TJX	5.94
9	•	Republic Industries	5.68
10	2	Toys "R" Us	5.30

FOOD AND DRUG STORES

Rank	Last Year	Company	Score
1	3	Safeway	7.49
2	2	Publix Super Markets	7.48
3	1	Walgreen	7.27
4	4	Albertson's	7.21
5	5	Kroger	7.04
6	8	CVS	6.53
7	9	Food Lion	5.70
8	8	Winn-Dixie Stores	5.65
9	6	American Stores	5.26
10	10	A&P	4.51

FOOD SERVICES

Rank	Last Year	Company	Score
1	1	McDonald's	7.01
2	5	Brinker International	6.99
3	•	Outback Steakhouse	6.82
4	3	Wendy's International	6.68
5	4	Host Marriott Services	6.16
6	8	Darden Restaurants	6.01
7	•	Performance Food Group	4.93
8	10	Advantica	4.66
9	7	Viad	4.25
10	9	Shoney's	3.61

WHOLESALERS

Rank	Last Year	Company	Score
1	1	Cardinal Health	7.74
2	2	Ingram Micro	7.08
3	4	McKesson	7.02
4	3	Sysco	6.92
5	8	Supervalu	6.46
6	5	Arrow Electronics	6.19
7	7	Bergen Brunswig	6.08
8	•	AmeriSource Health	5.63
9	•	Bindley Western	5.59
10	10	Fleming	5.07

GENERAL MERCHANDISERS

Rank	Last Year	Company	Score
1	1	Wal-Mart Stores	7.66
2	3	Dayton Hudson	7.18
3	2	Nordstrom	6.89
4	5	May Department Stores	6.56
5	6	Federated Department Stores	6.32
6	4	Sears Roebuck	6.27
7	•	Harcourt General	5.75
8	7	J.C. Penney	5.33
9	8	Dillard's	5.32
10	10	Kmart	4.38

Rank	Last Year	Company	Score
1	2	Jacobs Engineering Group	6.80
2	3	Halliburton	6.66
3	7	Pulte	6.31
4	9	Turner	6.29
5	4	Centex	6.13
6	•	Emcor	5.90
7	1	Fluor	5.89
8	10	Kaufman & Broad Home	5.81
9	8	Fleetwood Enterprises	5.75
10	6	Foster Wheeler	5.72

BUILDING MATERIALS, GLASS

Rank	Last Year	Company	Score
1	1	Corning	8.24
2	2	Armstrong World Industries	6.89
3	4	USG	5.66
4	5	Owens-Illinois	5.62
5	3	Owens Corning	5.45
6	6	Johns Manville	5.14

METAL PRODUCTS

Rank	Last Year	Company	Score
1	1	Fortune Brands	6.94
2	1	Tyco International	5.98
3	2	Illinois Tool Works	5.64
4	3	Newell	4.94
5	4	Danaher	4.86
6	5	Masco	4.63
7	9	Ball	4.60
8	7	Stanley Works	4.56
9	8	Crown Cork & Seal	4.47
10	10	U.S. Industries	4.10

METALS

Rank	Last Year	Company	Score
1	1	Alcoa	7.45
2	2	Nucor	6.90
3	4	Phelps Dodge	6.36
4	3	Allegheny Teledyne	6.23
5	5	Reynolds Metals	6.11
6	•	AK Steel Holding	5.97
7	10	Bethlehem Steel	5.25
8	7	LTV	4.99
9	9	Maxxam	4.94
10	8	Inland Steel Industries	4.92

ELECTRIC AND GAS UTILITIES

Rank	Last Year	Company	Score
1	•	Duke Energy	7.89
2	2	Southern	7.31
3	1	FPL Group	7.22
4	3	Edison International	6.84
5	4	PG&E	6.76
6	6	Texas Utilities	6.63
7	•	Dominion Resources	6.24
8	9	Consolidated Edison	6.04
9	•	UtiliCorp United	5.89
10	10	Unicom	5.67

MINING, CRUDE OIL

Rank	Last Year	Company	Score
1	1	Burlington Resources	6.72
2	•	Apache	6.69
3	•	Unocal	6.40
4	3	Vulcan Materials	6.27
5	•	Newmont Mining	6.13
6	4	Cyprus Amax Minerals	5.93
7	6	Freeport-McMoRan Copper & Gold	5.75
8	7	Asarco	5.60
9	•	Union Pacific Resources	5.45
10	8	Oryx Energy	4.90

PETROLEUM REFINING

Rank	Last Year	Company	Score
1	2	Exxon	7.60
2	3	Mobil	7.38
3	1	Shell Oil	7.22
4	4	Chevron	6.99
5	6	BP America	6.86
6	7	Texaco	6.43
7	5	Amoco	6.21
8	9	Phillips Petroleum	5.90
9	8	Atlantic Richfield	5.73
10	10	USX	5.59

PIPELINES

Rank	Last Year	Company	Score
1	1	Enron	8.11
2	2	Williams	7.63
3	7	El Paso Natural Gas	6.65
4	•	KN Energy	6.12
5	5	Dynegy	6.00
6	•	TransMontaigne Oil	5.71
7	4	Sonat	5.61
8	•	Equitable Resources	5.44
9	8	Western Gas Resources	5.02

PHARMACEUTICALS

Rank	Last Year	Company	Score
1	2	Pfizer	8.27
2	1	Merck	8.13
3	3	Johnson & Johnson	7.45
4	5	Eli Lilly	7.37
5	4	Bristol-Myers Squibb	7.31
6	8	Schering-Plough	6.96
7	7	Warner-Lambert	6.85
8	6	Abbott Laboratories	6.44
9	9	American Home Products	6.39
10	10	Pharmacia & Upjohn	5.55

RUBBER AND PLASTICS PRODUCTS

Rank	Last Year	Company	Score
1	1	Goodyear Tire & Rubber	7.76
2	2	Rubbermaid	7.15
3	4	Cooper Tire & Rubber	7.10
4	5	Tupperware	6.93
5	10	GenCorp	6.91
6	•	First Brands	6.89
7	3	M.A. Hanna	6.74
8	8	Mark IV Industries	6.54
9	9	Bridgestone/Firestone	6.51
10	•	Carlisle	6.14

CHEMICALS

Rank	Last Year	Company	Score
1	1	Du Pont	7.85
2	3	Dow Chemical	7.02
3	2	Monsanto	6.79
4	4	PPG Industries	6.55
5	5	Bayer	6.54
6	7	BASF	6.39
7	6	Union Carbide	5.97
8	•	Sherwin-Williams	5.94
9	•	FMC	5.46
10	10	Occidental Petroleum	5.05

TEXTILES

Rank	Last Year	Company	Score
1	1	Unifi	7.14
2	3	WestPoint Stevens	6.94
3	4	Interface	6.93
4	6	Mohawk Industries	6.76
5	5	Shaw Industries	6.64
6	2	Springs Industries	6.52
7	7	Burlington Industries	6.35

FOREST AND PAPER PRODUCTS

Rank	Last Year	Company	Score
1	1	Kimberly-Clark	7.26
2	3	Weyerhaeuser	6.56
3	2	Mead	6.40
4	4	International Paper	5.98
5	5	Union Camp	5.96
6	8	Fort James	5.72
7	6	Georgia-Pacific	5.27
8	7	Champion International	5.07
9	9	Boise Cascade	4.50
10	10	Stone Container	4.10

ENTERTAINMENT

Rank	Last Year	Company	Score
1	1	Walt Disney	7.41
2	2	Time Warner	7.22
3	4	Viacom	6.56
4	5	News America Publishing	5.88
5	3	CBS	5.20

PUBLISHING, PRINTING

Rank	Last Year	Company	Score
1	1	Tribune	7.50
2	3	New York Times	7.24
3	2	Gannett	6.71
4	4	Knight-Ridder	6.50
5	5	Times Mirror	6.47
6	8	Dow Jones	6.41
7	7	McGraw-Hill	6.37
8	6	R.R. Donnelley & Sons	6.24
9	9	American Greetings	6.02
10	10	Reader's Digest Association	4.86

HOTELS, CASINOS, RESORTS

Rank	Last Year	Company	Score
1	1	Mirage Resorts	7.76
2	2	Marriott International	7.44
3	•	Host Marriott	6.70
4	4	Harrah's Entertainment	6.60
5	•	Promus Hotel	6.50
6	3	Hilton Hotels	5.75
7	•	Starwood Hotel & Resorts	5.32
8	5	Circus Circus Enterprises	4.90
9	•	Trump Hotels & Casino Resorts	3.20

COMPUTER AND DATA SERVICES

Rank	Last Year	Company	Score
1	2	Automatic Data Processing	7.12
2	6	America Online	6.92
3	3	Equifax	6.89
4	41	Computer Sciences	6.44
5	5	Comdisco	6.09
6	1	First Data	5.89
7	10	Unisys	5.75
8	•	Electronic Data Systems	5.50
9	9	Micro Warehouse	5.35
10	7	Dun & Bradstreet	5.29

COMPUTER, OFFICE EQUIPMENT

Rank	Last Year	Company	Score
1	3	International Business Machines	7.49
2	1	Hewlett-Packard	7.42
3	4	Dell Computer	7.35
4	5	Sun Microsystems	7.06
5	2	Compaq Computer	6.98
6	6	Xerox	6.88
7	8	Gateway 2000	6.46
8	7	Canon U.S.A.	5.71
9	10	Apple Computer	5.37
10	•	NCR	5.03

COMPUTER SOFTWARE

Rank	Last Year	Company	Score
1	1	Microsoft	7.73
2	2	Oracle	6.95
3	3	Computer Associates International	6.58
4	5	Novell	5.86
5	6	Sybase	4.77

TELECOMMUNICATIONS

Rank	Last Year	Company	Score
1	5	Sprint	7.39
2	•	Tele-Communications	6.34
3	2	BellSouth	6.33
4	3	Ameritech	6.23
5	4	Bell Atlantic	6.05
6	1	SBC Communications	5.83
7	8	AT&T	5.82
8	•	MCI WorldCom	5.51
9	6	GTE	5.43
10	9	US West	4.95

Rank	Last Year	Company	Score
1	1	EMC	7.59
2	7	Storage Technology	6.73
3	5	Lexmark International Group	6.71
4	3	Seagate Technology	6.58
5	6	Quantum	6.46
6	•	Imation	5.98
7	2	Western Digital	5.57
8	4	Iomega	5.30

Rank	Last Year	Company	Score
1	1	Cisco Systems	8.32
2	2	3Com	6.78
3	5	Bay Networks	5.92
4	4	Cabletron Systems	4.35

Rank	Last Year	Company	Score
1	1	General Electric	8.21
2	•	Lucent Technologies	7.78
3	3	Emerson Electric	7.28
4	4	Honeywell	6.68
5	2	Motorola	6.39
6	7	Raytheon	6.22
7	4	Siemens	6.17
8	9	Whirlpool	6.07
9	5	Rockwell International	5.95
10	8	Eaton	5.93

Rank	Last Year	Company	Score
1	2	Medtronic	7.70
2	1	Minnesota Mining & Manufacturing	7.65
3	7	Eastman Kodak	6.59
4	8	Baxter International	6.34
5	3	Thermo Electron	6.13
6	6	Becton Dickinson	6.12
7	10	Bausch & Lomb	5.90
8	5	Tektronix	5.76
9	9	Polaroid	5.58
10	•	Boston Scientific	5.54

ELECTRONICS, SEMICONDUCTORS			
Rank	Last Year	Company	Score
1	1	Intel	8.37
2	3	Texas Instruments	7.29
3	2	Applied Materials	7.29
4	4	Analog Devices	6.60
5	6	LSI Logic	6.00
6	8	Advanced Micro Devices	5.01
7	7	National Semiconductor	4.68